My Journey from Marxism-Leninism to Nehruvian Socialism

C.H. Hanumantha Rao holds a PhD from the Delhi School of Economics, University of Delhi (1962). He was Post-Doctoral Fellow, Department of Economics, University of Chicago (1966-67) and Fellow, Institute of Economic Growth, University of Delhi (1961-1992). He has been Hon. Professor, Centre for Economic and Social Studies, Hyderabad since 1992. His areas of interest are: Agricultural Economics, Development Planning and Policy. He has been a member of the Planning Commission, Finance Commission, on the Board of Directors of the RBI; Member, National Advisory Council; and Chancellor, University of Hyderabad. He was awarded 'Padma Bhushan' by the President of India in 2004 in the field of literature and education.

My Journey from Marxism-Leninism to Nehruvian Socialism

Some Memoirs and Reflections on Inclusive Growth

C.H. HANUMANTHA RAO

ACADEMIC FOUNDATION
NEW DELHI

www.academicfoundation.org

First published in 2018
by

ACADEMIC FOUNDATION
4772-73 / 23 Bharat Ram Road, (23 Ansari Road),
Darya Ganj, New Delhi - 110 002 (India).
Phones : 23245001 / 02 / 03 / 04.
Fax : +91-11-23245005.
E-mail : booksaf@gmail.com
www.academicfoundation.org

Cataloging in Publication Data--DK
Courtesy: D.K. Agencies (P) Ltd. <docinfo@dkagencies.com>

Hanumantha Rao, C. H., author.
My journey from Marxism-Leninism to Nehruvian socialism : some memoirs and reflections on inclusive growth / C.H. Hanumantha Rao.
pages cm
Includes bibliographical references and index.
ISBN 9789332704350

1. Economic development--India. 2. Socialism--India. 3. India--Economic policy--1947- 4. Hanumantha Rao, C. H. I. Title.

LCC HC435.3.H36 2017 | DDC 338.954 23

Typeset, printed and bound by The Book Mint, New Delhi.
www.thebookmint.in

To
My Parents

Contents

Introduction 11

PART ONE

I-A

Journey from Marxism-Leninism to Nehruvian Socialism: Some Memoirs

1. My Early Years: Participation in the Struggle for Freedom, Democracy and Socialism 19
2. From Marxism-Leninism to Nehruvian Socialism: An Introspection 35
   Appendix
3. Four Years (1982-1986) in the Planning Commission: The Leadership of Indira Gandhi and Rajiv Gandhi 55
4. Economic Reforms and Continued Relevance of Nehruvian Model of Equitable Development 71
5. Challenges of Post-Nehru Era 81
   Epilogue
6. Indian Development: Options and Choices 91
   Epilogue
7. Fighting Religious Fundamentalism: Role of Ideology and Social Policy 105
8. Conditions Favourable to Economic Reforms in the Early 1990s 109

9. Twenty Five Years of Economic Reforms: Remembering Shri P.V. Narasimha Rao 113

10. From PhD Student to Board Chairman: My Experiences at the Institute of Economic Growth, Delhi 119

11. Professor P.N. Dhar 127

12. Professor Dharm Narain 129

13. Delhi School of Economics Annual Day Address 131

I-B
From Vishal Andhra to Telangana

1. Letter to the Editor on Telangana (National Herald, 20 July 1969) 139

2. Statehood for Telangana: The Current Stalemate 141

3. Release of Ghanta Chakrapani's Book "Telangana Jaitra Yatra". 147

4. Major Development Challenges to Telangana State 151

5. Telangana Agriculture Performance, Policy and Research Strategy 157

6. Development of Telangana: Policy Concerns 163

PART TWO
II-A
Some Reflections on Inclusive Growth

1. Crisis in Economic Theory: Implications for Indian Economy 171

2. Marginalised Groups and Inclusive Growth: Implications for Indian Economy 175

3. Future of Indian Children. 183

4. A Study on Young Lives 187

5. Division for Sustainable Development Studies at the CESS 191

6. India Labour and Employment Report 2014: Workers in the Era of Globalisation 195

7. Dynamics of Rural Labour Markets in India: Recent Trends and Policy Concerns 199

8. Some Major Issues Related to *Adivasis* 205

9. Governance, Resources, and Livelihoods of *Adivasis* in India: Strengthening Tribal Leadership for Effective Implementation of PESA and FRA. 211

10. Poverty as an Element in Priority Setting for Agricultural Research at International Research Centres' Level 215

11. Key Aspects of State-level Planning 221

12. Language Question: A Key to Educational Reform. 231

II-B
Comments on Some Books and Papers

1. Michael Lipton: Why Poor People Stay Poor: Urban Bias in World Development. 239

2. K.N. Raj: Organisational Issues in Indian Agriculture 252

3. Deepak Nayyar: Economic Liberalisation in India—Analytics, Experience and Lessons . . . 259

4. Ester Boserup: The Conditions of Agricultural Growth—The Economics of Agrarian Change under Population Pressure 265

5. Yujiro Hayami: Japanese Agriculture under Siege—The Political Economy of Agricultural Policies 269

6. N. Subba Reddy: Cultural Diversity and Common Humanity 273

7. Indira Hirway: Abolition of Poverty in India, with Special Reference to Target Group Approach in Gujarat. 277

8. B.M. Bhatia: Indian Agriculture—A Policy Perspective 283

9. Pulapre Balakrishnan: Economic Growth in India—History and Prospect 289

10. Raj Krishna: A Study on the Marketable Surplus Function for a Subsistence Crop 293

11. Dharm Narain: Distribution of the Marketed Surplus of Agricultural Produce by Size Level of Holding in India in 1950-51. 299

References 303

Index. 305

Introduction

"My Journey from Marxism-Leninism to Nehruvian Socialism" is a story of my changing perceptions on major socioeconomic developments in the country since the mid-1940s, when I became an activist in the student movement in the wake of political upsurge in the old Hyderabad state. These changes in my outlook have been marked by serious introspections in the light of contending ideological positions, including in the period of 1980s and 1990s characterised by paradigm shifts in the former socialist countries.

In the first phase of 12 years ending in 1957, when I completed my postgraduation in economics from the Osmania University, my participation in the freedom struggle and the student movement was inspired by the Marxian ideology, even as I was becoming introspective and critical of the stand taken by the communist movement on several issues. This is portrayed in the first chapter of the book.

The second phase began with my joining the Delhi School of Economics for pursuing PhD. I got disillusioned in this phase with the applicability of Marxist-Leninist theories under Indian conditions and found the Nehruvian approach relevant for addressing the socioeconomic problems in India. This approach combined with my Marxian orientation has been a source of inspiration for the research work I pursued at the Institute of Economic Growth for over three decades. The second chapter analyses how the belief by the Indian communist movement in the basic tenets of Marxism-Leninism,viz., Proletarian

Internationalism, Proletarian Dictatorship and Democratic Centralism has been responsible for its inability to take a proper stand on many issues by formulating strategies and policies in keeping with the socioeconomic realities in India.

The third chapter discusses the issues I faced for four years in the Planning Commission under the leadership of Prime Ministers Mrs Indira Gandhi and Shri Rajiv Gandhi. These relate to economic planning and policies in India in the light of the Nehruvian perspective of a mixed economy with socialist orientation within a democratic set-up where private sector and markets have a significant place. The strengthening of resources position of states in general and of the poorer states in particular as a result of the recommendations of the 7th and the 8th Finance Commissions is brought out in the fourth chapter. Globalisation and economic reforms in India in the wake of the breakdown of centralised bureaucratic planning in the former socialist countries and the relevance of the Nehruvian model of development for evolving a balanced approach to reforms by adequately addressing the problems of poverty, inequality and backwardness are discussed in this chapter. The same issues are dealt with in the remaining chapters of this section.

As a student activist, I had participated in the movement for the formation of Vishal Andhra or undivided Andhra Pradesh. But the year 1969 was a turning point in my thinking on this when there was a widespread agitation for carving out a separate state of Telangana. I visited Hyderabad to understand the reasons for unrest which led to my writing on the desirability of constituting smaller states wherever they are viable. After the state of Telangana was carved out in June 2014, I have had opportunities to speak and write on development challenges facing Telangana. These essays are included in the section "From Vishal Andhra to Telangana".

Part II of the book contains essays on inclusive growth written for certain important occasions over the last three years. But I also include the three earlier essays, one on Priority Setting in Agricultural Research, written as member of the Technical Advisory Committee (TAC) on International Agricultural Research; another on State-Level Planning written when I was in the Planning Commission; and the third on the Language Question written as a graduate student for the college magazine at the Nizam College in 1954, when controversy on the language question was raging in the country. Some of my friends who read it recently told me that the language issue continues to be relevant to this day. The last section in Part II contains my comments on certain important books and papers covering agriculture, rural development and poverty alleviation which have a bearing on strategies and policies for achieving inclusive growth.

Comments and suggestions from S. Mahendra Dev, R. Radhakrishna, Y.V. Reddy, Burgula Narsing Rao, and senior journalists Ch. Rajeshwara Rao and Kumar Sharma were helpful in organising the material in the book for a better focus and sequence. I also received help from S. Galab, E. Revathi, G. Haragopal, N. Chandrasekhara Rao, CESS Librarian Murali Prasad, Assistant Librarian P. Sudhakar, other staff in the library, B. Sankara Reddy in the Administration, and Computer Engineer Narasimha Raju. I am grateful to all.

—C.H. Hanumantha Rao
Centre for Economic and Social Studies,
Hyderabad.

PART ONE

I-A

Journey from Marxism-Leninism to Nehruvian Socialism

Some Memoirs

1

My Early Years

Participation in the Struggle for Freedom, Democracy and Socialism

When Transferred from Third to Second Standard

At the age of nine, in June 1938, I was admitted to the third standard in the government primary school (*Madarsae-Tahetania*) at Karimnagar town where I was staying with my sister and brother-in-law, near the imposing clock tower. A couple of days after my admission, the head master sent word to my brother-in-law that I was not eligible for the third standard and that I had to be placed in the second standard. I benefited very much from this start with the second standard. I did well since then and could pass in the first division in the fourth standard, the final year in the primary school.

Those days, caning the 'erring' students used to be a common practices, though I escaped it except once or twice in the second standard in the primary school. This practice was found to decline as we grew up and moved from the lower to the higher classes in the high school and was quite rare from the eighth standard onwards. Still many teachers considered the cane as the potent instrument for maintaining 'discipline'. Once we had a head master who was endowed with powerful voice and used to announce his arrival every morning by loudly calling for 'silence' by banging the cane which could be heard at every nook and corner of the school.

Such practices notwithstanding, the teachers in general used to take great deal of interest in teaching and came to the classes very well prepared. Some of the teachers were acknowledged scholars in their subjects even at the high school level. We benefited a great deal from the high quality of their teaching. I never found the need for availing private 'tuition'.

Impact of Leftist Views

My brother-in-law Polkampalli Venkata Rama Rao garu was a highly reputed lawyer in Karimnagar. Though a 'nationalist', he had good relations with the communist leaders like Baddam Yella Reddy and A. Prabhakar Rao who used to visit him frequently for political gossip. Many distinguished political and social figures from Hyderabad and other places used to visit him for discussions. In those days Andhra Mahasabha, led mainly by the communists, came to be organised in all the districts of Telangana.

Immediately after the Second World War, the influence of socialist ideology increased in Hyderabad and other neighbouring districts. Communist leaders used to come to Karimngar and hold meetings. These meetings had a considerable impact on me. I became a student activist and secretary of the Karimnagar unit of the All Hyderabad Students' Union (affiliated to the All India Students' Federation). We used to organise meetings of the students, sometimes numbering as many as a thousand with almost equal participation from Hindus and Muslims. The issues for discussion used to be Freedom, Peace and Progress. 'Freedom' had a wider connotation—freedom not only from the British rule but also from the Nizam's rule. 'Peace' was necessary for the whole world as well as for our society, for example, between Hindus and Muslims. The impact of the progressive movement in general—against feudalism, communalism and casteism, and for democracy, secularism and socialism—could be seen clearly in these meetings.

Urdu over Telugu

During those days, textbooks mostly in Urdu used to be available in book stores. Being the state language and medium of instruction right from the primary school, Urdu acquired importance in the villages and towns alike. I was good in Urdu, but very weak in Telugu—my mother tongue!

For eighth standard onwards I could have chosen Telugu as my optional subject. Instead, I chose Higher Mathematics (*Aala Riazi*). This was also the advice given to me by our Telugu teacher because of my poor performance in Telugu.

When I started participating in political activities at the age of 15, there was hardly any literature available in Urdu on political issues. Almost all the magazines and political literature used to be available either in Telugu or English. My growing interest in political issues actually contributed to the revival of my Telugu! All such Telugu literature used to be from Prajashakti Publications, Vijayawada, the authors being Puchchalapalli Sundaraiah, Chandra Rajeshwara Rao and Khambampati Satyanarayana, among others. Although leaders like Makhdoom Mohiuddin, Ravi Narayan Reddy and Baddam Yella Reddy were from Hyderabad, most of the leaders and the authors of the communist literature were from Vijayawada.

When Rusticated from the School

The activities of our student movement were stepped up. A summer school was organised for two weeks at our residence (*Somiah Bunglow*) in Karimnagar in May 1946, where the meetings were addressed by student leaders from Hyderabad like Jawad Razvi, Bhalchandra Paranjape, besides Dr Raj Bahadur Goud, a veteran communist leader. The government's attention was then drawn towards us. Our head master Azeezullah Durrani *saheb* called me and J. Madhusudhan Rao, a colleague of mine, and said that he was fully in the know of our participation in 'political' meetings, and advised us to stop participating in them. He also asked us to resign from the membership of our organisation and give him a written apology. We mustered enough courage to ask him to give this to us in writing. On

High School, Karimnagar

this the head master shouted at us by banging the cane on his table. We then quickly left his room.

Subsequent to our meeting with the headmaster, we were absolutely clear that there was no question of submitting an apology or resigning from the Students' Union. But some of the elders in my family tried hard to persuade me to submit an apology as they thought it was not advisable for me to jeopardise my education at such an early stage.

On our refusal to apologize, we were rusticated from the school by withholding the results of our examination in the ninth standard in June 1946. Before leaving the school for good, I paid a courtesy call on the head master at his residence. He had a liking for me as a good student and was in tears when he saw me.

Completing Higher Secondary from Aligarh Muslim University

Those of us rusticated shifted to Hyderabad to continue our studies as private candidates for Higher Secondary Examination (HSE) at the Aligarh Muslim University where we had the advantage of Urdu as medium of instruction. We also had the advantage of good learning in subjects like higher mathematics and science in 8th and 9th standards through Urdu medium at high school in Karimnagar. We joined a Tutorial College in Sultan Bazar on the second floor of a building, where the office of the All Hyderabad Students' Union (AHSU) was also located on the first floor. We used to visit the AHSU office frequently and discuss with the leaders who helped us to get free accommodation and meals at a hostel in Hyderguda run for the freedom fighters.

There was an interesting episode at the time of my registering for the Aligarh exam by paying fees. I was told that one of the conditions of eligibility for the exam was that the candidate should have completed 18 years of age before the date of exam. There was no record in our family about my date of birth but my parents and other elders used to recall that I was born in August (Shravan) 17 years ago. To avoid the risk of being rejected as ineligible, I decided to declare in the form my date of birth as 15 May 1929, so that I would be exactly 18 years by 15 May 1947, the date of examination. Since then this continues to be my official date of birth! Thanks largely to my learning at the high school in Karimnagar, I could pass HSE from Aligarh Muslim University by missing first division narrowly by four marks.

In Hyderabad, led by the leader of the All Hyderabad Students' Union, Shri Omkar Prasad, we met eminent persons like Qazi Abdul Ghaffar, Founder-Editor of '*Payam*', the leading Urdu Daily, nationalist leaders Swami Ramanand Teerth, Shri Govindas Shroff and Shri Vyshempayen, to appraise them of the events in Karimnagar.

The country achieved independence in August 1947. Following Police Action in September 1948, Hyderabad State was merged with the Indian Union. Despite this, the Communist Party continued its armed struggle. I was studying intermediate science in the City College with a view to pursuing medical course, while staying with my brother Ch. Rajeshwara Rao *garu* in Chikkadpalli.

Professor Alam Khundmiri

In the City College I had the privilege of taking a course in 'Ethics' (*Aqlaqyat*) taught by Prof Alam Khundmiri. He was one of the Founders of the legendary "Comrades' Association" along with Com. Ibrahim, Com. Makhdoom Mohiuddin and others in December 1939. Formation of Comrades' Association was a unique initiative at that time, at once visionary and courageous, committed to struggling for freedom, democracy, secularism and socialism in a Princely State. Prof Alam Khundmiri later became a professor in Philosophy at the Osmania University. His lectures at the City College in chaste Urdu marked by great clarity and analytical rigour, left a lasting impression on me.

Arrest and Detention

Those days my brother Ch. Rajeshwara Rao *garu* was underground along with Com. Makhdoom Mohiuddin. One day in February 1949, a few months before my exam, police came to our house in search of my brother and arrested me after getting hold of some hidden documents and asking me whether I was a member of the Communist Party to which I said 'yes'. Apparently, this was made one of the grounds for my arrest as the Communist Party was banned. After a few months of detention in Chanchalguda Jail, I and some of my associates were shifted to the 'Concentration Camp' in Jalna where over 2,000 detenues suspected to be communists or their sympathisers were placed in barracks.

I was made a member of the Jail Committee of the Communist Party of which Com. Kondapalli Gopala Rao was the secretary, Com. Dharma Biksham and Com. Kokil being the other members. At that time the Communist Party in the country was following a radical line under the leadership of Com. B.T. Ranadive. There were instructions to wage struggles even inside the jails by observing hunger strikes and holding demonstrations by facing *lathi* charges and firing. Hunger strikes used to be observed by us lasting for five days or even more at a stretch. There were *lathi* charges by the police, but no firing although such a risk did exist.

Around this time, the Inspector-General of Police, one Mr Jaitley, visited the Jalna Concentration Camp. We were made to sit on our beds in a row in the barrack and were allowed to make representations, if any, to the I.G.P. When he was passing through our row, Com. Gopala Rao who was seated before me stood up to make the representation on our behalf. One of the demands he made by pointing to me was to release me so that I could resume my studies. At this Mr Jaitley asked why we were keen for study when we were against 'bourgeois education' and were bent upon overthrowing the government. At this Gopala Rao without the slightest hesitation replied what we learnt through the Marxist literature: "we do join the government institutions, get bourgeois education, carry out struggles and eventually overthrow the bourgeoisie." At this Mr Jaitley got angry and hit Com. Gopala Rao with his hand stick and briskly walked out of the barrack, apparently to avoid any 'violent' reaction from the prisoners.

Release and Recuperation

Hunger strikes and living conditions in the Concentration Camp began to tell on my fragile physique and my health deteriorated. The jail authorities in September 1949 took me to the railway station at Jalna, left me on a bench and went away. Luckily, a railway gangman's son who had known me in the village when they were employed by my father, Srinivasa Rao *garu*, recognised me. He took me to their house near the railway station, gave me meals and put me in the train proceeding to Hyderabad.

When I got down at the Kachiguda Railway station in Hyderabad, the only house I remembered was that of N. Dharma Rao *garu* (nephew of my brother-in-law) located at Narayanguda. Seeing my condition he took me to my maternal uncle J. Anand Rao *garu*, who promptly put me under medical care. My condition was critical as I could not even speak. My elder sister Satyamma *garu* with whom I had stayed in Karimnagar and my father joined me soon. After a few days when I recovered slightly, my father took me to the village for rest and recuperation.

Because of constant company and interactions with co-detenus inside the jail, my political commitment to the party and its cause became stronger. Even though I was still unwell and recovering, I used to engage myself in spirited arguments with my father on the principles of the communist party and the armed struggle. He thought I was under the spell of '*shani*' for a year or so! Despite my ill-health, I felt ashamed that I was living 'comfortably' at home while my colleagues were fighting in the forests. I was oppressed by the feeling that I was betraying the cause of revolution and the party. I decided to leave the house and join the armed squads of the party in the forests. My father, mother Chandramma *garu* and the elder sister tried hard to persuade me against my leaving the house. My mother wept and, for the first time, I saw my father in tears. My sister said in disgust that she would have a head bath after I leave because she was certain that I would be shot dead in the armed struggle that I was going to join.

Going Underground

Using my underground contacts I proceeded to the forests via Sircilla to join the armed squad (*Dalam*) led by Com. Amrit Lal Shukla, secretary, Sircilla unit of the Party, whom I had known since my student days in Karimnagar. Weapons in hand, I and other members of the squad had to walk 10 to 15 km. per day from place to place, while getting training in the use of arms, and holding meetings of the villagers during the nights to find out their problems and grievances. One day our squad leader Com. Amrit Lal Shukla received a letter addressed to me by Com. Makhdoom Mohiuddin, secretary, Hyderabad City Unit of the Party. He wrote, "Hanumantha Rao, you are a member of the Hyderabad Unit of the Party but you did not take any permission from the Unit to join the *Dalam*. Therefore, you should immediately return to Hyderabad." He also wrote that I was showing a 'Narodnik Deviation' (a term often used those days in the Party alluding to some 'errant' revolutionaries in Russia showing 'pro-peasant' politics deviating from the 'working class' approach). I was to learn later that Ranadive's political line sought to restore the 'vanguard' position of the working class in bringing about the revolution as in the 'Russian model' contrary to the pre-eminent position assigned to guerilla warfare by the peasants in the 'Chinese model'. After reading Com. Makhdoom's letter, Com. Amrit Lal Shukla quietly but firmly suggested that I should immediately leave for Hyderabad to join Com. Makhdoom Mohiuddin.

While proceeding to Hyderabad, I stopped for a day at my village (Nagaram) for meeting my father and uncle against whom I heard some complaints concerning disputes over land made by the aggrieved villagers in the course of the meetings of our squad with the people in other villages. On account of this, my father and uncle could be targeted by the armed squads. I stayed at the house of our domestic help in the village and went in the night to meet my father and uncle to tell them about the complaints asking them to settle these amicably. They at first got angry over my intervention but relented after I explained the position.

I reached Hyderabad and after a few days of waiting and exploration I could meet Com. Makhdoom at a house near Sabzimandi in the old city. This was my first meeting with him. Among others staying with him were my brother and sister-in-law. A few days after reaching there I learnt that my brother Rajeshwara Rao *garu*, who is six years older to me, also had a hand in getting me back from the *Dalam*. His fear was that I might fall ill again in the difficult terrain there. Pending assignment of regular work for me, one of my immediate assignments in the 'den'—the house where we lived underground—was getting provisions from the market as, being quite young, I could not easily be suspected by the police.

While underground, Com. Makhdoom went by the name 'Amrit'. Like others, I too had to change my name. I decided to name myself as 'Ranga Rao', who was my class-mate, a close friend and a top ranking student at Karimnagar High School.

The Personality of Makhdoom Mohiuddin

Among the leaders I met, I was highly impressed by Makhdoom Mohiuddin and Ravi Narayan Reddy. Makhdoom had read widely on the basic theory and principles of communism. I found him reading new books and articles in journals every day. He knew the views of prominent leaders, right from Stalin to Indian leaders, on important issues. He was a poet, of course, and had earned distinction as such, but his contributions as a communist leader in building up Trade Union movement in Hyderabad State were no less significant.

He had a special affinity with the working class and, according to him, working class alone could bring about the revolution because they are very industrious and selfless. He did not equally subscribe to the view that peasants can also bring about the revolution. He had a liking for the utterances of the labourers and even abuses by them! He once narrated to me one such incident gleefully with a sense of humour characteristic of him: Once he was returning from Delhi travelling by train. Those days this travel used to take two days and two nights. He became restless and anxious as to when he would be reaching Hyderabad. One morning when the train halted at a station, the voices of labourers outside selling tea could be heard. Some of them while talking to each other were using choicely abuses. Then, he said, he had a sigh of relief sensing that he had at last reached his '*watan*' (home town)!

Ravi Narayan Reddy

After a few months my brother and sister-in-law along with me were shifted to another den in the old city where Com. Ravi Narayan Reddy (R.N.) and his wife Sita Devi *garu* were staying. R.N. had taken a bold stand against the continuance of armed struggle which, according to him, should have been withdrawn after the Police Action on Hyderabad State and its merger with the Indian Union. R.N. had joined the freedom movement first as a nationalist inspired by Mahatma Gandhi. He was among the first batch of *satyagrahis* from Hyderabad. He had independent views with a broader, liberal outlook and was an inspiring orator in Telugu. It was fascinating to listen to his account of the freedom movement and peasant struggles in Telangana spearheaded by the Andhra Mahasabha of which he was the president twice.

He was, without doubt, the most popular mass leader in Telangana. This was evidenced by his election to the Lok Sabha from Nalgonda in the first general elections in 1952 when he polled the highest number of votes in the country, those polled by Pandit Jawaharlal Nehru being next to him. It was under his influence that I could realise for the first time that even the Communist Party could go wrong! Since then a critical approach to received theories, whether in the political or economic sphere, got ingrained in me. Largely inspired by his views I wrote two articles in *Payam*, the Urdu Daily, analysing the factors leading to the Police Action on Hyderabad and the consequences, in the summer of 1951 under a pseudonym 'B. Ramachandram', a close friend of mine during my school days, who changed from a 'nationalist' to communist under the impact of constant discussions between us, fell a martyr in the Telangana armed struggle. Unfortunately, despite the attempts made recently by my journalist friend Ch. Rajeshwara Rao, the issues of *Payam* containing those articles could not be traced.

Free Movement, Arrest and Release

While still underground, I had an opportunity to visit and meet students at Janagaun and other places. This was an eye opener as I could see an increasing demand for developmental activities including new schools and colleges, and rising expectations from the existing system under the democratic set-up. I could also attend, along with my colleague Burgula Narsing Rao, a meeting of the working committee of the All India Students' Federation held at Madras.

I was arrested again in November 1951 and placed in Chanchalguda and Musheerabad jails. During this round of my detention, the political atmosphere outside was becoming normal as the preparations for the first general elections were in full swing. The facilities inside the jail improved somewhat, and I could read a number of news papers and books, including the *Autobiography* and *The Discovery of India* by Pandit Jawaharlal Nehru, which contributed to widening my intellectual horizons and openness of mind.

In May 1952, I was brought to Karimnagar Jail and released there with the condition that I should report to the collector every week. After some time I came to Hyderabad and resumed my activities in the student movement while staying at the old MLAs quarters with my maternal uncle J. Anand Rao *garu* who was elected from Sircilla constituency, as a candidate of the Peoples' Democratic Front (PDF) led by the communists.

Hyderabad of Those Days

Hyderabad, particularly the Telangana region, was known for religious harmony and brotherhood. In the Osmania University and colleges mutual relations among students used to be very friendly. The population of Muslims was large in Hyderabad, their proportion being relatively less in the districts. In the course of Police Action there were some incidents of communal disturbance in the Karnatak and Marathwada regions but Telangana, by and large, remained peaceful. Because of Razakars the situation deteriorated in certain places but owing to the growing strength of the movement led by the communists, a large number of these leaders being Muslims like Makhdoom Mohiuddin, Jawad Razvi and others, the atmosphere remained secular.

There used to be meetings organised by the Urdu Progressive Writers' Association. Kaifi Azmi, Ali Sardar Jafri and several other litterateurs used to participate in these meetings. Such meetings had a profound impact on the younger generation inspiring them with the ideals of secularism, democracy and socialism. When the first general elections were held in 1952, many of those elected to the Hyderabad State Assembly from Telangana were candidates from the PDF led by the communists.

Intermediate Education as Private Candidate

I passed intermediate examination (with Economics, Civics and History as my subjects) as a private candidate from the Board of Secondary Education, Ajmer. Apart from my own study of selected books before going to Ajmer, my preparation for the exam included listening to the lectures in Ajmer given by Amrit Nahata by using microphone to a large gathering of candidates in an open ground every evening on the answers to questions expected the next morning! About two and half decades later it was a pleasant surprise for me to meet him by chance in a flight where I could easily spot him because one of his hands was incapacitated. When I checked with him he immediately affirmed that he is the same Amrit Nahata who gave pre-exam lectures in Ajmer 25 years ago. He was elected now as a Member of Parliament, after the Emergency was lifted, having authored the famous book *Kissa Kursi ka*!

Nizam College and Arts College

I took admission into the Nizam college in June 1953 for doing BA while, at the same time, participating in the student movement. Nizam College turned out to be quite a new world for me. Because I resumed my studies after a gap of four years, most of those studying there were much younger to me but, being city-bred, were very knowledgeable, their English being particularly good. Having been in jails or underground for over three years, my interactions with these young friends was an eye opener and connected me to the emerging society under freedom, democratic set-up, with prospects for bringing about development and social change through peaceful methods.

After completing BA, I, along with Waheeduddeen Khan, my class fellow, who was later to become the Director of the Centre for Economic and Social Studies, decided to shift to the Arts College, Osmania University, for doing MA in Economics inspired by Prof A.M. Khusro who, fresh from the University of Leeds (UK), was teaching Economics there. There was also a push factor as one of our senior professors at the Nizam College felt hurt by the activities of the student movement and had shown the potential to harm the academic prospects of those active in the movement. When I met Dr Syed Hussain, Principal of Nizam College, he was not happy at my decision to leave the College. By this time, he had known me well as the Vice-President of the College Students' Union. He instantly offered me a scholarship for pursuing post-graduate studies at the College, obviously to induce me to continue, but I had already made up my mind to shift to the Arts College.

The sprouting ambitions in me to take to academic profession started taking a shape with my decision to do MA in Economics in the College of Arts and Commerce, Osmania University. But my commitment to participate in the student movement as the General Secretary of the AHSU persisted. I could not yet see clearly the conflict involved between pursuing the academic and political goals simultaneously, beyond a point. This explains my decision to contest for the position of president of the college union. But I was defeated in the election with a narrow margin of seven votes.

I did not quite anticipate the intensity of organised opposition to me from certain political quarters (not from the side of the candidate who won the election) because of my pronounced Leftist background. Attempts were made to divide the votes by putting up a 'dummy' candidate. In the course of the campaign, a common friend of mine and the candidate who won was in a dilemma as to whom to vote and canvas for, as he had a large following. He came to me and frankly asked me to make a choice between his vote and his canvassing for me. I told him that his vote is precious for me. I was aware that this choice meant losing a large number of votes that he would have mobilised for me. Even so, the general impression was that, but for the complacency on our part in the campaign, the election result would have been different.

The responsibilities of the president of the University College Union were onerous and it is doubtful that, in the event of winning the election, I could have done as well in the MA final year exam as I did by concentrating on my studies immediately thereafter.

After completing MA, I was encouraged by Prof A.M. Khusro, who became a professor at the Delhi School of Economics only a few months ago, to pursue my PhD work there. Prof V.K.R.V. Rao with whom I had an opportunity to interact during a seminar in July at the College of Arts and Commerce, Osmania University, also encouraged me to do PhD at the Delhi School. While I was excited at this rare opportunity, some of my family members thought it would be beneficial for me as well as the family if I took up some job at Hyderabad itself, especially in view of my father's deteriorating health, and made a concerted attempt to dissuade me from going to Delhi. Fortunately, my bedridden father was forward-looking and reacted favourably to my plans saying that I must have taken a right decision.

In August 1957, I left for Delhi to pursue PhD at the Delhi School of Economics. Thanks to being a Hyderabadi and Urdu-speaking, I could easily mix with people in Delhi and was spared from being called a *Madrasi*! Many people thought I was a '*Hindusthani*', implying one belonging to Hindi-speaking North India, but no one knew that I could neither read nor write Hindi!

Based on the interview for the series entitled "Hyderabad That was Yesterday" (*Hyderabad Jo Kal tha*), published in *The Siasat*, Urdu Daily, Hyderabad, 24 August 2014 (Interviewer: F.M. Saleem).

2

From Marxism-Leninism to Nehruvian Socialism

An Introspection

Towards Marxian Ideology

I was attracted towards Marxian ideology when I was barely 15, studying in eighth standard in Karimnagar High School (*fokania*) in the year 1944-45. Although I was staying with my brother-in-law who was a staunch nationalist and Gandhian, I came under the influence of Andhra Mahasabha led by the communists. An equitable social order in India and the world at large espoused by Marxism was far more inspiring, as it went much beyond the goal of national independence. Besides, a nationalist party like the Congress was not prominent in Telangana those days which was reeling under feudalism. On the other hand, Communist Party was well-organised and their offices as well as Andhra Mahasabha libraries used to have quite a few books on Marxism and socialism in English and Telugu.

The prevailing social inequalities and injustices also predisposed me towards Marxian influences rather spontaneously. As a child from a landlord family, I frequently saw the villagers and domestic servants being treated roughly, often cruelly, by the landlord families. This inequality and injustice was puzzling to me until my brother once explained that it arises from the power and wealth these landlord families enjoy. Untouchability was rampant and whenever I went to the field escorted by farm servants, immediately after my return I had to take bath and change the clothes. I found that most of those observing religious rituals rigorously also strictly practiced untouchability. Due to this and many other superstitions and irrational beliefs, I distanced myself from our religion. Later, when I joined the school in Karimnagar, I had opportunities to mix freely with fellow students irrespective of their religion and caste.

As a young communist I was exposed almost exclusively to Marxian literature and interactions with communist leaders and workers for six years, including the period spent in jails and underground, until 1951-52 with hardly any exposure to other streams of thought. When I was released from jail in 1952 and resumed my studies, first for taking intermediate exam from Ajmer and later joining Nizam college for graduate studies, even as I continued to participate in the student movement as All Hyderabad Students' Union (AHSU) activist, I was exposed to a different world. With the first general elections over, democracy had become a functioning reality in the country and discussions on development through economic planning were in full swing. As activists in the student movement, we used to face questions from the students on the prospects of development through democratic and peaceful methods and the policies of the CPI on such issues. I found quite a few of them very well read on the ideologies and policies of different parties in India and in other countries.

The CPI's Position on Major Issues

Having taken the position for quite some time that the country did not really achieve independence in August 1947, but saw a mere 'transfer of power' without effective independence, the CPI had slowly come to admit publicly by the mid-1950s that the country had indeed achieved independence. This resulted in the alienation of the party from the people.

Again, the Party failed to take an independent view, based on ground realities, on the continuance of the armed struggle in Telangana even after the feudal rule ended as a result of police action by the Union Government and the broad masses of people celebrated the event. The advice given by Ravi Narayan Reddy, the foremost leader of the Telangana movement, favouring withdrawal of armed struggle was rejected and finally the decision for withdrawal was taken, reportedly after the discussions with Com. Stalin by a group of Indian leaders who went to Moscow to seek his advice towards the end of 1951, after hundreds of party leaders and workers were lost. Apparently, this decision was taken on logistic and tactical grounds whereas Com. Ravi Narayan Reddy's advice was based on an understanding of the changing political situation which had long-term implications. Com. Ravi Narayan Reddy in his autobiography observed that it was 'indeed ridiculous' that these leaders had to go to Moscow and meet Com. Stalin on this issue instead of resolving it themselves in the light of the conditions obtaining in Telangana.[1]

During 1950-51, while underground, I was witness to the animated 'inner-party' debates on how the political line of the former general secretary of the CPI, P.C. Joshi was 'reformist' and B.T. Ranadive's line was truly 'revolutionary' and 'correct'. Very soon, this line was denounced as 'left-wing adventurism' and the 'Chinese line' of guerilla warfare in the countryside espoused by Chandra Rajeshwara Rao and others was considered appropriate to Indian conditions. These changing positions within a short period, claimed each time to be 'correct' and appropriate to Indian conditions, were mostly based on the interpretations by the party ideologues of the writings in 'authoritative' journals such as *New Times* of the Communist Party of the Soviet Union (CPSU-B), *For a Lasting Peace, For a People's Democracy* (LPPD) of the Cominform, and *Peoples' Daily* of the Communist Party of China. Very often, there used to be hair-splitting arguments on each sentence and some times even each word from these articles. I recall one such occasion when

---

1. See his *Naa Jeevana Pathamlo*, Ravi Bharathi (ed.), Moosi Publications, Hyderabad, 1992, p.91.

a particular article in the Soviet journal after debating it intensely was treated virtually as a directive to the Indian party but later was found to have been a report by a theoretician of the CPSU to the Soviet Academy!

The CPI's Approach: Ideological Roots

I realised by the early 1960s that the real sources for this attitude were the concepts of 'Proletarian Internationalism', 'Proletarian Dictatorship' and 'Democratic Centralism'—the guiding principles of the party arising from Marxism-Leninism. 'Proletarian Internationalism' meant not just solidarity between the workers of different countries or deriving inspiration from revolutions brought about by workers around the world such as the October Revolution in the Soviet Union, but was reduced in practice to seeing all the political wisdom in the pronouncements of the Soviet Communist Party and treating its formulations as authoritative interpretations of Marxism-Leninism and, therefore, as directives with a willingness to follow them. Even after the fall of the Soviet Union, it appears that Marxism-Leninism in its pristine form continues to be the guiding ideology and framework for the communist movement in the country. The greatest casualty of this attitude has been the independence of approach towards a proper understanding of the prevailing social structure in the country and analysing the evolving socio-political situation for addressing the emerging problems. (For a critique of the concept and practice of Proletarian Internationalism by the communist movement, see the chapter "Internationalism and Revolution: China and Indian Revolutionaries" in *Red and Green: Five Decades of the Indian Maoist Movement*, by Manoranjan Mohanty, Setu Prakasham, Kolkata, 2015.)

Internationalism was also interpreted to mean that a socialist country could never commit aggression against another country. It was not recognised that even a socialist country could be guided primarily by its own national interests in dealing with other countries, especially because there can be differences of perception even among the socialist countries in view of divergent history and circumstances in which they are placed. This became evident from the violent events that unfolded subsequently between the Soviet Union and Hungary, India and China, followed by serious differences and tensions between the Soviet Union and China, and between China and Vietnam. Inability to take an independent stand in the face of such developments landed the communist movement in India quite often in highly embarrassing situations. On the other hand, I could observe in Vietnam assertion of nationalism vis-à-vis China during the visit of the Indian Council of Social Science Research (ICSSR) delegation to Vietnam at the invitation of the Social Science Committee of Vietnam in December 1987. While in Langson province, northern-most hilly region bordering China, we were given a presentation with maps and other illustrations showing in detail how the Vietnamese culture is different from that of China and the expansionist tendencies of China.

'Proletarian Dictatorship' first became a reality in the special circumstances of the Soviet Union after the October Revolution, but turned into a perpetual one-party rule. This continued there until the collapse of the Soviet Union, and still continues in the Peoples' Republic of China. Other communist parties around the world, except possibly those from France and Italy, placed in different historical contexts and circumstances and struggling to establish a new social order rarely took an independent view on this question until recently and proceeded as though one-party rule through dictatorship would be indispensable to protect the gains of revolution.

A consequence of this approach and mindset has been that even in a country like India with multi-class social structure and a functioning democracy with multi-party political system, the mainstream communist movement which committed itself to bringing about a change in the existing social order through peaceful and democratic means tended to regard democracy as essentially a bourgeois institution designed to protect the vested interests and not as a desirable political system, in principle, which could be appropriately reformed for effectively serving the interests of the poor and the marginalised sections of society.

This became evident when the CPI strongly defended the promulgation of Emergency in India in the mid-seventies. During that period, I happened to go to Ajoy Bhavan in Delhi to see my brother Ch. Rajeshwara Rao, who had come there for attending a meeting of the CPI National Council. The top leaders present there, e.g. Chandra Rajeshwara Rao, General Secrtary, CPI, and Mohit Sen, Member, National Council, whom I had known over a long period, argued with me that Emergency became necessary to curb the 'reactionary' and 'anti-people' movement led by Jaya Prakash Narain, but I argued that common people could become the greatest sufferers because of suspension of civil liberties. They were aware that I was, otherwise, an enthusiastic supporter of the progressive policies of Mrs Indira Gandhi like the nationalisation of leading commercial banks and the 20-Point Programme for the alleviation of poverty. Subsequently, even the CPI workers in many places became victims of the excesses of Emergency. The party changed its position, in response to public criticism, much later after the Emergency was lifted by admitting that its promulgation was a mistake.

The practice of 'democratic centralism' defined as decision-making by the majority through debate and discussion and implementing such decisions by the central authority within the party or polity is, in a way, common to all the democratic political systems. However, its practice in the communist countries has been criticised for being more centralised than democratic. But this does not happen through day-to-day coercion and intimidation. It is really an outcome of the all-pervading impact of Marxism-Leninism, the ruling ideology, on the members combined with one-party rule. The decision-making is smooth, despite full-length discussions, assiduously encouraged in the communist system, because most members tend to think alike at any point of time. The sessions on 'Criticism' and 'Self-Criticism' rarely become introspective in the sense of questioning the basic ideological positions. Instead, such criticisms are focused on the 'deviations' from the entrenched ideological positions. One-party rule ensures that decisions taken are implemented effectively without much opposition. The practice of democratic centralism is thus sustained by the first two principles of proletarian internationalism and proletarian dictatorship.

The Lost Opportunities for Introspection by the Communist Movement

A big opportunity for introspection and reappraisal of the above fundamentals viz., 'Proletarian Internationalism', 'Proletarian Dictatorship' and 'Democratic Centralism', by the communist movement in India was provided by the revelations of Nikita Khrushchev on the excesses committed by Stalin and the de-Stalinisation drive undertaken by the CPSU in the mid-1950s. But what we saw instead was the disappearance of Stalin's pictures from the communist party offices and the homes of the party leaders! Much later, when I found Stalin's picture missing in the home in our village, I remember telling some of my family members present there that, notwithstanding the excesses committed by him, Stalin made great contributions towards building modern Russia and defeating Fascism in the Second World War.

I am not aware that the party ever saw that Stalinist excesses reflected basically a systemic and ideological failure and not purely an individual failure. In fact, such targeting of the individual wholly for 'excesses' is itself not quite Marxian because Marxism gave pride of place to history and circumstances in explaining the events. This became abundantly clear when Michael Gorbachev, the greatest liberaliser in the Soviet Communist Party, in his effort to save the system through his reforms had to virtually preside over its collapse. This demise is explained basically by the failure of the Soviet system over a long period to get rid of its authoritarian and isolationist or inward-looking traits to become an open and democratic polity for deriving full benefits from changes in technology and institutions which became major sources of growth in Western economies. Interestingly, thanks to their openness and democratic institutions, these countries, especially in Europe, learnt a great deal from socialist countries on the need for achieving social equity and matured, in course of time, as strong welfare states which contributed to the survival of capitalism from periodic crises.

Distancing from the Received Doctrine

After the resumption of my studies in the early 1950s, my interactions with fellow students and teachers on issues concerning ideology intensified extending into early 1960s when I completed my PhD at the Delhi School of Economics. The field work I did in the villages for PhD turned out be an important milestone in this journey as the facts gathered on the agrarian situation seemed to contradict many of my beliefs nurtured by the ideology I was wedded to. My ceasing to be active in the political movement and concentrating on studies, together with exposure to different streams of thought, provided the necessary environment for a detached and critical thinking on issues of ideology.

But I found some of my Marxist colleagues in the Delhi School of Economics still nurturing the idea that their research work would contribute to more effective application of the received Marxian doctrines towards addressing problems of poverty and development in India and would help to advance the communist and the Left movement in the country. They were unwilling to examine the relevance of some of the basic premises of such theories to the socioeconomic conditions in India in a changing world. Surprisingly, a few of them even after spending a number of years on assignments abroad and getting exposed to different streams of thought returned with the same mindset. Such instances speak as much about the power of such doctrines, embraced when young, as the closed nature of the minds imbibing them.

In the early 1960s on the suggestion of Prof P.C. Joshi, a colleague close to me, I met Com. P.C. Joshi, a legendary communist leader of the 1940s to discuss the current political scenario and also share my research interests. He was known for his nationalistic approach, his thoughts being close to those of the mainstream political movement in India. In the course of a fairly long discussion, I found his thinking to be essentially within the known ideological parameters of the CPI. He advised me in some detail as to how my research work should throw more light by providing empirical support to some of these well-known positions. I came back rather disappointed and frankly told my friend Prof P.C. Joshi that research work in its very nature has to be open-ended with readiness to examine and question even the well-accepted propositions rather than merely trying to provide support to them. I realised then that even some of the most liberal leaders in the communist movement could not fully come out of the stranglehold of their ideological framework.

This is not to undermine, in any way, the historic contributions of these leaders towards building up the communist and progressive movement in general in India. In fact, much later in the early 1990s when I was invited by the organisers of the P.C. Joshi Archives at the Jawaharlal Nehru University, New Delhi, to speak on the occasion of his Birth Centenary, I had an opportunity to recount the contributions of such leaders as builders of the communist movement in India, as those relentlessly trying to relate this movement with the mainstream national movement for independence, and who tried to save the communist movement from the sectarian path.

Towards the Nehruvian Model of Democratic Socialism

Distancing from Marxism-Leninism, imbibed in my younger days, was, no doubt, facilitated by my pursuit of higher studies in a wider intellectual environment of Delhi. But the attraction of an alternative ideological framework, viz., Nehruvian socialism through planning in a mixed economy under democracy proved to be decisive in this process. As a student of economics I became actively interested in the subject of planning in a democracy. Nehruvian model appeared eminently desirable as well as feasible under Indian conditions. What appealed to me most was its emphasis on openness and democratic framework which provided ample scope for alterations in the model in response to changing needs.

I was aware of the limitations imposed by the prevailing social structure in achieving the avowed objectives of socialism, already evident from the failure of land reforms to redistribute land to the landless, and cooperative farming initiated by Nehru with great expectations. Subsequently, the government took advice from Dr Wolf Ladejinisky of the World Bank, whose reputation rested on the successful implementation of land reforms in South Korea by Gen Mac Arthur with his advice. I learnt in a seminar held in Tokyo that in Japan land reforms had a chequered history of a hundred years but ultimately they could be implemented successfully only after the Second World War by the occupation forces.

I had occasions to discuss these issues with Dr Ladejinisky in Delhi. Clearly, it was naïve to expect to achieve in India what was accomplished by the occupation forces under Gen Mac Arthur after the Second World War. Resistance to change and pressures exerted by the vested interests in India have been evident from the inability of even some of the communist-led state governments to implement radical measures. Even so, Nehruvian vision of equitable development and the possibilities provided by the democratic framework for mobilising large sections of people for implementing progressive measures continue to hold promise under Indian conditions. For example, even though redistribution of land from the rich landowners to the landless was not a success, the implementation of the legal ceiling on the ownership of agricultural land prevented the accentuation of rural inequalities through the concentration of land in a few hands by expropriating land from the smallholders.

Despite my whole time involvement in research in economics, my interest on issues of political economy continued mainly because of my earlier participation as an activist in the student movement for over a decade. I have always felt that economic policy to be relevant and vibrant has to be based on the full awareness of socio-political goals as well as a proper understanding of the underlying political economy. As for the forces of the Left in Indian polity, notwithstanding their mistakes, I have always seen their extreme relevance, given our objectives of equitable or inclusive development within a secular and democratic polity. This has been vindicated time and again through the vicissitudes of Indian politics. Therefore, despite my preference for the Nehruvian model of development, I have retained my personal regard for the forces of the Left by interacting with them occasionally, not least because it is this past of mine which has prompted me to devote myself to research work on issues of equitable development.

Strengthening Nehruvian Model

Prime Minister Mrs Indira Gandhi's progressive policies beginning from the late 1960s such as nationalisation of major commercial banks, launching of Green Revolution for ensuring food security (which corrected the inadequate priority to agriculture in the earlier Plans), second round of land reforms undertaken in the early 1970s and poverty alleviation programmes strengthened the Nehruvian model of socialism by imparting greater social equity to the development process.

However, the decision to nationalise wholesale trade in wheat in the early 1970s, as a means for controlling inflation, became controversial as it had a potential for bureaucratisation without achieving the avowed objective. In the wake of this controversy and raging inflation, Prime Minister Indira Gandhi invited a Group of economists headed by Prof V.K.R.V. Rao from the Institute of Economic Growth to give suggestions on the ways to control inflation, which were discussed at the full meeting of the Cabinet with the Group. Among other things, the Group strongly recommended freeing of wholesale trade in wheat in order to prevent misallocation of resources, shortages and rising prices (Rao et al. 1973). The government accepted these recommendations which gave due place to the functioning of markets—a desirable feature of Nehruvian model of development in a mixed economy.

Nehruvian Vision under Stress: Imposition of Emergency

But very soon there was a set-back to the Nehruvian vision of democratic socialism because of imposition of Emergency by the government on 26 June 1975. Upset by this development, I wrote a letter to Prof V.K.R.V. Rao, the very next day, requesting him to excuse me for my inability to join him for submitting a note to the Prime Minister on measures for ensuring food security, as contemplated by him earlier.

I used to freely share my reservations on the imposition of Emergency with my friends and colleagues at the Institute of Economic Growth and the University Campus. In fact, when Prof V.P. Dutt, M.P., Pro-Vice-Chancellor of the University of Delhi, who came from a distinguished family of freedom fighters and considered close to the Prime Minister, organised a meeting of the teachers in the University on the progressive agenda of the government, I had an opportunity to suggest, amidst positive response from the teachers, that civil liberties including freedom of expression are essential to successfully implement and sustain the government's progressive agenda.

Around the time I was appointed as Director of the Institute of Economic Growth in October 1976, Shri V.B. Raju, M.P., General Secretary of the Indian National Congress, whom I had known well in Hyderabad as a student activist in the 1950s, invited me and my colleague Prof P.C. Joshi for a discussion on the political framework required for initiating and implementing pro-poor policies. In the course of the discussion he hinted at the need for amending the Constitution for carrying forward the progressive agenda smoothly. At this I told him that, as it is, the Constitution provides ample scope for moving forward in the desired direction and any step to amend the Constitution at this stage would create avoidable misunderstanding, suspicions and opposition. Presumably, this discussion with us was a part of a series of consultations he was holding on the issue with 'friendly' intellectuals.

Subsequently, I received a letter from Shri U.S. Rathia, M.P., dated 29 December 1976, regarding a special publication proposed on "The Emergency: Its Impact", which was to include various aspects of the achievements under Emergency—PM's 20-Point Economic Programme as well as the 5-Point national programme of Shri Sanjay Gandhi. On behalf of a Group of about 25 distinguished Members of Parliament and Union Ministers who agreed to be on the Board of Editors being constituted for this Project, he requested me to be a member of this publication.

This came to me as a big surprise. Apparently, the members agreeing to be on the Board were not aware of my views on Emergency. In all probability, they were guided by my strong support for the progressive policies of Mrs Indira Gandhi over a long period ever since she became Prime Minister. In any case, this letter had considerable potential for embarrassment.

Shri Rathia in his subsequent letter of 11 January 1977, requested me to write a comprehensive paper for the volume on "Emergency and Economic Development in India." He sent a reminder on 29 January requesting me to send my paper immediately, saying that the Prime Minister had decided to seek a fresh mandate from the people and they would soon get busy with elections. I then sent a reply on 2 February 1977, regretting my inability to prepare a paper. After this I did not keep track of this Project (See the Appendix to this chapter for the text of correspondence on special publication, *The Emergency: Its Impact*).

Appendix

Correspondence on Special Publication—The Emergency: Its Impact

U.S. RATHIA.
MEMBER OF PARLIAMENT
(LOK SABHA)
EDITOR.
'THE EMERGENCY : ITS IMPACT'.

Phone : 373673

15, North Avenue,
New Delhi - 110001.

December 29, 1976.

Dear Dr. Hanumantha Rao,

I am writing in regard to a special publication of national importance - 'THE EMERGENCY : ITS IMPACT'. This Research manuscript was presented to the Prime Minister on 7th August, 1976. Shri P.V.N.Rao, the then General Secretary of the AICC had gone through the manuscript and found it a fact oriented document worth publication.

This document, in a revised and enlarged version, is now ready for publication and will be presented to the Prime Minister on 26th January, 1977. 'THE EMERGENCY : ITS IMPACT' includes various aspects of the achievements under Emergency - PM's 20-Point Economic Programme as well as the 5-Point national programme of our youth leader Shri Sanjay Gandhi. Shri Fakhruddin Ali Ahmed, President, Indian Republic, has been requested to write a foreword for our publication. Shri Yash, Minister for Excise and Taxation, Punjab and Editor of Anushasan Parva, 75th Plenary Session, Indian National Congress, has accepted to

(.....2.....)

be the Editor-in-Chief. The other public spirited men and women, Shri V.B.Raju MP, General Secretary Indian National Congress, Shri Chandrajit Yadav, Minister of Steel & Mines India, Shri Shah Nawaz Khan, Minister of State Agriculture & Irrigation India, Prof.Siddheshwar Prasad, Union Deputy Minister of Energy India, Shri Prabhudas Patel, Union Deputy Minister of Agriculture & Irrigation, Shri B.Bhagavati MP, President INTUC, Shri Sat Pal Kapur MP, Shri S.R.Damani MP, Shri Khursheed Alam Khan MP, Smt. Amarjit Kaur MP, Smt. Lakshmi Kumari Chundawat MP, Shri Mohd. Yunus MP, Shri Mulka Govinda Reddy MP, Prof. Dr. Lokesh Chandra MP, Syed Nizamuddin MP, Shri Vasant Sathe MP, Prof. R.C.Mehrotra, Vice-Chancellor, University of Delhi, Dr. V.P.Dutt MP, Shri D.D.Puri Ex.MP, Smt.Leela Damodara Menon MP, Dr. Rajat Kumar Chakrabarti MP, Prof. P.N.Bisi MP, Shri Amar Nath Chawla, President DPCC, Dr. K.L.Nadir, Professor, Department of Humanities, I.I.T. Delhi, and Dr. Ram Mohan, Education-ist, have agreed to be on the Board of Editors for this Project.

(....3.....)

The 'Board' unanimously feels that a leader of your eminence would be aptly suited to be member of this prestigious publication of national importance. We shall feel highly obliged if you would kindly send us your consent.

With warm personal regards,

Yours sincerely,

U. S. Rathia

(U.S. RATHIA)

Dr. C.H.Hanumantha Rao,
Director,
Institute of Economic Growth,
University Enclave,
DELHI - 110007

SPECIAL PUBLICATION

THE EMERGENCY : ITS IMPACT

K-4, SOUTH EXTENSION-I, NEW DELHI-110049 TEL : 618450

January 29, 1977.

Dear Prof. Rao,

We request your attention to our letter of January 11, 1977,(copy enclosed for your ready reference). We are disappointed to have heard nothing in this regard from you so far.

The situation has slightly changed, as our beloved leader, Smt. Indira Gandhi has decided to seek a fresh mandate from the people. This publication must be ready for release before all of us settledown for the election work. We want Madam Prime Minister to release the book by the 3rd week of next month, as most of the members of the Board of Editors will soon get busy with their elections.

We would, therefore, request you to kindly send us a paper on the subject immediately so as to help us to keep to the new schedule.

With respects and regards,

Yours sincerely,

U. S. Rathia

(U.S. RATHIA)

Prof. Hanumanthayya Rao,
Director, Institute of Economic Growth,
University Enclave,
Delhi-110007.

SPECIAL PUBLICATION

THE EMERGENCY : ITS IMPACT

K-4, SOUTH EXTENSION-I, NEW DELHI-110049 TEL : 618450

January 11, 1977.

C O P Y

Dear Prof. Rao,

I have great pleasure in writing to you about the special publication of national importance THE EMERGENCY : ITS IMPACT. The purpose of this publication is to highlight the achievements of the Prime Minister's 20-Point Economic Programme as well as 5-Point National Programme of Shri Sanjay Gandhi. It will cover political, constitutional, social as well as economic aspects of our national developments. Besides, it will dwell upon the need for promulgation of emergency in India and the role that our Prime Minister is playing in the vital task of national re-construction.

Shri Fakhruddin Ali Ahmed, President, Indian Republic has been approached to write a foreword for the publication which is proposed to be presented to the Prime Minister. The first draft of the manuscript has already been presented to the Prime Minister a few months earlier. Shri P.V.N.Rao, the then General Secretary of AICC had gone through the manuscript and found that it merits an early publication in the national interest. With a view to make an

.....2/-

authoritative estimate of the impact of emergency on our national life and to portray emergency in its proper perspective, we are approaching you to help us by writing a comprehensive paper on Emergency and Economic Development in India. It should deal with Economic Policy of India : emergency and its impact on national economy.

This publication is meant to be circulated widely in India as well as abroad. We feel that without the help of known scholars of your eminence we would perhaps not be able to bring out the publication of national importance to an academic level that it really deserves. I may mention here that the subject is merely indicative of the broad based objectives, does not purport to define the range of issues that you may like to cover in your paper.

We had planned to present the publication to our beloved Prime Minister, Smt. Indira Gandhi on the Republic Day, but it may not be possible to keep to the schedule for various reasons. Now it is proposed to delay the presentation ofthe same by a month at the most. We will convey you the exact date of presentation as soon as the PM's office confirms the same.

With personal regards,

Yours sincerely,

Sd/-
(U.S. RATHIA)

Prof. Hanumanthayya Rao,
Director,
Institute of Economic Growth,
University Enclave,
Delhi-110007.

C.H.HANUMANTHA RAO

2 February 1977

Dear Shri Rathia,

Thank you for your letter dated January 29, 1977 and a copy of your letter dated January 11, 1977. I am surprised to find that your letter of January 11 did not reach me.

The time now left is too short for me to be in a position to write a comprehensive paper on 'Emergency and Economic Development in India'. I am, therefore, extremely sorry for my inability to prepare a paper.

With kind regards,

Yours sincerely,

C.H.Hanumantha Rao

Shri U.S.Rathia,
Editor,
The Emergency : Its Impact,
K-4, South Extension I,
New Delhi-49

3

Four Years (1982-1986) in the Planning Commission

The Leadership of Indira Gandhi and Rajiv Gandhi

I

Indira Gandhi

I felt a lack of enthusiasm, if not fatigue, at the Economic Administration Reforms Commission headed by L.K. Jha, to which I was appointed as a member in April 1981, even before I completed a year there. This was primarily due to my reservations on some of the reforms being recommended which I thought were too radical and did not also feel comfortable with a negative role in which I found myself for most of the time, even though those reforms appear, in retrospect, as too mild and timid! Nevertheless, despite my personal relations with L.K. Jha being cordial, I had made up my mind to leave the Commission after the completion of one year and get back to the Institute of Economic Growth (IEG). I had even conveyed this informally to Dr Arjun Sengupta, Secretary to the Prime Minister.

A little later, when Prof M.S. Swaminathan left the Planning Commission to take over as Director-General, International Rice Research Institute (IRRI) at Manila, I was invited to join the Planning Commission. I joined the Commission with a measure of enthusiasm as the idea of development planning had been a source of inspiration for all my research work in economics, and subjects like Agriculture, Rural Development, Welfare of SCs (scheduled castes) & STs (scheduled tribes), Backward Area Development, etc., which I was asked to deal with in the Commission were close to my heart.

When I met Prime Minister Indira Gandhi immediately after I joined the Planning Commission in April 1982, she expressed her happiness over my joining the Commission. A few days later she convened a meeting at the Prime Minister's Office (PMO) where she asked me and Pranab Mukherjee, who was appointed as Finance Minister around that time, to make a presentation on the resources position. I learnt later that she expressed her satisfaction about my presentation in which I had emphasised the need for raising public investment by mobilising resources through widening the tax base and reducing inessential subsidies.

Emotional integration among diverse groups is possible when they can experience a sense of belonging to the

Planning Commission Meeting in 1982 with Mrs Indira Gandhi as Chairperson

larger entity. This comes about when every one has a stake in nation-building, giving rise to the feeling that their aspirations can be fulfilled within the system through democratic and peaceful means. The feeling of alienation is bred when there is a sense of neglect and discrimination; and, worse, when there is no hope of redressing through democratic and peaceful means.

A sense of belonging and possibility of redressing and, therefore, confidence in the system was promoted during her tenure by giving a broad-based developmental orientation to the goal of national integration, involving, among others, the far-flung Himalayan and north-eastern regions, and the poorer and the under-privileged sections at large in the country.

Recall the events of the mid-1960s when national sovereignty came under severe stress because of 'ship-to-mouth' existence by having to import as much as 10 million tonnes of foodgrains annually. She brought the country out of this crisis through her bold decision to usher in 'green revolution', and by extending it to the states in the eastern zone in 1980s, for consolidating food security.

Economic integration of North-Eastern states and the Himalayan region with the rest of the country was achieved through their rapid development by according them the status of Special Category States, whereby 30 per cent of total plan outlay of the country was preempted for them. They are increasingly becoming part of the national mainstream. We now find quite a few boys and girls from these regions studying in several colleges and universities in different parts of the country and employed in different departments, especially of the Central government.

Another major contribution by her towards national integration was to align the aspirations of the poor and the under-privileged with the national development effort. Her decision to nationalise commercial banks and to expand banking to the hitherto un-banked areas, particularly rural areas, contributed significantly to raising the saving rate in the economy, and helped to provide resources for innumerable small entrepreneurs, farmers and artisans. Apart from the second round of land reforms undertaken in the early 1970s and programmes for the uplift of small and marginal farmers, a number of poverty alleviation programmes, e.g., Integrated Rural Development Programmee (IRDP), National Rural Employment Programme (NREP), Rural Landless Employment Guarantee Scheme (RLEGS), Minimum Needs Programme (MNP), etc., were launched from time to time during her long tenure.

Scheduled Caste Component Plan (SCP) and Integrated Tribal Development Projects (ITDP)—which have been in the headlines recently for their severe neglect and diversion of resources meant for them—were started and their performance rigorously monitored during her tenure. As one dealing with these subjects in the Planning Commission, I was a witness to her spending long hours, some times till late in the evenings, reviewing the implementation of these programmes with the representatives of the Central and state governments. I recall one such meeting she held with Chief Ministers to review the implementation of programmes for tribal development, on 13 July 1984, where she expressed concern over the lack of involvement by the voluntary organisations in these areas; suggested the involvement of tribal labour cooperatives in place of the contractor system; and stressed the desirability of land allotment for the rehabilitation of displaced tribals.

I recall an occasion when Gopi Arora, her adviser in the PMO, suddenly dropped at the Planning Commission to tell me that the PM read my Tour Report of Bihar in which I had pointed out that the actual or market wages in rural Bihar were much lower than the minimum wages fixed by the government, and that she is keen to know the measures needed for raising market wages. I explained to Gopi Arora that rural wages are highly sensitive to the demand for labour in agriculture and that policy measures to step up agricultural growth in Bihar would be the best way to raise market wages.

It is, therefore, no exaggeration to say that the greatest contribution of Indira Gandhi in the field of economic planning was to make the whole planning process relevant to the common people of the country, whose expectations and enthusiasm were aroused and whose active involvement in the movement for social justice became real.

She was not oblivious to the ecological degradation caused by reckless denudation of forests and the resulting problems of floods, soil erosion and loss of livelihoods of the poor, especially tribals. Development without destruction became a guiding principle of planning with her active intervention and guidance. Denudation of forests slowed down because of special measures undertaken for afforestation of degraded areas and social forestry. Clearance of development projects from the environmental angle became mandatory and a separate Ministry of Environment was created with necessary institutions to oversee the observance of mandatory provisions.

Such development activities undoubtedly helped to isolate the fundamentalist forces, whether religious or Left-Wing extremism. If the latter has emerged as the biggest threat to national security now, it is for introspection whether these programmes have been pursued with the same vision and commitment as Indira Gandhi had done. It is on the strength of the performance of such programmes that she came back to power in 1980. It appeared then that the whole nation stood as one behind her, the core support coming from the poor and the underprivileged.

Economic Planning in India and the Seventh Plan

Administering licenses and various controls on trade and industry—partly a wartime legacy—can not be regarded as essential to the planning process. Except for this, however, planning as such in India has never been as bureaucratic and centralised as in socialist countries like the Soviet Union. Thanks largely to the democratic framework and the multi-party system, planning in India has never been more than indicative in practice. The achievements, whether in respect of growth or social indicators, have invariably fallen short of the targets for most states as well as the centre. Expenditure targets were rarely adhered to and have been subject to changes through discussions and negotiations between the centre and the states on the one hand, and between the central ministries and the Planning Commission, on the other.

Over a period of time, economic planning, especially in the post-Nehru era, increasingly acquired bureaucratic overtones. States and Central ministries were required to turn to the Planning Commission frequently for the allocation of resources through the approval of their plans and projects, although this was not an essential ingredient of planning.

Like many of my colleagues in the Planning Commission, I subscribed to the view that there is a need to step up public investment in physical and social infrastructure, particularly because this would stimulate private investment. For this to happen, the expenditure on subsidies had to be reduced by targeting them to the deserving sections. Public enterprises needed to made competitive by ensuring to them autonomy in decision-making in respect of pricing, investment and management in general. Raising plan size by mobilising resources, reducing subsidies and other inessential expenditure could lead to broad-based development by stepping up investment in the less developed regions and enlarging benefits to the weaker sections of society. These considerations were kept in view while preparing the Seventh Five Year Plan and determining its size.

But the Finance Ministry thought that it would be difficult to finance a 'large' plan of the size proposed. In the full meeting of the Planning Commission where a number of cabinet Ministers were present, members of the Commission explained how the plan size as contemplated was possible and necessary to achieve the targets in respect of growth as well as social development. At this

R. Venkataraman, then a Cabinet Minister and a former Finance Minister, suggested that the growth targets as contemplated can be achieved even without the increase in plan size as proposed if productivity from the existing resources is increased. Responding to this, I pointed out that improving productivity and efficiency in resource-use was built into the projections made by the Planning Commission, so much so, lowering plan size without lowering the growth targets will not carry credibility. Persuaded by the presentation from the Planning Commission, the Prime Minister approved the size of the Seventh Plan as proposed.

On the morning of 31 October 1984, when I was having bath at 3, Safdarjung Lane, New Delhi, where I and my wife were staying, I could spot through the window some unusual running about in the Prime Minister's house, only a few yards away across the lane. Within minutes, our domestic help came running to us breaking the shocking news of her assassination. I was scheduled to meet her soon to discuss the Plan for extending green revolution to the Eastern Region which she had asked me to prepare in the Planning Commission. Instead, sadly, I had to give a talk at the All India Radio on Indira Gandhi's Contributions to Economic Planning in India.

II

Rajiv Gandhi

I first met Rajiv Gandhi when I was in the Planning Commission and he, as General Secretary of the All India Congress Committee (AICC), invited me to deliver the Keynote Address at a seminar on "Development of Agricultural Sector with Specific Reference to Small Farmers" organised by the AICC on 20 May 1983, at Vigyan Bhavan, New Delhi. I found him very courteous and warm, and keen on clarifying issues confronting agriculture and the role of small farmers. In his own presentation, among other things, he emphasised the need to extend green revolution to new areas like the Indo-Gangetic Plains

Planning Commission Meeting in 1985 with Shri Rajiv Gandhi as Chairperson

and bringing banking to the doors of farmers. Giving the example of his own constituency (Amethi) where recovery of credit was 65 per cent, he thought recovery would not be a problem when credit is productively utilised. He also thought that our education system must be geared to the farmers' needs. Otherwise, they would leave farming when educated.

Immediately after he assumed office as Prime Minister, following general elections, I felt that, perhaps, members of the Planning Commission should submit their resignations, as the new PM may like to reconstitute the Commission. But there was also a different opinion that there was no need to do so, as the new PM belongs to the same party which has been in power. I then hurriedly consulted Nitin Desai who has been Advisor in the Planning Commission for a fairly long period. He was very clear and categorical that propriety demands submission of resignations. He even pointed out that such occasions did arise in the past and members had to resign. Without losing time and in order to make doubly sure, I immediately telephoned Krishnaswamy Rao *saheb*, Cabinet Secretary, and told him that I am thinking of sending my resignation. He immediately said "you are doing the right thing." Upon this I told him that my resignation letter would be there within a few minutes. The same day in the evening I received a call from P.C. Alexander, then Principal Secretary to the PM, saying "the PM would like to continue you in the Commission" and whether I would be willing, upon which I conveyed my acceptance.

Within a few weeks of taking over as Prime Minister, Rajiv Gandhi held an informal meeting with the members of the Planning Commission. He was forthright and appeared very concerned and restless. He said he would like to fully speak out his mind now and members can have their say on a later occasion. What he said then with some passion can be summarised briefly as follows: Planning Commission is basically involved in the routine work of moderating the proposals from Ministries and putting them together as a Plan. As such, Planning Commission does not do planning. Planners ought to be looking ahead at future scenarios for sectors like energy, water, etc., for choosing the efficient path among different alternatives, considering their relative costs and benefits and other relevant issues. Planning Commission should become a think tank rather than reduced to a bureaucratic machinery.

It was clear from his utterances at this very first encounter with the Planning Commission that he was forward-looking, highly technology-conscious, keen on inducting talent and expertise in the processes of Planning and decision-making, and moving fast by cutting down delays. His vision was one of managing the economy in a better and more efficient way. In this sense he anticipated economic reforms of the early 1990s, but with a zeal for technological change, raising productivity and efficiency, decentralisation and peoples' participation. Very soon it became clear that he had high hopes from the introduction of new technologies like information technology and biotechnology, on the one hand, and from decentralised management by empowering people at the grass roots, on the other. He was deeply suspicious of power brokers and middlemen, as they caused leakages of resources as well as distortions in their allocation.

It was also clear that he was no ideologue, and was pragmatic. For instance, at the first full meeting of the Planning Commission after he took over, held on 7 February 1985, he stated that there was a need for re-look not in terms of basic ideologies but in terms of translating effectively ideologies and policies. There was a need to think big and ahead, and to provide outlets for individual initiatives. He was not against subsidies as such. He said food and fertiliser subsidies were a fact of life and so it would not be practical to remove them altogether.

His vision for achieving social justice was to integrate growth with equity without sacrificing productivity. For example, he was against emphasising 'labour-intensive' methods but favoured employment generation through higher, broad-based growth by reorienting employment in those areas which are efficient and productive.

There was a concerted move by some of the new members to reopen the question of the size of the Seventh Plan with a view to scaling it down, which would have adversely affected the allocations for agriculture, irrigation, rural development, area development and social sectors, even though the Plan was approved by the National Development Council with Mrs Indira Gandhi as Chairperson. But at a meeting of the Commission to discuss the plan size Rajiv Gandhi, after listening to the views of the members and comparing the increase in the size of the Seventh Plan with the increase in the Sixth over the Fifth Plan, said there was no basis for pessimism and cutting down plan size by scaling down the goals would only build frustration. Thus the size of the Seventh Plan (1985-1990), as originally proposed, was approved again. Prof Manmohan Singh, the then Deputy Chairman of the Planning Commission, in his Preface to the Seventh Plan document wrote:

> As regards the financing of the Plan, in broad macro terms, the Plan is eminently bankable and credible, as it projects only a modest increase in the rate of investment and domestic savings during the Plan period.

Of the two major initiatives taken by Rajiv Gandhi, viz., introduction of information technology and PRIs (panchayati raj institutions), the former met with great success whereas the latter is still moving at a snail's pace. When he first talked of information technology in the mid-1980s, the skeptics far outnumbered the votaries even in the Yojana Bhavan, though skepticism was confined largely to private gossip! I remember Prof Yash Pal, the Chief consultant in the Planning Commission, quietly dropping into my room one day to sensitise me on the benefits of using information technology in the execution of anti-poverty programmes like IRDP involving millions of poor households, and explained to me how the whole programme can be monitored right from the Yojana Bhavan. Within less than quarter of a century, this technology has become a major driving force for Indian economy engulfing millions of enterprises, households and even 'unskilled' labour throughout the country! This is obviously explained by the strength of the technology itself—its immediate, tangible benefits with low cost, without any adverse effects on health and environment.

Decentralisation of development through PRIs, on the other hand, was destined to be a slow process because of resistance from the entrenched interests in our society and polity. At one of the meetings of the Task Force on this constituted by the Prime Minister, which included L.C. Jain, Pai Panandikar and B.K. Chandrashekar, finding him and some members quite optimistic about the prospects for decentralisation through *panchayats*, I tried to put in a note of caution by saying that empowering the rural poor is not easy because of the stranglehold of vested interests like big landowners, moneylenders and contractors. Mani Shankar Aiyar, who was the convener of this Task Force, also intervened to suggest that initiatives are needed simultaneously to weaken the hold of vested interests, if PRIs are to succeed in rural areas. To be sure, thanks to the 72nd and 73rd Amendments to the Constitution, following the lead given by Rajiv Gandhi, we now have millions of elected representatives at the grass roots level who, by themselves, are becoming a major driving force for rural transformation. But political will to empower them through the devolution of adequate functions, finances and functionaries is called for.

A number of initiatives were taken during Rajiv Gandhi's tenure towards liberalisation of the economy and its market orientation by dismantling unnecessary controls and regulations in the sphere of industry and trade. For this, the recommendations of the Economic Administration Reforms Commission (EARC) headed by L.K. Jha were implemented. In fact, it was widely rumoured that the appointment of the Jha Commission by Mrs Gandhi in 1981 was itself prompted by the wishes of Rajiv Gandhi when he was General Secretary of the AICC. If Rajiv Gandhi was a pioneer among the Prime Ministers in initiating and implementing economic reforms, L.K. Jha was tenaciously so among civil servants.

With the measures for liberalisation of economy getting implemented in quick succession and with hardly any new initiative visible for removal of poverty, the impression was gathering momentum that Indira Gandhi's pro-poor policies were getting a short shrift and the government was becoming increasingly pro-rich. This was becoming evident from the attitudes, approaches and utterances of the political leaders as well as the senior bureaucrats. Around this time I was about to complete five years in the government, including a year at the Jha Commission. By this time, I was overtaken by fatigue and a lack of enthusiasm to continue. I decided to resign from the Planning Commission to resume my academic work at the IEG.

My responsibilities at the Planning Commission together with my membership of the Eighth Finance Commission and Economic Advisory Council to the Prime Minister kept me fully occupied. All these responsibilities culminating in the finalisation of Seventh Plan in the second round left me in a state of total exhaustion. In fact, Prof V.M. Dandekar in the course of a meeting with me at the Commission those days, seeing me tired, sarcastically remarked, "You should leave the Planning commission before you are fully drained!"

Apart from fatigue and lack of enthusiasm, I could never think of asking the IEG to extend my leave beyond five years, having implemented such rules myself strictly when I was Director there, even though Dr Manmohan Singh, the Deputy Chairman, wanted me to continue in the Commission and offered to try for the extension of my leave from the IEG. Thus, while my decision to leave the Planning Commission was driven by a number of factors, including, of course, the prospect of pursuing research work using my exposure to policy making in the government, I was struck by the general tendency to attribute such decisions to a single factor, in my case this being my unhappiness with the new economic policies or differences with the Planning Commission! After sending my letter of resignation to the Prime Minister I had to wait for quite some time to get his response, and there were indications from him, then in circulation, that I may have been driven to this step because of some problem within the Commission. This was evident from a telephone call I received from Sarla Grewal, Secretary to the Prime Minister, enquiring whether I was leaving on my own, to which I said 'yes' and requested for an appointment with the PM.

When I met him he was very cordial and pointedly asked me whether I have any problem in the Commission. At this I told him that I have no such problem, that I have already spent five years in the government, and now that the Seventh Plan formulation is complete, I am keen to get back to academic life, adding that I would be happy to assist him from outside. He immediately nodded with a gentle smile and began discussing the importance of technological change for raising productivity and efficiency. On my part I tried to supplement his observations with the need for institutional changes for ensuring peoples' participation and accountability in governance.

Well after I returned to the IEG, one could sense popular discontent in the country with economic policies, as they focused almost exclusively on liberalisation and market orientation. The emerging unrest led to the revival of policy interest on issues of social equity. As part of this renewed interest, Rajiv Gandhi tried to revive Indira Gandhi's 20-Point Programme by appointing an expert Advisory Committee on its implementation, asking me to be its Chairperson. He also constituted a National Commission on Rural Labour.

While his charm and earnestness were disarming, he also occasionally showed impatience, especially when he saw resistance to change from entrenched attitudes. Otherwise, he used to be quite informal and jovial in meetings and enjoyed an occasional friendly dig at colleagues, but with a sense of humour. On one occasion in the company of the members of the Planning Commission he said, "with all respects to the senior economists present here, I would like to mention a saying that economists are those who are heavily paid for making forecasts which often go wrong!" At this Dr Raja Chelliah who was equally forthright and relaxed gently retorted, "Sir, since we are not paid heavily, our forecasts can never go wrong!" The PM greeted the remark with a hearty laugh.

A very genuine and eloquent piece of appreciation for Rajiv Gandhi's personality came from N. Sanjeeva Reddy after he retired as President of the Republic, when I and my wife, while on a visit to the drought-stricken areas of Anantapur District in March 1986, paid a courtesy call on him at his native village. He and Mrs Reddy received us warmly and in the course of the conversation he mentioned about the visit of Rajiv Gandhi to their place only a week ago on his way to Tirupati. Pointing to the place where Rajiv Gandhi sat, described him as a very sincere young man who had inherited the great qualities of Pandit Jawaharlal Nehru!

The last time I and my wife met Rajiv Gandhi was at an investiture ceremony where Shyam Benegal and Dilip Kumar were awarded Padma Bhushan by the President of India. This was when he had been out of power for some time while Chandra Shekhar was the PM. When we saw him standing alone in a relaxed mood, we moved towards him. He immediately recognised us, gave a warm hand shake, and enquired from me about the progress of work on the National Commission on Rural Labour which I was chairing, and whether we are able to come out with useful recommendations. I told him we have made good progress and are busy giving final touches to our recommendations.

The first part of this chapter is based on the presentation made by the author at the meeting on the occasion of the Twenty Fifth Anniversary of Mrs Indira Gandhi, organised by the Intellectual Cell of the Andhra Pradesh Congress Committee, in Hyderabad on 30 October 2009; published in *Hans India*, Hyderabad, 30 October 2012.

4

Economic Reforms and Continued Relevance of Nehruvian Model of Equitable Development

Economic Reforms: Winds of Change in Planned Economies

Economic reforms in India in the sense of moving towards greater integration with the global economy by liberalising trade and investment and ensuring greater role for the markets with the role of the state in the economy restricted to certain essential activities, were very much in the air in the decade of 1980s before large-scale reforms were undertaken in the early 1990s in response to the BoPs (balance of payments) crisis. As a member of the Economic Administration Reforms Commission, headed by L.K. Jha, appointed in April 1981, I was party to a series of recommendations towards liberalisation of the economy, especially in respect of pricing and taxation.

In socialist countries like the Soviet Union, Peoples' Republic of China and Vietnam where centralised planning was rigorously practised, definite steps were taken in the 1980s to break away from the past and move towards liberalisation. In the Soviet Union, where the economy was relatively well developed and the urge for political freedom under the impact of democracy in Europe was intense, reforms towards political liberalisation (*glasnost*) assumed top priority, economic restructuring (*perestroika*) left to be determined by the emerging political framework. Political democracy, eventually established there, resulted in the demise of the socialist system itself and the development of capitalism, quite unanticipated by the leadership which initiated reforms. For instance, even as Michael Gorbachev initiated measures for free expression of views and debate, they were still discussing the 'Crisis in Capitalist Economies' quite oblivious of the simmering crisis in their 'Socialist Economy' which was to come into open very soon. This was evident from the discussions at the International Seminar on "Modern Peculiarities of the General Crisis of Capitalism" held at Moscow between 17-19 March 1987, to which I was invited by the Institute of World Economy and International Relations, Academy of Sciences, USSR. In retrospect, a plausible reason for this complacency appears to be blindness to ground realities due to the persisting communication gap for decades, sustained by the ruling ideology at different levels and the authoritarian political set-up.

Pre-reform China presented a picture of very low levels of living and low productivity of resources prompting the communist leadership there to give top priority to stepping up private investment and technological change through globalisation and the development of capitalism, ironically, under the authoritarian political set-up led by the communist party. My visits to China and Vietnam in the second half of 1980s provided opportunities to witness this compelling urge for change as well as the definite transition taking place, though in an embryonic form.

The drive towards economic liberalisation was already eight years old in China by the time I visited as leader of the Indian delegation from the Indian Council of Social Science Research (ICSSR) in October 1986 to participate in the joint ICSSR-CASS (Chinese Academy of Social Sciences) Seminar on Planning held in Beijing. In the course of the discussions at this Seminar as well as field visits thereafter, it was clear that the motive force behind liberalisation was the total disenchantment with what they called 'egalitarianism' practised for over two decades, including through the communes, to the utter neglect of growth and modernisation of the economy. They derided 'egalitarianism' openly and voiced frequently the dictum:

"Let some people become rich so that others can follow." This unprecedented development under the communist rule reflected the extremes to which communisation had been carried, to the neglect of growth.

For example, a disastrous consequence of one of their campaigns undertaken during the period of Great Leap Forward was the decline in agricultural output at the rate of nearly four per cent per annum consecutively for four to five years because of official prescription and enforcement of farm practises like the type of seeds to be sown and the amount of fertiliser to be applied, resulting in severe famine in the early 1960s. This was confirmed at a get-together in the course of the seminar in Beijing when an interpreter responded to my question about the extent of lives lost in this famine saying 'millions' in a hushed tone. The extent of this loss became debatable in India earlier when Prof Amartya Sen mentioned a similar high figure as vindication of his proposition that famines can not take such a heavy toll in a democracy like India.

This period was also characterised by the gross neglect of education and skills. In a flight to Shanghai, after the Seminar, I found a retired university professor seated by my side. Introducing himself, he explained to me how a whole generation of students lost education and training in skills during the 1960s and 1970s because of their participation in one campaign or the other. He also narrated how he was made to sweep the floors at the university under the supervision of his students!

The way forward towards reform they set for China was clear from what we saw in Shenzhen, a Special Economic Zone, in South China near Hong Kong. They had joint ventures there with foreign companies in the private sector from many countries. They were designed mainly to import technology, create employment opportunities and improve the skills of local labour (Rao 2005a).

I could sense a similar vision of policy shift towards growth and technological change during my visit to Vietnam as leader of the delegation from the ICSSR at the invitation of the Social Science Committee of Vietnam, in

December 1987. In Vietnam they were busy consolidating their gains from agrarian reform by measures to raise agricultural productivity. There were clear indications of improvement in the levels of living in rural areas. After visiting the countryside, we had a rare honour of calling on the legendary General Vo Nguyen Giap, who was elected Vice-Chairman of the Council of Ministers of the Socialist Republic of Vietnam in 1976, after the complete liberation of Vietnam and reunification of the country. As students at Nizam College in 1954, we used to talk with great admiration about his leadership in the historic battle of Dien Bien Phu when the French were decisively defeated in May 1954.

After the formal exchange of greetings and messages, as we were moving for tea, General Giap took me aside and said, "We have just now talked much about the greatness of our cultures and traditions, but all that is past; we are very underdeveloped and poor. We have to move fast now for modernising our economies through technological change and new ways of doing things." It was obvious that he did not want me to return home by taking too seriously all that was said about the greatness of our cultures and traditions but think in radically different ways for removing poverty and underdevelopment! His hurried utterances full of concern summed up his vision for reform and development for both the countries. It was indeed a unique moment to listen to the great General, fresh from the life-long battle for liberation, talking about the need for new ways of working for development.

Integrating Economic Efficiency with Social Equity: Groping for a New Approach to Economic Reforms

The growing awareness among the policy makers in India over the 1980s about the need for economic liberalisation was boosted further by the far-reaching changes witnessed in the socialist economies. But, in the wake of the debate on economic reforms and the implementation of some of these measures in India, in response to the BoPs crisis in the 1990s, apprehensions were expressed about the possible adverse impact on poverty and inequality, particularly on account of the speed, intensity and sequence of reforms being implemented. On the other hand, those in favour of speedy implementation of reforms contended that downsizing the role of the state considerably and relying on market forces would raise the growth rate of the economy significantly, which would lead to the alleviation of poverty and reduction of inequality through 'trickle-down' mechanisms. They regarded the collapse of the Soviet Union and the vigorous implementation of market reforms in China as vindication of their proposition.

Despite the absence of a broad consensus in the country, a number of market oriented reforms could be pushed through in the early 1990s primarily because of the immediate need to overcome the BoPs crisis by complying with the conditions required by the international financial institutions. In the Economic Administration Reforms Commission headed by L.K. Jha during 1981-82 as well as subsequently in the Planning Commission (1982-1986), my own plea on the need to proceed gradually and cautiously on economic reforms rested on two basic considerations. First, downsizing public investment in physical and social infrastructure would adversely affect the growth rate of GDP (gross domestic product) itself, especially because public investment would crowd in private investment. Secondly, the less developed regions and weaker sections of society who are already starved of essential infrastructure would be pushed behind further. Thus, release of market forces without strengthening the socio-economic position of weaker segments would worsen the poverty situation by widening the inequalities.

Prime Minister P.V. Narasimha Rao who piloted economic reforms in the early 1990s was himself conscious of the pitfalls in pursuing reforms hastily under Indian conditions. This was evident from his advocacy of 'middle way' while pursuing economic reforms at the international economic summit in Davos, and 'reforms with human face' in the country together with his resolve to focus on rural development and employment generation. But economic reforms continued to be implemented sporadically by the successive governments without any coherent strategy for integrating considerations of economic efficiency with those of social equity. In the process, agriculture, rural development, and social sectors like health and education suffered from neglect.

Intellectually, I was confronted with the basic issue of development strategy appropriate to Indian conditions in the context of on-going reforms and paradigm shifts witnessed in many of the countries, especially in the former socialist economies practising centralised planning. This exploration appeared difficult to me as against my earlier experience of a relatively smooth and spontaneous change from adherence to Marxism-Leninism to Nehruvian Socialism. This is because the Nehruvian Model was based on a proper understanding of the prevailing social structure in India which militated against social equity. Hence, the emphasis of this model on the need for social action and greater role assigned to the state.

This was vindicated by my field visits to various parts of the country and interactions with different sections of the population, as member of various Commissions and Committees constituted by the Government of India, in particular, as member of the Planning Commission and Seventh and Eighth Finance Commissions. In the Planning Commission, I was entrusted with the work on Perspective Planning, Agriculture, Irrigation, Rural Development, Area Development (including Himalayan Region and Western Ghats), and Development of SCs (scheduled castes) and STs (scheduled tribes). These responsibilities involved extensive interactions with people at the grass roots through field visits. I also had an opportunity of extensive visits and discussions with various stake holders in the course of the preparation of a Special Programme for Breakthrough in Rice Output in Eastern Sates, as asked by the Prime Minister Indira Gandhi.

My participation as a member of the Seventh and Eighth Finance Commissions, enabled me to take a view on the resource prospects for the Seventh Plan for the Centre as well as the states. There was a significant step-up in the devolution of revenues to the states as a result of the recommendations of the Seventh Finance Commission. The devolution of revenues to the states recommended by the Eighth Finance Commission was distinctly progressive, per capita transfers to the poorer states becoming significantly higher than the average per capita transfers. This pattern stood the test of time and continues to this day.

In the light of the experience of centrally planned economies I was convinced about the need for economic reforms, but the alternative of an almost exclusive reliance on market forces espoused by the exponents of reform, especially from the international financial institutions, did not appear to suit the Indian conditions. I was, therefore, keen to understand the process of economic reforms implemented and its consequences in other countries, especially in countries of the East and South-East Asia, particularly because high growth achieved by many of these countries over a number of decades with a relatively equitable distribution of gains was attributed by the votaries of reform almost entirely to the economic reforms implemented in these countries.

Before I could undertake such a study, I got an opportunity to have a fresh look at Indian agriculture in the context of economic reforms when the International Food Policy Research Institute (IFPRI), Washington D.C., invited me and Prof Ashok Gulati to work jointly on a paper "Indian Agriculture: Emerging Perspectives and Policy Issues" in September-October 1994 (Rao and Gulati 1994). Our findings from this study were two fold: first, agriculture would benefit from liberalisation and opening up of the economy through improved prospects for exports and favourable terms of trade, especially because reforms would result in removal of protection accorded to domestic industry. Second, agriculture can derive benefit from favourable demand, only if supply side factors like irrigation, power, roads, provision of institutional credit, marketing, etc., are strengthened through public investment in infrastructure. Clearly, reforms that

Meeting of the Seventh Finance Commission, headed by Justice J.M. Shelat, in 1977

Meeting of the Eighth Finance Commission, headed by Shri Y.B. Chavan, in 1982

undermine public investment by reducing the role of the state would adversely affect agricultural growth.

Subsequently, in November 1995, I was invited by the Economic and Social Commission for Asia and the Pacific (ESCAP), at Bangkok, to work as a consultant for four months to coordinate a study on "Rural Poverty Alleviation and Sustainable Development in Asia and the Pacific" (ESCAP 1996). This turned out to be a fruitful experience as I could study the individual country experiences in the region in the wake of economic reforms (Rao 1996). It was clear from this study that several countries in East and South East Asia could successfully embark upon economic reforms because of relatively well-developed initial endowments of physical and social infrastructure like irrigation, power, roads, education, health, and institutional credit and markets. Also, land reforms had been implemented effectively in many of these countries well before economic reforms were introduced. These initial advantages enabled these economies to derive full benefit from economic reforms resulting in high growth rate in GDP as well as speedy removal of poverty (Rao 2005b).

Involvement in this research project, completed in 1996, proved to be an eye opener for me, as it helped to clarify my thinking on major issues of economic reform after 15 years of intellectual churning beginning from 1981 as a member of the Economic Administration Reforms Commission.

From my experience of this research project, I realised that whereas I was vindicated about my understanding of the socio-structural constraints to equitable development in India in the wake of globalisation, I was rather slow to see the overall benefits of liberalisation and globalisation to the economy. In retrospect, I attribute this slow perception partly to the ideological hang-over from my adherence to Marxism-Leninism since my student days. Second, my specialisation in and dedicated application to the study of a particular subject like agricultural economics meant inadequate attention to the study of macroeconomic issues and policies.

In India, exclusive attention to market-oriented reforms in the 1990s with a fragile infrastructure, far from leading to high GDP growth, as anticipated, resulted in sharp deceleration of agriculture growth, widespread rural unemployment and distress for over a decade. The mass discontent, so accumulated, manifested itself after 15 years of economic reforms when, in the general elections held in 2004, the government of the day suffered an electoral defeat despite a high GDP growth rate of over 8 per cent achieved in that year! This brought home the adverse consequences of pushing through economic reforms with an eye solely on raising the GDP growth rate to the utter neglect of the pattern or content of growth.

The new government was quick to realise the need for pursuing growth with social justice. Achieving 'inclusive growth' became the prime goal of the Eleventh Five Year Plan. Interestingly, around the same time, China too which had pursued economic reforms vigorously, changed focus in its Eleventh Five Year Plan to achieving 'social harmony'. In India, for ensuring inclusiveness in growth, the National Advisory Council headed by Sonia Gandhi (where I was a member during the tenure of UPA-I), constituted by the new government, recommended a series of measures like Employment Guarantee Act, Right to Information Act, Forest Rights Act, Food Security Act, and The Right to Fair Compensation and Transparency in Land Acquisition, Rehabilitation and Resettlement Act, etc.

These developments underscore the continued relevance of Nehruvian Model of Development for India in the post-reform era. In the Nehruvian model, private enterprise and markets had a significant place, within a democratic setting, since the beginning of economic planning in India. Only the relative roles of the State and market had to undergo a change with the role of markets and private enterprise increasing. The role of the state and public policy towards ensuring social equity or inclusiveness in growth continues to be important and challenging, as before.

5

Challenges of Post-Nehru Era

Jawaharlal Nehru laid the foundations for a secular, democratic and socialist state in India, in keeping with the basic goals of the national movement for independence. The constraints under which Nehru worked were many and serious: a highly stratified, multi-class, multi-caste, multi-lingual and multi-religious social structure; a society largely bound by traditional values and attitudes; enormous regional diversity characterised, among other things, by differences in regard to the levels of socioeconomic development and the degree of modernisation. As a superstructure, we inherited numerous political parties wedded to diverse sets of goals and patterns of functioning. The bureaucracy and the administrative system inherited from the colonial era were faced with the challenge of adjustment to the requirements of new India.

Amidst such diverse constraining factors, the unifying factors holding prospects for social change were the national goals of secularism, socialism and democracy, and the forces committed to these goals. As a leader, Nehru himself became a symbol as well as a rallying point for these ideals and forces. He was the biggest unifying factor for the movement to achieve these goals. He was as much a rallying point in the movement for the realisation of aspirations after independence as Gandhi was in the struggle for independence. In both cases, there was direct rapport between the leader and the masses and the party they led became increasingly an instrument in the hands of the leaders to organise the people and work for the achievement of the goals.

Nehru's biggest asset was the broad consensus that was built in the country around these goals even before Independence; and his own stature, built largely in the course of the struggle for independence, enabled him to put this consensus into shape by launching plans for economic development with accent on social welfare, within a democratic and secular framework. His work during the 17 years after Independence was concerned essentially with initiating and strengthening institutions for achieving these objectives.

Considering the constraints under which Nehru had to work, his achievements were spectacular. The policy of peace and nonalignment in international affairs and the path of planned economic development stand out prominently among these achievements. The Five Year Plans under his stewardship were mainly concerned with building up the necessary institutional and physical infrastructure for self-reliant growth with social justice. It is now clear that the rate of growth of GNP (gross national product) was higher in the Nehru era when compared to the 15 years of post-Nehru era. Also, the inequalities in income—in both the rural and urban sectors—seem to have increased in the post-Nehru era. Shortage of food, foreign exchange and savings were regarded as the three major constraints to growth in the 1950s and the 1960s. But, thanks to the infrastructure built and the imaginative policies followed in the Nehru era, we have now achieved near self-sufficiency in food, the saving rate has gone up to a level comparable to that in the middle and high income countries, and foreign exchange is no longer as serious a constraint as it used to be in the early phase of planning.

However, except for the measures to abolish princely states and intermediaries like *zamindars* and *jagirdars* almost at the dawn of Independence, no significant institutional changes were effected towards the redistribution of assets. The impressive legislation in regard to the ceilings on agricultural landholdings, for instance, remained largely on paper without any direct impact on the distribution of land. The policies of the

Nehru era, concerned as they were essentially with the development of infrastructure, appeared class-neutral. In practice, however, the affluent and the influential sections in rural as well as urban areas, who have better access to resources, knowledge and power, benefited proportionately more than the weaker sections from this growth of infrastructure. In particular, the rural rich and the dominant castes were very much strengthened economically as well as politically. They became 'vote banks' and were virtually in power in most of the States in the 1960s. This explains, more than anything else, the failure to redistribute land from the big landowners to the landless and the marginal farmers.

The superstructure of 'politics of consensus', which was the characteristic of the Nehru era, was built on economic policies which were apparently 'class-neutral' but in effect strengthened the affluent segments. The 'politics of consensus' and the economic policy restricted largely to infrastructure development pushed the goal of 'social justice' or 'socialism' very much under the carpet. The 'politics of consensus' itself came under severe strains with the exit of Nehru. The emergence of the rural rich who increasingly sought alliance with obscurantist forces in urban areas was a natural outcome of the 'politics of consensus' and economic policy confined to infrastructure development.

The emergence of the poor, the downtrodden and the underprivileged sections (scheduled castes and scheduled tribes, minorities, etc.) as a force for social change has been the dominant characteristic of the socio-political scene in India for a decade now. Population growth, the rise in inequalities in income which has increasingly demonstrated to the poor the cornering of benefits by the rich, the growth of education and general awareness have contributed to sustaining and deepening this awareness among the poor over this period. In terms of opinion formation and consciousness, it is remarkable that the poor and the underprivileged have emerged on the Indian scene decisively as a dominant force cutting across all the known diversities from North to South and from East to West. Thus, the greatest event of the post-Nehru era so far has been the rise of the poor and the underprivileged of this country against economic and social injustices with expectations for their betterment through the instrument of state power.

It should be recognised that the 'politics of consensus' was not the product of the post-Independence period, but was inherited from the national movement for independence and lasted as long as Nehru lived and worked. The logic of development in post-Independence India has been such as to put such politics under severe strain. A new consensus has to be built around the national goals of speedier economic growth, removal of poverty and national unity and integration. The aspirations of the poor and the underprivileged constitute the single largest force which can bind the country together despite its innumerable diverse and conflicting interests. In fact, the country is held together today by such a force. Therefore, for a country as diverse as India, the emergence of the poor and the underprivileged as a dominant force has become a necessity for its survival and growth as a nation, in the absence of the 'politics of consensus' handed down from the movement for independence.

Despite the three decades of planned economic development, the per capita income of India is among the lowest in the world. Worse still, the rate of growth of per capita GNP, which is a mere 1.5 per cent per annum, is about the lowest among all countries. Except Bangladesh, Burma, Nepal and Bhutan bordering us in the sub-continent, we are surrounded by countries which have been experiencing a much higher rate of growth in per capita income. Also, despite the differences in political and social systems, economic as well as social inequality and the proportion of people below the poverty line in these countries are lower than in India. It is, therefore, clear that we have failed so far to exploit the tremendous opportunities available for a large country like ours to step up the rate of economic growth and consolidate the forces for economic and social justice. Without these, it is impossible for the country to occupy its rightful place in the comity of nations.

The increase in inequalities is leading to deficiency of demand even in regard to essential commodities like foodgrains. Owing to deficiency in domestic demand, export orientation to the economy is becoming increasingly necessary to sustain even the limited growth we have been able to achieve. 'Self-reliance' in the true and fundamental sense implies increasing absorption of food, labour, equipment and skills within the domestic economy for achieving rapid and self-sustaining growth.

The slow growth as well as the adverse distribution of benefits is attributable to the emergence of a small minority of privileged groups which are able to avail of the opportunities for growth and corner the benefits. These groups consist of big business interests, traders, contractors, rich farmers, the highly paid and highly organised workers in the strategic sectors of the economy, etc. These groups are able to benefit despite extreme inefficiency in the utilisation of the available resources and the resulting slow growth, because of their bargaining power and access to resources and subsidies. The vast majority of the poor in the country consisting largely of the rural poor are unorganised and have, therefore, benefited least from economic growth. There is thus a conflict between the objective of speedier economic growth with better distribution of benefits on the one hand, and the interests of these privileged groups on the other.

The biggest challenge in the 1980s in India is to evolve an institutional framework which can ensure effective management of the infrastructure built and a proper flow of benefits to the vast masses of the unorganised poor. In the ultimate analysis, the latter can be ensured through rise in consciousness and unity among the poor themselves. The spread of education, particularly adult and primary education, development of the language press on an autonomous basis with state support, use of the public communication media for education of the masses and, above all, the democratic process of periodic elections for the formation of popular governments are indispensable for this purpose. However, the role of the state as vanguard in this process is extremely important.

The question of institutional framework is not one of democracy versus dictatorship. The problem is essentially one of undertaking a critical review of existing political arrangements and the bureaucratic system with a view to identifying the elements which have served to retard growth and prevent institutional changes for the improvement of the lot of the poor. It is only through such identification that it will be possible to think of viable alternative arrangements. It is clear, however, that no system is sacrosanct forever and a dynamic system has to adapt itself, to the extent necessary, to the requirements of growth and social justice.

Certain imperatives are, however, clear from the experience of the working of the socio-political system in India in the last three decades. The foremost lesson is that the three goals of democracy, secularism and socialism are inevitable as well as indivisible. Given the social structure as well as the nature and magnitude of the problems faced in India, there is no alternative to pursuing these goals simultaneously. In view of the prime importance of the goals of speedy economic growth and removal of poverty, the democratic framework has to be appropriately strengthened, for example, by empowering the common people through effective decentralisation of governance, to subserve these goals.

Experience has shown that these goals are indivisible. For instance, it is not possible to ensure justice to the poor by dismantling the democratic framework. Such a step can harm the very poor for whose service the authoritarian framework is employed. The greatest danger inherent in such a framework is the loss of communication channels between the vast masses of the poor and those in authority. The communication gap feeds on itself and becomes increasingly serious and, in a large and diverse country like India, such a gap can inflict the greatest harm on the poor themselves. Similarly, experience has also shown that obsession with the goal of democracy to the neglect of other goals can inflict the greatest damage on the democratic framework itself. If, in the name of democracy, the privileged classes derive maximum benefits to the neglect of the poor, then this is the surest way of destroying the democratic framework.

Mainstream, 15 November 1980.

Epilogue

Mrs Indira Gandhi's initiatives towards removal of poverty and protection of environment amounted to carrying forward Nehru's legacy in the changed circumstances, as her policies were quite in keeping with Nehru's vision of equitable development. Even as she pursued measures for the removal of poverty, Indira Gandhi pioneered economic reforms in the country by appointing Economic Administration Reforms Commission headed by L.K. Jha in 1981, with me and R. Tirumalai, a retired IAS officer of the first batch, as members. Rightly, she did not believe that there was any inherent conflict between the goals of equitable development and liberalisation and de-bureaucratisation of economy.

L.K. Jha Commission made a series of recommendations for liberalisation of the economy through deregulation in the spheres of taxation, pricing, investment etc., within the framework of a mixed economy. The pursuit of these reforms was continued with greater vigour by Prime Minister Rajiv Gandhi culminating in far-reaching reforms undertaken by Prime Minister P.V. Narasimha Rao and the then Finance Minister Dr Manmohan Singh, in the wake of BoPs (balance of payments) crisis of the early 1990s.

These reforms released the latent potential of our entrepreneurs for enterprise leading to an acceleration in the growth rate of GDP (gross domestic product). However, for a little over a decade, policies and measures for poverty removal and social development in general took a back seat resulting in deceleration in employment growth and rise in rural distress. These developments brought home the need for a balanced approach to economic reforms, after pursuing them for 15 years. Since 2004 pursuing 'reforms with human face' and the strategy of 'inclusive growth' became the guiding principles of economic policy.

The rise of GDP in the wake of economic reforms led to the bulging of middle class in the country, the upper echelons of whom are generally wedded to the philosophy of free market economy and insensitive to the plight of the poor and destruction of their livelihoods on account of unregulated exploitation of natural resources.

Of late, there has been a growing concern, world-wide, about the rising inequalities in income and wealth, global financial and economic crisis and global warming because of unsustainable use of natural resources. These are attributable to excessive reliance on the market forces. These concerns have served to emphasise the need for increasing role of the state and social action towards mitigating such imbalances and crises. They thus point to the continued relevance of Nehruvian vision in the post-Nehru India. For, the core of this vision is equitable development through appropriate state intervention in a mixed economy within a secular and democratic polity.

6

Indian Development

Options and Choices

The perspective of Indian development is fast becoming a matter of crucial concern for the polity of the nation. Taking into account the need for serious discussion on the state of our political economy and the options before the country, *Mainstream* (20 March 1982) published a contribution from a distinguished observer of the economic scene. It has roused considerable interest among opinion-makers. We publish here a response to that article from Dr C.H. Hanumantha Rao, eminent economist, who is at present member of the Economic Administration Reforms Commission. The discussion continues, and readers of *Mainstream* are invited to participate.

—Editor

The article "Indian Development: Options and Choices" (*Mainstream*, 20 March 1982), by a 'student of political economy'[1] has raised certain important issues concerning the alternative paths of development in India and the role of the Left movement. These issues have been debated ever since Independence and they seem to be eluding clarity even to this day. The Indian situation is so complex and unique that the received doctrines cannot provide ready-made answers and this is at the root of the so-called 'ideological crisis'. The author of this article has made a

1. The student of political economy whose article prompted the above debate was Prof Arjun Sengupta, then secretary to the Prime Minister, Mrs Indira Gandhi. He became Member, Planning Commission and later served as Chairnan, National Commission for Enterprises in the Unorganized Sector, 2004-2007.

significant and timely contribution by throwing fresh light on several pertinent issues.

Issues for the Debate

For the sake of convenience, let me summarise the main contents of the above article as I understand them before proceeding to offer my own comments on the formulations contained in the article.

The author argues that there is an inherent tendency for large industrial houses, monopolies and oligopolies to perpetuate and strengthen themselves, within the prevailing socioeconomic framework, if there are no restraints on them through public regulation. These monopolies may perpetuate high prices despite the continuous adoption of new technology, with a view to maintaining a high rate of profit. Owing to the limitations of domestic absorption at such high prices, they may increasingly find outlets in the markets abroad with the help of export subsidies. This may inevitably involve them in collaborations with multinational corporations on the one hand, and with surplus producing large farmers in the countryside on the other, with all the adverse economic and political consequences on the domestic front. According to the author, such an 'export-dependent' growth is to be distinguished from 'export-led' growth: the former is the consequence of a particular pattern of growth associated with monopolies whereas the latter would be characteristic of a situation where exports become a leading sector because of inherent comparative advantage.

The author makes a basic point in this context when he observes that in view of the large size of the country with a large segment of affluent population, general deficiency of domestic demand cannot be a constraint to overall growth in India, although this may be so for particular sectors. The author, therefore, suggests that a reasonably high rate of economic growth is possible through domestic absorption provided costs are reduced with appropriate regulations and development is made broad-based. The author underlines the crucial role of public sector not only as a countervailing power to the private monopolies and multinational corporations but also as a means for widening the industrial and agricultural base and for reducing inequalities.

Such a pattern of development, according to the author, is necessary for furthering the goals of independent foreign policy of peace and non-alignment, economic self-reliance, and reduction of poverty. As against this, 'enclave development' which would inevitably emerge under a neutral economic policy with a weak public sector, would generate socio-political forces which would work against an independent foreign policy, rapid economic development and wider distribution of benefits. Here is an opportunity for the Left to intervene and contribute towards the consolidation of the forces working for national goals of self-reliance, speedy economic growth and social justice. The failure to perceive and seize such an opportunity by the Left and other progressive forces could well lead to a major setback for the national endeavour to achieve the above goals and, therefore, for the future of the Left itself.

Development Experience

It is interesting to reflect on why the line of independent foreign policy, self-reliance through planned economic development and wider distribution of benefits of growth with accent on the removal of poverty, has come to stay. I would like to place these goals as national imperatives for a developing country like ours, which became free from colonialism. The goals of peace and non-alignment, democracy, secularism and socialism emerged out of the very process of our achievement of independence. These goals, which are in the nature of national imperatives, are also indivisible in the sense that one cannot be achieved to the exclusion of the others. A clear perception of imperialist manoeuvres and dangers to independent foreign policy is probably the most vital element contributing to the effectiveness with which leadership is provided.

India's survival as a strong nation-state capable of preserving its integrity is the foremost requirement on which depends the prospects of all development—whether of the capitalist or non-capitalist type. Indian history is full of instances when the rulers and society at large got lost in narrow internal grooves and became completely complacent and insensitive to external threats until the doors were knocked. Even those who subscribe to 'internationalism' as one of the principal tenets of their ideology have a tendency to become occasionally insensitive to external dangers and imperialist manoeuvres. In the Marxian analyses pertaining to the developing countries emerging to freedom from colonial rule, the primacy of the role of nation-state in its survival and development has been highlighted. Lenin was in the forefront in the debate on the role of nation-states, especially in the Asian countries, in preserving their freedom and integrity as a necessary condition for development. It was also recognised in those debates that imperialist manoeuvres would continue in various forms to destabilise these young nation-state so as to keep them economically weaker. It must, therefore, go to the credit of our present national leadership for perceiving clearly the imperialist manoeuvres to keep India weaker and for showing the necessary courage to face the challenge.

To give primacy to foreign policy and to consider internal policies in an integrated framework, has been part of our tradition handed down from the national movement for independence. This tradition has been very much marked in the case of certain Leftist parties subscribing to 'internationalism'. However, it is surprising to find the tendency to see the internal policies as being distinct from and unaffected by foreign policy. There can be some inconsistencies here and there for some time between the anti-imperialist postures and internal policies. But for a developing country like India, there cannot be any basic inconsistency between the two in the long-run.

As pointed out by the author, deficiency of internal demand is related to the pattern of development itself;

a broad-based industrial and agricultural development with adequate emphasis on the generation of employment would have a redistributive bias and would generate the necessary demand for goods and services. Enclave type of development, on the other hand, can yield a certain rate of growth, but would soon face an internal absorption problem and can be sustained only through export promotion. As rightly pointed out by the author, such a situation has to be characterised as export dependency rather than reflecting inherent comparative advantages that underlie spontaneous export-led growth.

Whereas the author believes that even under the existing socioeconomic framework, growth need not be constrained by the deficiency of internal demand, he does concede that enclave or elitist type of development can result in deficiency of demand and exports may become increasingly necessary to sustain such a growth. This would mean that improved income distribution is indispensable for sustained and viable development. It is, therefore, necessary to emphasise that there would be a complementarity between improved distribution of income and growth in our situation rather than a trade-off as is often believed. The author seems to concede the existence of a trade-off between growth and social justice in our situation, when he says that under the alternative path of the maximum spread of growth involving increasingly larger number of people, "the overall rate of growth of gross national product may not be as high as the model of monopolist-capitalist growth outlined above, but it can still be a reasonably high growth with social justice, with increasing emphasis on providing subsidies and incentives to the weaker sections and generating indigenous capacity for self-reliance".

The proposition that improved distribution may result in slow growth because of a decline in savings rate rests on static considerations. Diffusion of development in so far as it draws in larger sections of society into the growth process may contribute to the deployment of part of the savings for productive purposes which would otherwise be frittered away in consumption. Moreover, absorption of new technology and improvement in labour productivity through improved nutrition, health and diffusion of skills may be facilitated better in a pattern of growth where benefits are widely distributed. A more equal distribution of income and wealth can facilitate the acceptance of alternative institutional arrangements for mobilising larger savings, for increasing labour productivity and for disseminating new techniques.

The experience of agricultural development in India in the recent period fully bears out the proposition put forward by the author that the elitist pattern of development may cause a deficiency in domestic demand necessitating export orientation and that such a development may unleash forces which may articulate demands of the rich to the detriment of the interests of the rural poor and may eventually lead to political formation supporting obscurantist tendencies. The Green Revolution in India has been concentrated in a few prosperous pockets and among large farmers. Although the achievements have been substantial and we have achieved near self-sufficiency in foodgrains, per capita availability of foodgrains has not increased significantly because the gains represent essentially import substitution in respect of wheat. Despite the per capita availability remaining nearly the same, we had piled up foodgrain stocks of about 20 million tonnes for two to three years and it was seriously felt that it would be difficult to sustain agricultural growth without finding export outlets. This is because the growth process failed to generate necessary purchasing power for the rural poor, particularly in the less developed regions. The rural rich emerged as a powerful lobby during this period, pressing for higher prices and subsidies. Politically they have increasingly sought alliance with those forces in urban areas who pose a major threat to the movement for speedy economic development and the removal of poverty. Public investment in agriculture, particularly in irrigation, and for providing essential inputs to small and marginal farmers, especially in the less developed regions, would raise employment, productivity and purchasing power among these large sections of rural population, and would thus serve to counteract the power of the rural rich.

Public Investment

This brings me to the crucial role of the public sector in giving a proper orientation to the pattern of development. The author has rightly emphasised the need for stepping up public investment so as to expand the activities of the public sector. Such a strategy can contribute to stepping up the overall rate of growth because of the essential complementarity between the public and the private sectors at the present stage of development in India. The benefits of growth under such a strategy would be distributed widely by drawing in less advantaged sections into the growth process.

However, it is important to emphasise the need for a major reform of public sector management in India. Without ensuring proper autonomy for public enterprises, and without improving their managerial capabilities through training, proper recruitment methods, etc., the public sector in India cannot play its crucial role as a countervailing power vis-á-vis the monopolies and multinational corporations. In fact, the continued neglect of managerial reform has only contributed to strengthening the bargaining power of the big industrial houses and multinationals. A mere expansion of public sector is not sufficient. It is equally important to make it function more efficiently.

Role of the Left

From the operational point of view, the most important point made by the author is the convergence of interests of the Left in India and the forces led by Indira Gandhi for the achievement of the common goals of peace and non-alignment by resisting imperialist manoeuvres, rapid economic development and the removal of poverty, within a secular democratic framework. This, I think, is the crux of the problem. While the national goals, which in my view are in the nature of imperatives, remain the same as were handed down from the national movement for independence, the organisational apparatus working for such goals has been under severe pressure and has weakened gradually in the course of the last 30 years. This was, perhaps, inevitable because a multi-class political apparatus inherited from the pre-Independence period cannot survive the pressures of new challenges which have brought out sharply the clash of interests. Secondly, the corrupting influence of power enjoyed over a long period in a social framework like ours cannot also be ignored. The goals can remain pure and fresh, but the apparatus working for it can get rusted and polluted. A continuous renewal of such forces by drawing in the fresh and progressive elements who have the greatest stake in the fight for such ideals becomes necessary.

There is today a large organisational vacuum between the wide masses of the poor whose expectations have been aroused, and the leadership. Bureaucratic machinery cannot fill in this vacuum which can be filled only by political forces. I think the author has sharply posed here a challenge to the Left: whether they would be willing to muster their resources of patriotism and commitment to the betterment of the poor, and come forward boldly to help fill this vacuum. Given the necessary imagination and courage, the Left is poised to play a historic role in the furtherance of the goals of national integrity, planned economic development and socialism. Failure to perceive these opportunities on the part of the Left could well turn out to be a tragedy for the democratic, secular and socialist movement at this point of time in our history. Such a set-back can and must be avoided.

Having fully endorsed the author's plea, I would however like to ask the question as to why the Left has time and again missed such opportunities, especially in the course of the last 30 years. This is an extremely important question from both the intellectual and practical points of view. Unless there is a frank debate on this question, it would be difficult to understand the tragedy of missed opportunities and in the absence of such understanding the appeals to the Left may have only sentimental value without any practical solution emerging.

I am afraid, the Left has been groaning under the weight of its received doctrines, which do not permit it to see the realities of the Indian situation with a clear and open mind. The absence of a breakthrough on their part is explained by this doctrinal tradition. In almost all the socialist countries the success of forces of socialism represented the culmination of an anti-imperialist or an anti-fascist struggle, where such forces actually spearheaded the anti-imperialist and anti-fascist movements. In our situation the bourgeoisie held the hegemony of such a movement, although the Leftist parties have had a strong base among the working class and peasantry and some sections of the middle classes in certain parts of the country. The 'economism' of sectional approach has probably been a handicap, as against a national approach that would, as a rule, result when one has the hegemony of the national movement.

However, it has been in the tradition of the Left that in ideological debates pride of place is given to foreign policy and the characterisation of the government of the day. This highly desirable approach, nevertheless, does not get translated into a practical line for building up the mass movement for the achievement of the objectives. Attention gets focussed on whether to support or to oppose the existing Government rather than on continuously striving for the goals by mobilising the maximum possible support, including from the ruling groups. In the latter approach, the onus would lie on those ruling groups which are opposed to such goals. The existing approach of the Left, on the other hand, pre-judges the attitudes and the role of the ruling groups and thereby runs a great risk of alienating those who can be potentially mobilised for the furtherance of these objectives.

Preoccupation with the characterisation of the existing ruling groups may have been reasonable in certain countries where the correlation of forces was such that capture of power by the Left was in the realm of possibility.

However, for the Leftist movement in India, the major task would appear to be gradually and patiently build up the mass movement in furtherance of the objectives of secularism, socialism, democracy, and independent foreign policy. In this task, certain progressive policies of the Government and the mass support that is already created around such policies can become a great asset for the Leftist forces. What is needed is a modest and positive approach of building up the movement rather than of characterisation of the ruling groups into a certain fixed frame. The existing approach of excessive preoccupation with the characterisation of the Government to decide one's attitude towards Government has several dangers. First and foremost, it runs the great risk of misjudging the ruling class and, therefore, of mis-directing the whole movement based on wrong characterisation. Secondly, even if one comes out with the characterisation that the existing ruling groups need to be supported, the whole policy is focused on supporting the rulers rather than patiently building up the movement around the common goals.

For the reasons mentioned above, I think it would not be an easy task for the Leftist movement in India to play a positive role at this historic juncture without shaking off the weight of received doctrines and looking at the realities of Indian situation with a clean and clear mind. What is needed, above all, is a deep commitment to the solution of the day-to-day problems of the masses of the people and a good deal of modesty in approach. It is surprising that in a country with such problems of mass poverty crying out for solution, the ideological debates for decades together do not bring clarity. In many of the socialist as well as West European countries the Left has learnt to shed much of the doctrinal weight and think creatively by responding more to the felt and crying needs of society rather than getting bogged down in theological debates. The Indian Left has lagged very much behind other socialist movements around the world in moving towards ideological independence.

In the case of the Left in India, one finds a coexistence of sophisticated ideological debates, though unresolved for decades together, with their ready involvement in parliamentary politics as well as in the genuine trade union and peasant movements. It is their dedicated and untiring efforts and the sacrifices made in building up trade union and *kisan* movements over half a century that have contributed not only to raising the consciousness of the masses of the poor but also to strengthening their organised power. This constitutes a great asset not only to the Left but to the whole national movement for achieving the common objectives. In view of their declared policies, the secular and progressive elements in the ruling groups cannot afford to remain indifferent to the vast organisational potential that the Left can offer in large parts of the country for furtherance of the national objectives. Given the necessary imagination and initiatives on the part of the progressive sections in certain ruling groups as well as the Left, it should be possible to build up a wide consensus in the country for achieving the national goals.

Mainstream, 10 April 1982.

Epilogue

For over three decades since the above debate was initiated, there has been a further fragmentation of the Left with no clear evidence of indigenisation and creative adaptation of its ideology. As a consequence, the political clout of the poor and the marginalised sections appears to have diminished further. On the other hand, over the same period, in several countries, especially in Latin America, the Left has demonstrated remarkable creativity in its thinking and followed distinctly new strategies and forms of struggle that are peaceful and democratic, through the wider mobilisation of people. They have been able to achieve electoral victories on quite a few occasions, form popular governments and implement pro-poor policies with the support and active participation of the common people

The development experience in India has clearly demonstrated that progress towards achieving inclusive or equitable development is determined by socio-political pressures brought to bear on the ruling establishments not merely through electoral outcomes but basically by the organised movements of the poor and the marginalised sections. The rising awareness among the people at large, the role of progressive elements in many of the established political parties, the united voice of the Left parties, participation of an increasing stream of NGOs (non-government organisations), and effective articulation of the issues and events by an independent and pro-poor media are critical to this process of change.

While the working of the existing democratic system holds the key to the progress on these lines, the system of democracy we have adopted needs to be reformed so that it can more adequately reflect the aspirations of the poor and the marginalised sections. However, bringing about the desired reforms in the present democratic system is bound to be time-consuming and may have a chance of materialising when the system itself faces the crisis on account of its failure to deliver the results. But the debate on the needed reforms has to be pursued, even as the existing democratic system is fully utilised for carrying forward the socioeconomic agenda for equitable development.

7

Fighting Religious Fundamentalism

Role of Ideology and Social Policy

The incidents of Ayodhya on 6 December 1992 have thrown a big challenge to the secular and democratic forces. The idea of joint action by the secular and democratic forces has been gaining strength. From all indications available so far, the campaign against religious fundamentalism and against the exploitation of religion for political purposes is to be carried on at the ideological level. People in the country at large are to be explained about the secular foundations of our polity and about the virtues of secularism in a multi-religious society set on the path of development and modernisation.

While all this is necessary, it seems far from adequate to rally the people against religious fundamentalism and for defeating those seeking to exploit religion for political purposes. The events of the last few years do not lend credence to the view that this battle can be fought successfully on the ideological front alone. Such an approach would amount to falling into the trap laid by fundamentalists who would like to fight on their chosen ground where a pandora's box has been opened regarding the future location of the *masjid* and *mandir* and a host of issues relating to other places of worship.

The resolve by the secular forces to fight it out on the ideological plane represents, at best, a weak response to the formidable challenge posed by the forces of religious fundamentalism. Indeed, there is a total lack of understanding as to why the situation has degenerated to the point where the secular forces find themselves virtually in a defensive position in large parts of the country.

Whether in the pre-independence or the post-independence period, secularism or equal respect for different faiths has never been preached as an abstract ideal, in isolation from other secular issues. Secularism has been inextricably linked with the goals of national independence, economic development, modernisation and social justice. These goals were attractive enough to inspire and enthuse people at large to become active participants in the movement towards realising such objectives. At the same time, the loftiness of these goals brought home the pettiness, meaninglessness and futility of pre-occupation with sectarian and obscurantist issues, and indeed served to wean the people away from those seeking the path of religious fundamentalism. The latter, on the other hand, having a vested interest in status quo have always been interested in diverting the people's attention and energies away from the secular issues on the socioeconomic plane towards sectarian and obscurantist issues.

This is amply borne out by the history of the freedom movement under the leadership of Mahatma Gandhi. The goal of national independence became inseparable from the goals of secularism, self-reliance and freedom from socioeconomic injustices. In the immediate post-independence period, under a different set of circumstances, Jawaharlal Nehru carried forward this movement with a call for modernisation and development, among other things, by undertaking giant projects which he called 'Temples of Modern India'. Secularism continued to remain inseparable from the drive for modernisation, development and social justice.

The early post-independence period of expectations gave place to the concern for the equitable sharing of the fruits of development in the 1970s. Indira Gandhi charted out a secular path in this new phase by placing the objective of poverty removal at the top on the national agenda. Economic planning became relevant to the common people of the country in this period through the launching of several programmes for the uplift of the deprived and downtrodden sections of our people. The forces of religious fundamentalism could not raise their head because of the powerful backing from the people for the drive towards achieving social justice.

It is not accidental that the obscurantist forces started gaining strength after the mid-1980s when the concern for social justice and people-centered development began to be diluted. The package of economic reforms that followed no doubt enthused the upper strata of our society but created serious misgiving among the organised working class and apathy and disillusionment among the unorganised sections constituting the large majority of our population. The severe cuts in public outlays on essential infrastructure, social development and poverty alleviation have only strengthened these misgivings.

The forces of religious fundamentalism have been happy with the existing package of economic reforms, because some of the groups which benefit most from such reforms constitute the social base for those seeking to exploit religion for political purposes. But it should not come as a surprise if they, in their bid to exploit the general economic discontent, hijack some of the secular aspects of the national agenda by calling for a 'sustainable' package of economic reforms, or even by tagging '*roti*' and '*rozgar*' with '*Ram*'. However, they have a vested interest in perpetuating the prevailing social and economic inequalities and may resist any far-reaching measures for social justice.

No one would seriously question the need for economic reforms and restructuring in our country, particularly in view of what has happened in the socialist countries. But economic reforms in those countries came decades after basic changes were effected in socioeconomic structures and after high rates of capital accumulation and high levels of human development were achieved. A package of reforms without regard to the socioeconomic realities of our country is bound to sharpen economic dualism and result in widespread social discontent.

Even among the aid-giving institutions, there is a serious debate now on the need to reconcile the goals of economic efficiency with considerations of social justice in countries like India characterised by socioeconomic disparities and widespread poverty. Certainly, a political democracy like ours cannot afford to run the risks arising from the implementation of reform packages which have failed to yield the desired results even in countries under authoritarian regimes.

Slowing down of the present pace of economic reforms is considered by some as a necessary 'concession' to the Left for forging a united front of secular forces. These analysts do not realise that, in a political democracy, the secular forces, whether Centrist or Leftist, may lose the battle if they fail to inspire the common people to identify themselves with, and actively participate in, the tasks of economic development and social transformation.

From times immemorial, great philosophers, sages and saints in India have been preaching religious tolerance based on the essential unity of purpose among all the religions. Yet, time and again, religious fanaticism held sway over the minds of the people. In a modern democracy, preoccupation with worldly or secular issues on the socioeconomic plane involving active participation of the people can be more effective in combating religious fundamentalism than a campaign merely on the ideological or philosophical plane.

Mainstream, 13 March 1993.

8

Conditions Favourable to Economic Reforms in the Early 1990s*

Both Dr S. Chakravarthy and P.V. Prabhakar Rao were perceptive in observing that successful implementation of economic reforms requires three preconditions: the idea of reforms, the opportune moment for reforms and the right person at the helm of affairs to implement the reforms. Let me first trace the genesis and evolution of the idea of economic reforms in India. The need for economic reforms was first felt seriously at least a decade before 1991 when Prime Minister Indira Gandhi appointed Economic Administration Reforms Commission (EARC) in April 1981, headed by L.K. Jha.

The next time a serious debate on the need for a radical change in economic policy was initiated was in the early 1985 when Rajiv Gandhi took over as Prime Minister with a massive mandate after the assassination of Indira Gandhi. Some of the reforms towards liberalisation of the economy were initiated at that time, including those recommended by the L.K. Jha Commission, but not pursued consistently as other concerns got prominence soon. The drive for economic liberalisation did not get much support either at the political level or from the bureaucracy. There were even popular misgivings that Indira Gandhi's pro-poor policies were being given up and economic policy was becoming pro-rich. The simmering discontent prompted Rajiv

---

*: Concluding observations as chair at the Panel Discussion on "25 Years of Economic Policy Reforms: A Retrospection", jointly organised by The Hyderabad Management Association and the Centre for Economic and Social Studies (CESS), at the CESS, Hyderabad, on 28 July 2016.

Gandhi to revive Indira Gandhi's 20-Point Programme by appointing an Advisory Committee. He also appointed the National Commission on Rural Labour. It was clear that although the idea of economic reforms was being debated and gaining strength, the time was not yet ripe for any serious move in that direction.

Prime Minister P.V. Narasimha Rao had inherited the BoPs (balance of payments) crisis in the early 1990s. It is tempting to argue that but for the severe BoPs crisis faced at that time, economic reforms could not have been pushed through. But this would be an incomplete and a very limited view to take. We did face BoPs crises earlier too, but did not implement economic reforms of a far-reaching nature. The early 1990s became an opportune moment for introducing wide-ranging economic reforms mainly because of a radically different international scenario. China under the communist rule had embarked upon economic liberalisation way back in 1978 and by the early 1990s she had implemented economic reforms at a much wider scale than we could ever do. Soviet Union had virtually collapsed by the early 1990s mainly because of centralised bureaucratic planning practiced there ever since its inception. Under these changed circumstances, the elite in India—political, bureaucratic and intellectual—was becoming more receptive to reforms than in the 1980s. All these developments enabled the Prime Minister P.V. Narasimha Rao and the then Finance Minister Prof Manmohan Singh to covert the severe BoPs crisis faced then into an opportunity to bring about far-reaching systemic changes in the management of economy, unprecedented since the days of Pandit Jawaharlal Nehru.

When the measures for far-reaching economic reforms were being undertaken in quick succession under the leadership of the Prime Minister P.V. Narasimha Rao, there was an element of surprise at the decisiveness because of his earlier image of a very cautious and halting decision-maker. I tried to find out the on-going process of decision-making from my friend Prof Deepak Nayyar, who was then Chief Economic Adviser in the government and was leading several high-level delegations for discussions with the International Monetary Fund (IMF) and the World Bank. He categorically told me that the Prime Minister was quite decisive in taking every major decision and was putting his foot down on unwarranted fears and prevarications. There is no doubt that he clearly saw the need as well as the opportunity for bringing about systemic changes and was confident of managing change politically despite the obvious limitations of a minority government.

Economic reforms have come to stay in India and there is no question of reversing them. There is, of course, an unfinished agenda for reform which needs to be addressed. To my mind, the most important issue of reform waiting to be addressed seriously is integration of economic efficiency with social equity. So far, economic reforms were concerned basically with attracting investment resources and raising their productivity. Concerns for social equity were addressed in an ad hoc manner through welfare programmes such as employment guarantee. Such programmes are essential in the short-run to mitigate the distress caused to the weaker sections of society. But a long-term and sustainable solution, consistent with efficiency, is to devise a development strategy that is broad-based with a view to ensuring benefits of economic growth for the less developed regions and lower income groups through greater employment generation in the process of economic growth, social development such as public provision of universal education and healthcare and social insurance. This fits well into P.V. Narasimha Rao's vision of 'reforms with human face' or his 'middle-path'.

9

Twenty Five Years of Economic Reforms

*Remembering Shri P.V. Narasimha Rao**

As we complete 25 years of economic reforms in the country, we remember P.V. Narasimha Rao for successfully piloting these reforms and, equally significantly, for his personal commitment to reforms with human face.

I could see in the Planning Commission in the mid-1980s how Rajiv Gandhi was restlessly looking for fresh initiatives for bringing about basic changes in economic policy framework being followed in the country. But the fate had snatched him away and this historic task fell on the shoulders of P.V. Narasimha Rao. Around this time in 1991, India faced a severe BoPs (balance of payments) crisis. P.V. clearly saw the writing on the wall and responded to the challenge of crisis with courage and equanimity with a surprising measure of decisiveness. For this task he chose Dr Manmohan Singh, an eminent economist with vast experience in the government, as his Finance Minister.

A democrat instinctively or by temperament, P.V. was consensual in his approach. For nearly 50 years before he became Prime Minister, as a Congressman he was oriented to Nehruvian outlook on socioeconomic policies. He was a disciple of Swami Ramanand Teerth, a Leftist within the Congress in the old Hyderabad state. P.V. identified himself with and participated in the anti-feudal struggle in Telangana.

---

*: Based on the author's observations on the occasion of the launch of Sanjaya Baru's book, *1991: How P.V. Narasimha Rao Made History* (Aleph Book Company, New Delhi, 2016), at the CESS, Hyderabad, on 13 October 2016.

To understand the evolution of P.V.'s views on economic reforms, and indeed of the Congress leadership, it is instructive to go through his Presidential address at the AICC Plenary Session at Tirupati in April 1992 (see the Appendix in Sanjaya Baru's book).

In this Presidential Address P.V. traces how "in Nehru's view, both the models of a totally free market economy and communism or fully controlled economy have failed. We had to strike a balance between the two. Democracy permits fine-tuning of the roles of market and state from time to time.... as we look to the future, the fundamentals of the Nehru's vision remain entirely relevant from every standpoint".

He points out that "the priority given to basic industries was one of the major contributions of Nehru. It is this which has brought us to the point today where we are able to consider other options with confidence. We believe, however, that the stage has now come when we could review our strategy. Import substitution can not be an end in itself.... The criterion of self-reliance today has to be not whether you can make whatever you need, but whether you can pay for whatever you need...India can now achieve this by integrating itself with the world economy....We have, therefore, to reorient our previous approach to foreign capital".

He cautioned, that: "There is, however, one danger which we must recognise and guard against in the 'opening up' process. This could lead to wider disparities within society. To meet the situation, we have to enable the under-privileged sections also to derive the benefits of the new opportunities. The process would naturally need some time to fructify. Until that happens, there has to be a by-pass arrangement whereby benefits reach the lowest rungs of the social pyramid directly from the State. We are doing this." This is consistent with what he told the top official of IMF: The government would be happy to accept all good advice from the IMF so long as 'not one worker is out of employment' due to those policies.

Hinting at the need for long-term solution he said, "it is regrettably true that in Plan after Plan, the outlays on education and health, the key areas of human resource development, have received inadequate attention... They need to get pride of place in our programmes".

In the brief interregnum after the assassination of Indira Gandhi and until Rajiv Gandhi took over as Prime Minister again after the general elections, P.V. was the Deputy Chairman of the Planning Commission, and I had opportunities of interacting with him as a Member. He was keen that we should give employment orientation to our plan programmes. I remember discussing with various divisions in the Planning Commission to explore the possibilities of giving employment orientation to the Seventh Plan.

Because he had earlier initiated bold measures for land reform as the Chief Minister of Andhra Pradesh, his credentials as one who would work for social justice were strong. However, despite such credentials, the impression persisted that while undertaking economic reforms, the concerns for employment generation and social equity were not being adequately addressed. I did express such misgivings on a number of occasions to both Prime Minister P.V. Narasimha Rao and Finance Minister Dr Manmohan Singh. The Prime Minister in the course of one such discussions tried to assure me that these concerns are being addressed. He said that he was quite alive to this problem and that was precisely the reason why he brought into the Prime Minister's office distinguished and committed officers like B.N. Yugandhar and K.R. Venugopal. His sincerity on this count is beyond question, as he realised the importance of rural development and was the first Prime Minister to keep this portfolio with him and also allocate a record amount of resources for rural development, when S.R. Sankaran, was the secretary in this Ministry.

The Scheme for Employment Assurance in the backward districts was introduced by him. He explicitly pleaded for the "Middle Way" in economic reforms at the World Economic Forum (international economic summit) at Davos. He successfully piloted 73rd and 74th Amendments

Hanumantha Rao Committee Presents its Report on DPAP & DDP

The Technical Committee Appointed by the Ministry of Rural Development to Review Drought Prone Areas Programme and Desert Development Programme, Presented its Report to the Prime Minister, Mr P.V. Narashimha Rao in New Delhi on 23 April 1994.

to the Constitution, initiated by Rajiv Gandhi, for empowering the local elected institutions. He promptly accepted and implemented the recommendations of the Technical Committee (with which I was associated as chairman) for conservation of land and water resources through participatory development of watersheds.

P.V. became quite critical and articulate about the reform process after the late 1990s. He spoke against the reckless drive for privatisation of public enterprises and instead argued for measures towards improving the efficiency in the working of public enterprises (See an unpublished paper by P.V. entitled "Liberalisation and the Public Sector" prepared in February-March 2001, recently published as Annexure 9 in the book by Jairam Ramesh, *To the Brink and Back: India's 1991 Story*).

P.V. also argued for greater concern for reducing regional disparities and for social justice in general. At a seminar he organised on Regional Disparities in Development under the joint auspices of National Institute of Rural Development (NIRD) and the Swami Ramanand Teerth Research Institute, which he headed, he invited me to speak on the subject as a panelist, where I found him very meticulously discussing measures for reducing regional disparities in development.

Thanks to the economic reforms initiated by P.V. Narasimha Rao 25 years ago, India is now the fastest growing economy in the world. But economic inequalities have been increasing beyond the acceptable levels in a democratic polity like ours, even though poverty has been reduced. Integrating growth with social justice continues to remain an unfinished task in economic reform agenda. The best tribute that we can pay to P.V. Narasimha Rao is to carry forward the reform process he had initiated, with a clear and strong orientation to social justice—with accent on universal access to quality education and healthcare, rural development, employment generation, and reducing regional disparities in development.

10

From PhD Student to Board Chairman

My Experiences at the Institute of Economic Growth, Delhi

In January 1958, I was selected for a PhD Fellowship in the Economic Development Section at the Delhi School of Economics (DSE), supported by the Ford Foundation, for undergoing training in Research Methodology for a year before I was registered for PhD. For my thesis, in addition to Prof Vikas Mishra, under whose supervision my work was done, I was lucky to get guidance from Prof V.K.R.V. Rao and Prof A.M. Khusro.

While I and my contemporaries started working for PhD with enthusiasm, many of our seniors already working for PhD at the DSE had spent several years—some nearly a decade—causing some pessimism among us. Apparently, their interaction with supervisors was inadequate. The situation changed soon with the successful completion of a series of PhD theses in the 1960s, notably under the supervision of Prof Khusro. Prof V.K.R.V. Rao made it a point since then to mention that Prof Khusro gives enough time to his students.

By the time I started working for my PhD, I had made up my mind to specialise in Agricultural Economics, as agriculture on all accounts appeared critical at that time for overall growth of the economy and eradication of poverty. My rural background and acquaintance with the agrarian movement prompted me to seek answers to the many questions facing the peasantry through research and learning. Moreover, for 12 years since the mid-1940s, I was active in the student movement led by the

Left, aimed at socio-political transformation, beginning with the campaign for civil liberties against the Nizam's government, which led to my rustication and arrests, causing frequent interruptions in my studies. Thus while my past did provide an inspiration and a sense of relevance and meaning in my research, it also brought me face to face with the need to improve my equipment in economics and also 'unlearn' quite a bit on the ideological plane if research is to be pursued with objectivity free from pre-conceived notions and other prejudices. Thus, my PhD work became a practice in 'running fast' to make up for the lost time! It cultivated in me respect for facts and readiness to question the settled ideas if facts so demanded. It also turned out to be an exercise towards precision in writing.

When the Agricultural Economics Research Section was started in 1961 at the Institute of Economic Growth (IEG), I was appointed as a Junior Fellow. After a few years, the authorities at the IEG thought of encouraging me to spend a year or so at some good University abroad. When the suggestion came to me in early 1966, instead of seeing in this gesture an opportunity for learning, I tended to detect a 'craze' for 'foreign credentials'! But it did not take much time to see the positive side, although shedding prejudices totally was to wait until I spent a few months in the library at the Department of Economics, University of Chicago, and completed auditing courses offered by stalwarts like T.W. Schultz, Milton Friedman, George Stigler and others. My wife Krishna was with me, herself working in the South Asia Library, and providing me, as always, full support for my academic pursuits.

The number of articles and books one could read in a year sitting in a corner in the library was simply unimaginable even in a decade in India. I could also complete my paper on 'sharecropping' which later appeared in the *Journal of Political Economy*. I felt so much stimulated, even excited, that I thought of staying on for a few months more! Accordingly, I wrote to Prof P.N. Dhar, then Director, requesting him to extend my Fellowship for another three months. This he did graciously, but with a rider that I should not ask for further extension!

The Author and Mrs. Krishna Hanumantha Rao at their flat in the IEG Campus.

A decade later, the IEG negotiated with the Ford Foundation to revive the programme for supporting its scholars to pursue post-Doctoral work abroad. A number of scholars availed of this and several of them, including Professors B.B. Bhattacharya, N.S. Siddharthan and S.C. Gulati, continued to work and make outstanding contributions at the IEG. The IEG's approach to scholars taking up academic assignments abroad for limited periods has been positive so long as they did not adversely affect Institute's own research and training activities.

Declining to accept long-term or regular assignments with international institutions is in line with Prof V.K.R.V. Rao's own practice. Such assignments, apart from depriving the country of much needed talent, carry the risk of alienating the scholars from the developments in the country leading to their analyses and prescriptions becoming sometimes out of tune with the situation in the country. On the other hand, exposure to the wider intellectual currents in the world at large through stay and interactions for limited periods abroad can be refreshing and rewarding for fruitfully addressing the country's problems by liberating oneself from the 'frog-in-the-well' mind set.

If most of the IEG Faculty preferred to remain at the IEG by declining offers from within the country and abroad, it is not only due to their commitment to the above values but also to the 'work culture' at the IEG. Freedom of thought and expression, a sense of social relevance in research and academic excellence are the foremost values nurtured by Prof V.K.RV. Rao. These have sustained us intellectually and spiritually over the decades. IEG's location in Delhi, adjacent to the DSE in the University campus, conferred unique advantages. Many from the Faculty had completed their PhD from the DSE before joining IEG. These and others have continued their beneficial interaction with the DSE, even as the life at the IEG remained quiet when the University was in turmoil! Easy interaction with visiting scholars from abroad, effective exposure to major policy initiatives and participation in the Expert Committees at the national level are enriched further by the insights from the field work by a number of IEG scholars, notably from the Population Research Centre. Accountability for their research work was sought to be ensured basically through the presentation of their work, in several stages of the project, at faculty seminars where experts from other institutions were also invited.

A National Seminar on Relevance in Social Science Research was organised at the IEG in 1980 to clarify and sharpen our understanding of the relevant issues. This resulted in an important publication from the IEG. Again, in the mid-1990s, there was an interesting debate at the IEG on the need for its research agenda to respond to the changing economic environment. Through the flood of emerging literature, exchange of visits and academic interactions, the IEG scholars are sufficiently exposed to the on-going intellectual currents in the world and are amenable to changes in thinking to the extent warranted. It is gratifying that the research community at the IEG not only responded positively to the changing economic environment but evolved, on its own, a balanced approach to economic reform much before the view 'economic reforms with human face' or 'inclusive growth' came to be officially accepted.

An issue needing exploration is the prospect for multi-disciplinary research. At the moment, when institutions like IEG claim to be multidisciplinary, it simply means scholars from different disciplines sitting and working under the same roof! They do exchange views occasionally, but on matters mostly outside their disciplines! Joint studies undertaken, for example, by sociologists, economists and demographers on subjects of common interest could perhaps serve as good experiments for seeing their usefulness and for advancing the collaborative efforts further.

In the early 1970s, Prof V.K.R.V. Rao took the initiative, by involving some of us, to restructure the management of the Institute with a view to making it democratic and self-governing through the participation of the senior faculty

Inauguration of the IEG Golden Jubilee Year by the Prime Minister Prof Manmohan Singh on 15 December 2007.

at various levels. Accordingly, the rules and regulations of the Institute were amended in several rounds to ensure, among other things, greater representation to the faculty in the Governing Body and the Committee of Administration and Finance. The Academic Committee takes decisions on all academic matters. A number of other committees have also been functioning well. Looking at the functioning of the Institute as Chairman, I find that IEG has evolved, over a period of time, procedures and practices that are well-settled by now with the widest possible participation by the faculty, without any populist overtones. The IEG has indeed matured!

An indirect but important contribution of the Institute, which can not find a place in the usual list of its achievements, is the education of the children of the

A view of the audience at the inauguration of the IEG Golden Jubilee Year.

faculty and other staff. These children—in many cases extremely well-endowed—are spread over in different parts of the country and the world, making a mark in their fields. The IEG can legitimately take pride in such human capital! No less significant is the social capital, for example, the successful functioning of the IEG Employees' Cooperative Credit and Thrift Society, Staff Welfare Committee, and the goodwill among different sections of the IEG community.

IEG at Fifty: Recollections, Retrospect and Prospect, Institute of Economic Growth, Delhi, Academic Foundation, New Delhi, 2008.

11

Professor P.N. Dhar

I came in touch with Prof P.N. Dhar closely only after he became Director of the Institute of Economic Growth in the early 1960s. I think, he was then admired more for his native abilities than for his achievements. Dr Dharm Narain told me that Dhar *saheb* (as he used to be called) is one of the top minds in the University of Delhi and that in the field of Economics he can be rated very high for his native gifts—perhaps next only to Prof V.K.R.V. Rao. My experience with Prof Dhar has borne out the accuracy of this remark. His mind was razor sharp. He could think very clearly and had an amazing capacity to sort out the essentials from a confusing array of ideas and facts. He was equally gifted with an impressive voice. He employed these rare gifts basically as a conversationalist—very lively and insightful.

Another close friend of mine used to tell me that Dhar *saheb* is extremely intelligent and shrewd. The research work he has done, especially the one on small scale industries (Dhar 1958)—which anticipated the need for the kind of structural reforms undertaken in the 1990s—is rated quite high.

He had his likes and dislikes but never ended up translating them into his conduct because he was a democrat and had a compelling sense of fairness and even a desire to please everybody. He was rarely straight in his utterances but always wished well and did what was only fair.

He had considerable experience of political movements in Kashmir. Indeed, he was the only person in the

University campus to whom most people turned for information as well as ideas on the current political problems facing the nation. He had a mature judgement—so rare among economists at the campus. But his style may very often conceal this basic maturity. I suspect that Dhar *saheb* played with his style which never interfered either with the strength of his ideas or with the maturity of his judgement.

Dhar *saheb* played an increasing role as a politically-minded and a mature economist. Regarded by some as an ex-Marxist, he was primarily a nationalist passionately devoted to the goals of national unity and economic progress.

Prof Dhar was over 90 when he passed away in 2012; he became the Principal Secretary to the Prime Minister Indira Gandhi in the 1970s and later served as Assistant Secretary-General of the United Nations; and after his return contributed significantly to the debate on the need for economic reforms in India in the 1990s. He was awarded the Padma Vibhushan by the president of India.

12

Professor Dharm Narain

During my career at the Institute of Economic Growth, Dharm Narain impressed me very much both as a scholar and as a person. A man about as short as I am, he nevertheless was gifted with a sensitive and impressive face and an imposing voice. His thick mustaches and *hukkka* (smoking pipe) added considerably to his exterior.

Prof P.N. Dhar once in one of his usual leg-pulling moods—at which he seemed to be equally effective when he is dealing with his closest associates—remarked in the presence of Dr Dharm Narain that Hindu society has a tendency to postpone growth because a typical Hindu always assures himself that he can achieve in his next '*janma*' (life) what he finds unable to achieve in his present life and then added as an instance that Dharm Narain would think that he would become a Ricardo in his next life! At this I jocularly remarked that Dr Dharm Narain was probably David Ricardo already in his previous life!

Narain indeed had the highest of academic ambitions. He had his training in economics from the University of Delhi and had a brilliant academic career throughout. His reasoning was very sharp and possessed of depth. He also believed in perfectionism both in regard to content and form which accounts for his very low rate of academic output. He rarely wrote for journals, not to speak of newspapers. He often used to advise his colleagues not to rush for publication when the paper is 'ready' but instead place it in the drawer for a week or two and read it again for possible revisions before it is sent for publication. Prof Dhar once remarked that fewer people can understand the very few things Dharm Narain writes! He wrote in a style compelling the reader to think for himself in the same manner as the author.

He combined his brilliance with his genial disposition. I was struck by his genuine academic abilities, intellectual integrity and a sense of fairness. But his sense of perfectionism held him down considerably. He was extremely balanced in his utterances and genuinely friendly to the people around him. In shrewdness he was excelled by none among the people I knew. He had a thorough grasp of good as well as weak aspects among each of the professionals closely known and had the capacity to tackle them appropriately.

He was a chronic gastric patient. I remember an incident in our tea-club at the IEG. Prof Dhar who had recently become a victim of gastric trouble began to feel some difficulty after tea. Unable to participate in conversation, he was trying to relax. Naturally Dharm Narain and myself began to talk about gastric trouble. I began narrating the story of a gastric patient whose protracted negligence had resulted in the growth of peptic ulcers and how he once vomited blood. Dr Dharm Narain could not bear this description and immediately got up in an effort to get rid of the 'onslaught' and signalled me to stop this narration. Prof Dhar was following all this, but appeared serene while fighting the gastric pressure that was oppressing him.

Dharm Narain passed away in 1980 at the age of 55 in Washington D.C., while he was with the International Food Policy Research Institute, Washington, D.C. For more about him and his writings, see *Dharm Narain: Studies on Indian Agriculture* (edited by K.N. Raj, Amartya Sen and C.H. Hanumantha Rao, Oxford University Press, New Delhi,1988).

13

Delhi School of Economics Annual Day Address

The Delhi School of Economics (DSE) was founded by Prof V.K.R.V. Rao with a high ideal of training economists and other social scientists for their effective participation in nation-building. The existence of the DSE on the pattern of the London School of Economics inspired many among the younger generation in different parts of the country to benefit from this opportunity opened up for advanced learning. The same inspiration brought me with a zeal to the Delhi School of Economics in August 1957 from the Osmania University. I was lucky to be registered for PhD at the DSE with encouragement from Prof A.M. Khusro.

My first opportunity to listen to Prof V.K.R.V. Rao at the DSE was in this Vivekananda Hall on the occasion of its Founder's Day on 14 November 1957. He spoke with great passion about the ideals of the DSE. First and foremost among these ideals he said was freedom of thought and expression. I came to know years later that his founding the DSE owed primarily to his own struggle for freedom of thought and expression. He narrated how, while speaking as a member of an official delegation in those days, he was interrupted by its head, a civil servant of the ICS cadre, by saying that economists are expected to 'produce' arguments in support of the official line and not air their 'own' views! This infuriated Prof Rao who decided to resign from his post in the government the very next day to start an autonomous institution where scholars can enjoy freedom of thought and expression to be able to contribute to policymaking in a fearless manner.

Achieving academic excellence was another great ideal for him. For this purpose, he recruited professors of great distinction from different universities in India and abroad. Apart from professors B.N. Ganguli and P.N. Dhar who together with him formed a trio in the then small department of economics working tirelessly towards shaping the DSE, he brought, in the first round, eminent scholars like professors K.N. Raj, B.V. Krishnamurthy, M.N. Srinivas, M.S.A. Rao, Tapan Raychaudhuri, A.M. Khusro, S. Sivasubramanian, George Kurian, V.L.S. Prakasa Rao and others.

The third ideal which he passionately exhorted the teachers and students to follow was social commitment which he thought was as important as technical competence. Drawing inspiration from the freedom movement, he felt that ensuring a just social order in the country was not possible without social commitment. Towards this end, he strongly believed in the need for inter-disciplinary approach in addressing socioeconomic problems. Therefore, in all the institutions he established, namely, Delhi School of Economics, Institute of Economic Growth (IEG), and the Institute for Social and Economic Change (ISEC) at Bangalore, he took great pains to accommodate different disciplines in social sciences to facilitate fruitful interaction.

Thanks to the functioning of our democratic set-up for over 60 years and the existence of institutions such as the University Grants Commission and the Indian Council of Social Science Research, we enjoy today far greater measure of autonomy and freedom of thought and expression when compared to the immediate post-independence period.

In respect of academic excellence too, we are today in a much better position than in the early years of the DSE. I was a witness to the virtually demoralising intellectual atmosphere in the room where the PhD scholars used to be seated. I found that quite a few of them had already spent 5 to 7 years or more groping for the subject. To a considerable extent, this reflected the research culture in a typical Indian university in those days. The emphasis

Address by the author at the Inaugural Session of the Annual Day Celebrations of the Delhi School of Economics, 16 January 2015.

then was on producing a bulky thesis after a great deal of reading and summarising the literature, with an objective of making a 'lasting' contribution to the subject! Happily, the focus gradually shifted to the quality of research questions addressed in the thesis, methods of analysis followed and the significance of the findings arrived at.

At the time of founding of the IEG in 1958, certain sections of the DSE, including the Economic Development Section, headed by Prof A.M. Khusro, and supported by the Ford Foundation, where I was a PhD scholar, were shifted to the IEG. Having been associated with the IEG in the neighbourhood for 50 years until its Golden Jubilee Celebrations in 2008, I can testify to the beneficial impact that the DSE had all along on the research work done at the IEG.

Nobel Laureate Prof Amartya Sen being honoured with a Doctorate by the University of Hyderabad on 19 December 2013

Many in the IEG faculty had completed their PhD from the DSE and continued their academic links with the parent institution. IEG faculty has had an active collaboration with the DSE in providing guidance to the MPhil as well as PhD students. The use of econometric techniques was virtually non-existent in the early years of DSE, but very soon became popular with the stalwarts in the subject like Prof A.L. Nagar and Prof K.L. Krishna coming on the scene. The IEG and DSE have had major collaborative projects in Macro-Econometric Modelling for India with Prof K. Krishnamurthy of IEG and Prof V.N. Pandit of DSE as leaders of the project. When academic institutions happen to be next door neighbours with common interest, scholars across these institutions easily walking into each other's rooms, not uncommon in both the institutions, for exchanging views and engaging in discussions could perhaps prove to be as fruitful as projects jointly undertaken.

The scholars of both the institutions are well-known for their broader approach to development. For example, the issues of sustainability and social justice have figured prominently in their research agenda. Besides, they have actively participated in shaping socioeconomic policies in the country as members of various expert committees and commissions. Prominent among economists well known for their broader approach to development are Professors V.K.R.V. Rao, P.N. Dhar and Raj Krishna who starting from the DSE made substantial contributions at the IEG. Similarly, the contributions made by scholars like K.N. Raj, Sukhamoy Chakravarty and Amartya Sen from the DSE on broader issues of development have greatly inspired scholars in both these institutions and in the country at large towards engaging themselves on socially relevant issues. We from the DSE and IEG are proud of the fact that Prof Manmohan Singh, the architect of economic reforms in the country as Finance Minister in the early 1990s had been a professor at the DSE before he joined the government, and is president of IEG. Again, as Prime Minister he brought in the perspective of 'inclusive growth' which has been widely supported in the country.

All these scholars have been open to interdisciplinary approach to development. Carrying this tradition forward requires harnessing satisfactorily the potential for collaboration between scholars working in different disciplines. Some interaction between such scholars is inevitable when they are working under the same roof, as, for example, when they meet every day at tea in the common room! A more serious exposure to each other's work takes place through participation in seminars. Attending each others' seminars apart, it needs a deliberate effort to formulate projects where scholars from different disciplines collaborate on issues of applied nature. Most of our failures on the policy front are traceable to the lack of such a broader inter-disciplinary approach.

Finally, I would like to express my sincere gratitude to the organisers of this event for remembering me as an old boy of DSE and providing me the opportunity of meeting so many friends at these celebrations.

Address at the Inaugural Session of the Annual Day Celebrations of the Delhi School of Economics, 16 January 2015.

I-B

From Vishal Andhra to Telangana

1

Letter to the Editor on Telangana[1]

(National Herald, 20 July 1969)

Sir—I am one of those who had actively participated in the movement for the formation of the present state of Andhra Pradesh in 1956. I have had an opportunity to observe the agitation for a separate Telangana during this summer as an outsider. There was a time when even a moderate political movement required a strong and highly motivated leadership. But the present agitation is unprecedented. The people themselves have spontaneously launched it.

Any person visiting Telangana now after a decade and a half would be struck by the emergence of a large organised and vocal class comprising NGOs (non-governmental organisations), students, teachers, engineers, lawyers, physicians, businessmen, etc. These sections strongly feel that their interests can be protected only in a separate state. They narrate how experience has convinced them that it would be difficult to ensure economic justice to Telangana, so long as political power is exercised by the Andhra region. The feeling for separation is so intense and widespread that in all probability the Union government will have to bow down to the wishes of the people, at any rate, after the general elections in 1972.

To understand the tensions brewing in Telangana, it is necessary to bear in mind the increasing role of Government or public investments and the crucial role of

---

1. This letter to the editor was carried in other major national dailies, including *The Statesman* (15 July 1969), *The Times of India* (15 July 1969).

education and skills in economic growth. Telangana failed to get even one-third of the Government outlays in the integrated state, despite the fact that Telangana accounts for 35 per cent of the population of the state and its per capita tax revenue is higher and per capita income lower than in Andhra. In view of the widely accepted fact that the revenue surpluses of Telangana have been diverted to the Andhra region, a general feeling persists that separation would enable Telangana to step up its investment. The discrimination against the Telangana personnel in regard to training, employment and promotion at various levels has demonstrated that it is far more difficult to ensure an adequate share in education and skills than in public outlays.

In these circumstances, it would appear that separation alone can ensure greater effort from the people of Telangana for the development of the region. The denial of the opportunity for the independent management of their affairs may breed persecution complex, thus undermining inter-regional solidarity without which no genuine socio-economic progress would be possible.

Those who decry the idea of separate Telangana in the name of national integration ignore that this agitation is motivated by the desire to ensure an equitable share in the fruits of socioeconomic growth. The Telangana agitators include, apart from Telugu-speaking people of the region, those speaking Urdu, Hindi, Marathi, Kannada, Tamil, Gujarati and several other Indian languages. Even those of the Andhra region who settled down in Telangana before the formation of Andhra Pradesh are active in this agitation. Thus, for the first time in the recent period, one finds rational economic considerations dominating over those of language, religion and caste. Therefore, the sooner our leaders grasp the nature of emerging forces, the better it would be for the balanced growth of the country on secular and democratic lines.

—C.H. Hanumantha Rao
Institute of Economic Growth,
University Enclave, Delhi - 7

2

Statehood for Telangana

The Current Stalemate[1]

The newly created smaller states, viz., Uttarakhand, Jharkhand and Chhattisgarh have achieved much higher growth rates in their GSDP (gross state domestic product) than the targets set for the Tenth Five Year Plan, whereas the growth rates achieved by their parent states, viz., Uttar Pradesh, Bihar and Madhya Pradesh fell significantly short of the targets (Planning Commission 2008, Rao 2009). Further, the growth rates achieved in the first two years of the Eleventh Plan, i.e., 2007-08 and 2008-09, by Chhattisgarh and Uttarakhand were significantly higher than those achieved by their parent states. Apart from releasing the creative energies of the people, viability of smaller states may have contributed to better governance, attracting greater private investment from outside as well as planning and utilising resources more efficiently (World Bank 2007).

An extremely encouraging development is in respect of Bihar, where the average growth rate achieved at 9.7 per cent per annum during these two years was significantly higher than for Jharkhand at 5.8 per cent per annum (Aiyar 2010, Rao 2010a). This may be explained by improved governance, of late, in this state, facilitated not the least by the fact that with the creation of Jharkhand, Bihar has become less heterogeneous and much smaller in area, with the size of its population getting reduced by about 25 per cent.

---

1. For my essays on Regional Disparities, Smaller States, and Statehood for Telangana written betweem 1969 and 2009, see Rao (2010b).

Experience has demonstrated the failure of regional planning to ensure adequate development of backward regions within the larger states. This is explained by the politics of planning in democracy inherent in such states characterised by regional unevenness in development. The experience of Maharashtra and Gujarat amply illustrates the failure to develop backward regions, despite the existence of constitutional provisions for setting up Regional Planning Boards and the powers entrusted to the Governor to review the progress of development under such regional plans. This experience underlines the need for conceding separate statehood for certain backward regions like Telangana and Vidarbha.

The observations of B.R. Ambedkar, the principal architect of our Constitution, on the desirability of smaller states are prophetic. He welcomed the recommendation of the States Reorganisation Commission in 1955 for the creation of Hyderabad State consisting of Telangana region and creation of Vidarbha as a separate state. Further, he envisaged the division of Uttar Pradesh into three states (Western, Central and Eastern); Bihar into two (North and South or present Jharkhand); Madhya Pradesh into two (Northern and Southern); and Maharashtra into three (Western,Central and Eastern). He was for linguistic homogeneity of a state in the sense of 'one state-one language' and not 'one language-one state'. He thus envisaged two Telugu speaking states, three Marathi speaking states and a large number of Hindi speaking states (Ambedkar 1979).

While arguing for smaller states, Ambedkar was guided basically by two considerations. One, no single state should be large enough to exercise undue influence in the federation. Drawing from the American experience, he thought that smaller states were in the best interests of healthy federalism. On this issue, his views were similar to those of K.M. Panikkar, set out in his note of dissent to the Report of the States Reorganisation Commission. Second, he thought that socially disadvantaged sections are likely to be subjected to greater discrimination in bigger states because of the consolidation of socially privileged or dominant groups (Ambedkar 1979).

Over the last half a century, two new dimensions have been added. Population growth and the multiplicity of developmental functions have rendered governance in large size states inefficient. Secondly, in the context of development planning under democracy, significant regional diversities with respect to the historically inherited levels of infrastructure and institutions within certain large states have given rise to severe tensions concerning the distribution of benefits from development. These tensions have reached a point where harmonious development seems no longer possible without their break-up into smaller states which are relatively homogeneous (Rao 2010b).

The agitations for separate statehood for Telangana in the Telangana region as well as for Samaikhya (United) Andhra Pradesh in the Andhra region are in full swing now. The agitation in Telangana is unprecedented in its sweep, being universal or, at any rate, far more widespread than in 1969, involving, among others, students, farmers, women and even children. The movement is virtually taken over and led by the students, all of whom were obviously born at least a decade after the agitation of 1969. It appears as if history is repeating itself or time is standing still for over four decades so far as this issue is concerned!

Curiously, in the case of the Andhra region, history appears to have been overturned. The 'Jai Andhra' or separate Andhra agitation of 1972-73 was triggered-off by the land reform legislation and the validation of Mulki Rules (preference for natives of Telangana in employment) by the Supreme Court, because of which the big landed sections as well as educated youth could lose in the integrated state. Over the last four decades, however, certain leading business sections including those involved in real estate business from the Andhra region developed a big stake in Telangana, particularly in and around Hyderabad city. Thanks to the lop-sided urbanisation and concentration of financial sector services and IT (information technology) industry in Hyderabad in the post-reform period, the educated youth—most of whom born after the 'Jai Andhra' agitation like their Telangana counterparts—could understandably have developed an emotional identification with the capital city and so a stake in Samaikhya (United) Andhra Pradesh.

Guided by the consensus among the major political parties in favour of the formation of separate Telangana state, as espoused in their election manifestos and reiterated by them as recently as 7 December 2009, the Central government on 9 December announced its decision to initiate the process for the formation of Telangana state. Within hours, this decision triggered off a counter-agitation in the Andhra region for united Andhra Pradesh, leaders of the major political parties taking sides by getting divided horizontally on regional lines. It is not clear whether these leaders did not mean what they promised earlier on Telangana in the expectation that no worthwhile initiative would come from the Centre or could not anticipate the adverse public reaction in the Andhra region in the event of any favourable move on the issue. In any case, this has placed the Centre in a difficult situation leading to the stalemate in the resolution of the crisis.

As it is, the Constitution fully empowers the Centre to carve out new states, the role of the state legislatures being limited to merely expressing their views on the proposed Bill by the Centre. While politics can not be wished away in a democracy and the Centre can not normally be expected to proceed against the wishes of the majority of legislators of a state, ultimately, politics in a democracy have to come to terms with the provisions of the Constitution and respect the universal demand of the people of a region for a separate statehood. Also, in the long-run, the youth of any region in the modern age, imbued as it would be with the democratic spirit, would come to respect peoples' wishes from the other region for separate statehood. Besides, a pride in the capacity to develop opportunities in one's own state is bound to come into play. Addressing the legitimate concerns of the stakeholders is essential to facilitate this process.

There is no alternative to the Centre as well as the leaders of both the regions taking initiatives for a constructive dialogue for resolving the outstanding issues by addressing the legitimate concerns of the stakeholders, to pave the way for separate statehood for Telangana and thus end the perpetual uncertainty undermining the harmonious development of both the regions. While agitations are necessary for the assertion of legitimate rights, in a democracy, constructive dialogue is indispensable for bringing such aspirations to fruition.

Published in *Mainstream*, 13 February 2010; Reproduced in *Mainstream*, 7 June 2014, on the occasion of the formation of the State of Telangana.

3

Release of Ghanta Chakrapani's Book "Telangana Jaitra Yatra"

This book is a collection of articles by Ghanta Chakrapani, published in the Telugu Daily *Namate Telangana*, on the major events covering Telangana movement over a crucial period of two and half years culminating in the passage of the Bill for the creation of Telangana state by both the Houses of Parliament. Chakrapani is at once a social scientist, a professional journalist, and a concerned social activist. Therefore, his articles are highly informative, readable, deeply analytical, and must have been a source of inspiration for the participants in the movement. The book is made lively by certain bits of sarcasm targeting where it is due, for example, his pointing to the myth propagated in Seemandhra that Sri Potti Sriramulu had sacrificed his life for the cause of 'Samaikyandhra'! (He had in fact sacrificed his life for carving out a separate Andhra state comprising the Telugu speaking areas of the erstwhile Madras state).

Chakrapani's portrayal of Telangana movement is telling. On the surprisingly high level of peoples' awareness, he says that even the school going children in the third standard in Telangana these days know what Article 3 in the Constitution of India says! A majority of A.P. legislators refused to read the Article for what it is when they insisted on passing a resolution in the state Assembly! He highlights the spontaneous nature of the Telangana movement which has had the widest possible involvement of the people because of greater awareness, better communication among participants and organisational skills. The leaders on many occasions were drawn to the movement because of its high tempo, unlike even in 1969.

The observations of Chakrapani are particularly striking on a very distressing aspect of the way our democracy has been functioning. This relates to its failure to cultivate democratic values or the democratic spirit among large sections of the elite. Development and modernity through education, employment, prosperity and security are expected to inculcate democratic values such as equal respect for the legitimate aspirations of those constituting a minority whether belonging to a particular region, religion or caste. Aggressive pursuit of self-interest is making some sections insensitive to the rights of many others guaranteed by the Constitution. One hopes that having been a victim of this lack of democratic spirit, the new set-up in Telangana will inculcate among its people respect for the legitimate aspirations of diverse sections of its society.

Over the last 60 years, Telangana was denied opportunities for inclusive and sustainable development through political empowerment. But, in the process of the protracted struggles and sacrifices made by the people for achieving statehood, Telangana has learnt a great deal for evolving its own path for development.

Moreover, Telangana is serving as a social laboratory for testing Dr B.R. Ambedkar's propositions on why smaller and relatively homogeneous states are essential for speedy and equitable development. Telangana's experience within the larger state and its success in achieving separate statehood is bound to give impetus to the reorganisation of states in the country where necessary, basically, by making the powers-that-be responsive to the democratic aspirations of the people for political empowerment. Telangana's experience also shows how prophetic our Constitution makers have been in shaping Article 3 under the leadership of Dr Ambedkar. In view of this experience, hopefully, the concerned law makers in future would adopt procedures that are more straightforward and honest.

The lessons thrown up by the Telangana movement for its own polity and society are clear. The social framework for development has to be secular, people-centric, participatory and accountable. It has to be kept in mind that in undivided Andhra Pradesh the experience in respect of ensuring peoples' participation in development as well as accountability of performance through grassroots level institutions like panchayati raj institutions has been dismal.

Opening remarks while releasing the book on 18 May 2014, at Saraswataparishath Hall, Boggulakunta, Hyderabad.

4

Major Development Challenges to Telangana State

It is a privilege for me to get this opportunity for meeting and interacting with the first elected representatives of the Telangana state. After its creation as a separate state, Telangana is better placed in several respects. It has the usual advantages of viability of a smaller state in terms of area and population as well as relative homogeneity of its history and culture. There is a predominance of weaker sections in the state, BCs (backward classes), SCs (scheduled castes), STs (scheduled tribes), and minorities together constituting nearly 90 per cent of its population. This underlines the need as well as possibilities of achieving inclusive growth because of political empowerment of weaker sections. They now have control over their resources and the power to shape their destiny.

The state of Telangana has the advantage of 'surplus' revenues on account of under-spending in the region in the past. On the basis of the data for the last 10 years, the projections made by the 14th Finance Commission show higher revenues and lower expenditure per capita for Telangana when compared to Andhra. The Bhargava Committee had brought out the same position for the 1950s and the 1960s. This position persisted over the last 60 years, but remained hidden so far because the accounts related to the undivided state as a whole. Now it has come into open because of bifurcation showing higher per capita revenue expenditure with revenue deficit for Andhra Pradesh state and revenue surplus with lower per capita revenue expenditure for Telangana state.

Therefore, the misinformation being spread, particularly in Delhi, that Andhra Pradesh is a victim of bifurcation whereas Telangana is an undue beneficiary will not carry any credibility. The real position needs to be explained effectively by the elected representatives of Telangana.

However, the greatest asset for the Telangana state is non-monetary, that is, the emergence of peoples' power out of protracted struggle, particularly over the last decade. This is exemplified by greater awareness among the people, their unity and capacity for community action. No doubt, they have high expectations from governance, but if their power is properly harnessed by securing their effective participation in PRIs (panchayati raj institutions), the results can be encouraging from better designing of the schemes as well as ensuring greater accountability of performance. The spontaneous response to the Mission Kakatiya from different sections of rural population for restoring and renovating tanks and the immediate positive response of the Chief Minister to the requests from the people for more grants towards restoration of certain tanks, as seen in Nalgonda the other day, is an encouraging development. The decline in surface irrigation and excessive dependence on well irrigation can be reversed by Mission Kakatiya.

NITI Aayog (National Institution for Transforming India) has been set up at the Centre for strengthening the planning process as a 'think tank' as well as Cooperative Federalism through greater participation of states. In fact, way back in the mid-1980s, when I was in the Planning Commission, the then Prime Minister Rajiv Gandhi had visualised making Planning Commission basically a 'Think Tank' working on long-term issues of development rather than becoming a bureaucratic machinery concerned with day-to-day issues. He had pioneered the introduction of IT (information technology) so as to benefit from globalisation and, at the same time, strengthening of PRIs by empowering the common people with a view to ensuring to them the benefits of development. As a member of the task force he had constituted for this purpose, I could see how difficult it is to strengthen such grass roots institutions because of resistance from vested interests, even as the spread of IT and globalisation was a resounding success.

NITI Aayog as a think tank at the national level can be effective in a large country like ours with enormous regional diversity, only if decentralised planning below the state level is taken up seriously by strengthening the state Planning Boards as think tanks with necessary competence and autonomy. But this issue was not even raised in the course of the recent debate when the NITI Aayog was constituted. Except in a few cases, state governments and their planning departments have always been lukewarm to the idea of strengthening state Planning Boards with necessary autonomy. Periodically, there has been a talk at the national level about strengthening decentralised planning in the country at the village, block and district levels. There was even a Centrally Sponsored Scheme (CSS) for strengthening state planning. I myself chaired a Committee on District Planning in the mid-1980s but the Reports, despite evoking much interest following their submission, are still gathering dust.

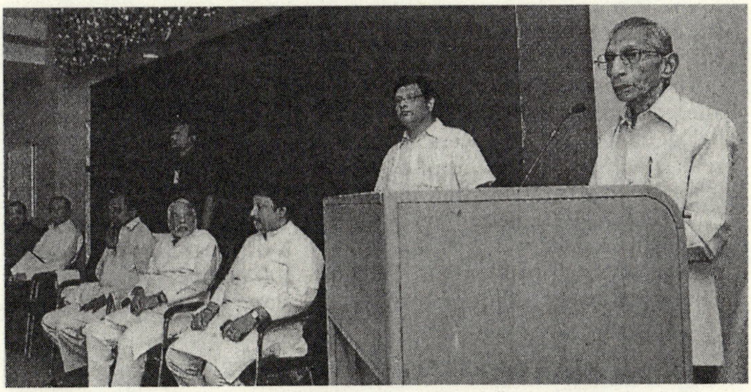

The author inaugurating Orientation Programme for elected representatives of the Telangana Rashtra Samiti of Telangana State, at Nagarjuna Sagar, 2 May 2015.

Resistance to decentralised planning by devolving functions, finances and functionaries from the state to local levels was conspicuous in Andhra Pradesh. A devolution index constructed by the National Council of Applied Economic Research (NCAER) showed this to be a mere 50 per cent for Andhra Pradesh as against 75 per cent for Kerala, 70 per cent for Karnataka and 67 per cent for Tamil Nadu. Contrary to Rajiv Gandhi's perspective, instead of empowering people at the grass roots, the Andhra Pradesh government preferred to float top-down schemes like 'Rajiv Palle Bata'!

Telangana state has emerged at a time when globalisation is in full swing, economies experiencing accelerated growth in their incomes with increasing inequalities. But increase in inequality in the context of globalisation is not inevitable, as theoretically there is no inherent 'cause-and-effect' relationship between them. If different regions and groups of people have equal access to infrastructure, assets, quality education, credit, etc., globalisation need not lead to the rise in inequalities.

Prevailing inequitable socioeconomic structure within the country and not globalisation as such is responsible for increase in inequalities. As it is, globalisation which could be initiated with a stroke of pen in India has moved at a much faster rate than social change, including decentralisation of development, which is a more difficult process. In China, for example, despite radical socioeconomic transformation achieved in the early stages of development, globalisation in the recent period has led to high inequalities, higher than in India and even higher than in the US, the land of capitalism. A study by the International Monetary Fund attributed this to unequal access to quality education in China in the post-globalisation period. Also, lack of democracy there results in special privileges being enjoyed by the limited groups of people having political clout.

There has been a great demand for education, especially from the poorer sections, as a means of employment in Telangana, particularly because of uncertain prospects from agriculture. I had noticed this way back in the early 1970s in the course of my exercise as a member of the Committee on the Perspective Planning for Telangana, and this trend continues as brought out recently by the Srikrishna Committee Report.

I would, therefore, like to conclude by suggesting that Telangana can derive maximum benefit from globalisation, in terms of growth as well as social equity, by trusting and empowering people through decentralisation of development and by ensuring universal access to quality education. The 'KG to PG' Scheme proposed by the Chief Minister is highly promising in this context.

Inaugural Address at the Interactive Orientation Programme for Elected Representatives (Telangana Rashtra Samiti) of Telangana State, Nagarjuna Sagar, 2-3 May 2015; published in *The Hans India*, Hyderabad, 11 May 2015; See also, *Mainstream*, 6 June 2015.

5

Telangana Agriculture Performance, Policy and Research Strategy

Professor K. Jayashankar

Professor Jayashankar was the foremost academic in the forefront of the movement for the creation of Telangana state right from the Mulki agitation of 1952. When he was barely 20, he met with the States Reorganisation Commission to plead for the creation of Telangana state. Confidence in the justness of his cause, steadfast commitment to it, and relentless intellectual effort armed with facts and arguments to convince even the staunch opponents to his idea in a persuasive manner were the hallmarks of his personality.

It is indeed a great privilege for me to be invited to deliver this lecture in honour of his memory. But I stand here this morning with a sense of personal loss to deliver this memorial lecture, as he was five years younger to me, and we always exchanged views on issues of statehood for Telangana with mutual regard and affection. It is sad that he passed away precisely at a time when there was every likelihood of his life-long dream of creation of Telangana state being realised soon.

It is a great honour for Telangana State Agricultural University (TSAU) to be named after Prof Jayashankar. This honour carries an immense responsibility in terms of social commitment, achieving technical excellence, and doing research relevant to Telangana. I have no doubt that the faculty and management of the University will live up to these expectations.

Agriculture Performance

Agriculture growth has been high at over 4 per cent per annum at the national level as well as in Telangana in the last decade following deceleration to a mere 2 per cent in the earlier decade. Agriculture GSDP (gross state domestic product) growth rate in Telangana in the last decade, at around 5 per cent, could well have been above the national average. Even in the last 5 years ending 2014-15, the growth rate for Telangana was only marginally lower than the decadal growth rate. This achievement is in line with the overall GSDP growth rates in Telangana as well as Andhra Pradesh rising above the All-India GDP (gross domestic product) growth rate nearly a decade ago after hovering below the national average for five decades of planning.

I recall as a member of the Expert Group for the preparation of the Perspective Plan for Telangana, constituted by the Government of Andhra Pradesh in 1971, that the exercises done then aimed at GSDP growth rate of Telangana rising above the national average in about a decade for reducing regional disparities in the levels of development. But the realisation of this dream had to wait for three decades. Thanks to the growth of services sector, including particularly the IT (information technology) sector, following economic reforms, the contribution of Telangana's own GSDP growth rate towards raising the growth rate of undivided Andhra Pradesh has been significant, leading to piercing national average growth rate.

This revival of farm growth at the national level as well as in Telangana in the last decade was made possible by stepping up public and private investment, adopting new technologies in an environment of improved terms of trade for agriculture, and, not the least, diversification of agriculture induced by the rising demand for high value products.

Sources of Agriculture Growth

Area increase during pre-green revolution period contributed to around half the growth; yield increase during green revolution phase became a predominant source of growth; and the contribution of TFP (total factor productivity) to growth in the current post-green revolution phase has been steadily increasing because of the shift from the exclusive emphasis on raising productivity per unit of land to raising productivity per unit of water and other inputs.

Achieving self-sufficiency, and even generating export surpluses, in foodgrains in the face of growing population is the major achievement of green revolution. But, neglect of water-saving techniques, excessive mining of soil nutrients through the unbalanced application of chemical fertilisers, and indiscriminate use of pesticides has brought the issues of TFP growth and sustainability to the forefront. Many of the present challenges in agriculture policy as well as research arise from such policy failures in the past.

Policy Failures

Major failures on the policy front are: deficiency of public investment and effort for water augmentation and its conservation; inadequate allocations for agriculture research, education and extension; neglect of marketing reforms and post-harvest infrastructure including agro-processing; and inadequate supply of institutional credit and provision of crop insurance.

Mounting subsidies on certain inputs have undermined productive investment, sustainability and incentives for the adoption of new technologies for conservation of resources. For example, excessive subsidy on urea, apart from undermining productive investment has prevented realisation of desirable NPK[1] ratio and led to indiscriminate mining of soil nutrients. Provision of free power for drawing ground water in semi-arid regions like Telangana became inevitable, no doubt, because of the decades-long neglect of surface irrigation leading to stagnation in agriculture and distress for farmers. Farm

1. Nitrogen (N), phosphorus (P) and potassium (K)

growth picked up in Telangana and very soon peaked to the All-India level, following the supply of free power since mid-2000s, but led to unsustainable extraction of groundwater and degradation of environment.

Hopefully, the current drive to augment surface water through Mission Kakatiya for reviving tanks as well as through a number of irrigation projects for harnessing Godavari water will bring about much needed balance in the supply of irrigation water from different sources. This can create necessary conditions for appropriate pricing of water and targeting of subsidies for ensuring their sustainable and equitable use.

Strategy for Agricultural Research in Telangana

Given the appropriate policy framework including the provision of necessary physical and social infrastructure, what should be the strategy for agricultural research and extension in Telangana? Even before the consequences of global warming and climate change began to be felt in terms of extreme weather events, Telangana being semi-arid, its agriculture has been characterised by high uncertainty and risk. Telangana accounted for over two-thirds of the total number of suicides committed by the farmers in the undivided Andhra Pradesh state. Therefore, raising farm productivity through methods that reduce output variability or risk while protecting environment has to be the foremost concern of agricultural research.

Apart from rainfall and irrigation, cropping intensity and diversification of agriculture contribute to growth as well as reducing variability in output and income. Some decline in the variability of output observed in the recent period could be explained by the increase in irrigation as well as diversification. Evolving cropping systems and farming systems, including livestock enterprises, suited to small farmers under varying agro-climatic conditions holds the key to such a strategy for making optimum use of farmers' own resources like land, labour and water and harnessing nature's bounty like sunshine.

The perspective on agricultural research drawn by the Faculty at the PJTSAU, in the light of the emerging challenges, is quite encouraging. Emphasis on soil health, water conservation and plant health through innovations in biotechnology are commendable. This perspective is relevant to the agro-climatic and socioeconomic conditions of Telangana, and is informed by the need to raise TFP in a sustainable manner.

Priority for Agriculture Research & Extension

But public funding for agricultural R&E (research & extension) in the country is far from adequate. Also, implementation of reforms recommended by high-level committees at the national level on de-bureaucratisation of management of research institutions and ensuring due autonomy in research is long overdue.

It is recognised that the area under cultivation in the country may decline due to pressures of urbanisation and industrialisation. Therefore, rising requirements of farm output have necessarily to be met through the rise in productivity of all the inputs (TFP). Agricultural R&E are the major determinants of the rise in TFP. Yet, the allocations for agricultural research, education and extension in the country have stagnated around 0.5 per cent to 0.6 per cent of Agriculture GDP for a long period, as against a minimum of 1 per cent of agriculture GDP recommended by the Indian Council of Agricultural Research (ICAR) over two decades ago.

State Agricultural Universities (SAUs) are greater victims of financial stress. In the undivided Andhra Pradesh, agricultural R&E received assistance, from the state and central government together, to the extent of only about 0.5 per cent of agriculture GSDP of the state. Agriculture extension was in total disarray, as allocation made amounted to a mere 0.05 per cent of agriculture GSDP. Despite increasing feminisation of agriculture, there was no special effort to reach the women farmers. Latest budgets of both the states of Telangana and Andhra Pradesh for 2014-15 indicate the provision for agricultural

R&E at 0.3 per cent of agriculture GSDP for Telangana and 0.26 per cent for Andhra Pradesh. The corresponding figures for extension and farmers' training are 0.04 and 0.03. Adding Center's allocation, the figure for each of them may go up to around 0.5 per cent.

Compare our position with China. China lagged behind India in respect of agriculture R&E during the green revolution period of 1970s and 1980s, but forged much ahead of India following economic reforms in the post-green revolution period. China is now allocating between 1.5 per cent to 2.0 per cent of its agriculture GDP for agriculture R&E.

I would like to conclude by wishing PJTSAU all the best in their research endeavours. I am aware that benefits from their effort will largely depend on public policy towards certain crucial tasks such as augmenting surface water, development of post-harvest infrastructure and adequate allocations for agriculture research and extension.

First Foundation Day Commemorative Lecture, Professor Jayashankar Telangana State Agricultural University (PJTSAU), 3 September 2015, Rajendranagar, Hyderabad; published in *The Hans India*, Hyderabad, 5 September 2015.

6

Development of Telangana

Policy Concerns

The revenue 'surplus' inherited by the new state of Telangana is spurious, as it arises because of under-spending in Telangana in the past. There is thus a considerable backlog of development in vital sectors like irrigation, power, education and health requiring huge investments.

In the last 50 years, there was a steep decline in area under tank irrigation and slow increase in irrigation under major and medium irrigation projects in Telangana, leading to the sharp rise in area irrigated through private wells. This has made farming costlier, highly uncertain and unsustainable. The new Government is trying to reverse this process through a big drive for the repair and renovation of tanks by involving the local people through Mission Kakatiya, as well as by stepping up public investment for tapping river water for irrigation, especially from Godavari, for which there is considerable potential. Towards this end, the government is actively engaged in negotiations with neighbouring states for clearing the projects by redesigning them wherever necessary.

The present supply-demand gap for power in Telangana, arising from long-standing neglect in the creation of capacity in the region, can be met, in the short-run, through special measures from the Centre. Surprisingly, contrary to the fears expressed, there have been fewer power cuts in the new state, because of prompt measures by the government to purchase power from other states.

Since irrigation water can not be so purchased, there has been acute distress in rural areas this year because of widespread drought.

There is a growing demand for education in Telangana, particularly at secondary and higher levels, as a means of employment. This is attributable mainly to the low and uncertain incomes from agriculture. Surprisingly, this phenomenon noticed way back in the 1960s continues to persist. But the cost of education in Telangana has been rising because of increasing privatisation consequent to inadequate public provision.

Hon. President of India, Shri Pranab Mukherjee inaugurating the 98th Annual Conference of the Indian Economic Association at Prof Jayashankar Telangana State Agriculture University, Hyderabad, 27 December 2016

What is worse, the rise in the cost of education has been associated with deterioration in its quality. The drop-out rates for students at primary level are quite high in Telangana. Indeed, the increasing demand for education through private institutions is explained basically by the deterioration in the quality of education in government schools and colleges. The major victims of this process of privatisation are students from low income groups, especially the SCs (scheduled castes) and scheduled STs (scheduled tribes), many of whom can not afford costly education. It has adversely affected their competitive position in the job market. This is reinforced by high spatial inequality, as, except in Hyderabad and Rangareddy districts, the provision of education is inadequate in the rest of Telangana.

The major challenge, therefore, is to ensure affordable and quality education to students at all levels in large parts of Telangana. This requires a significant rise in public expenditure on education. The proposed scheme of KG-to-PG education is promising in this context. It also calls for greater accountability of school management to the stakeholders through the local elected institutions for the provision of essential services like sanitation, ensuring attendance of teachers as well as their periodic training.

Telangana had inherited good health infrastructure from the former Hyderabad state. But, as in the case of education, there has been a concentration of facilities in Hyderabad, leaving the rest of Telangana far behind. There has been a neglect of health services on public account while private sector gained ascendance. Annual per capita government expenditure on healthcare is now well below per capita household expenditure on health services which accounts for a little over 70 per cent of total per capita expenditure on medical care.

Therefore, one of the major tasks confronting the Telangana state is to substantially step up public expenditure on health services, especially on primary healthcare in rural areas, by making them accountable to the stakeholders. At the same time, there is a need for the regulation of private corporate sector with a view to ensuring minimum standards and for preventing questionable practices.

As much as 60 per cent of the ST population of undivided Andhra Pradesh State is concentrated in Telangana. The issue of concern for them is to 'restore' to the original tillers land alienated illegally, apart from distribution of land to the landless poor, to the extent feasible. This includes checking further alienation of their land by reopening and re-examining of orders in favour of non-tribals and review of large number of cases of illegal occupation by non-tribals.

Finally, governance at the grass roots can be improved by ensuring greater accountability of performance through the panchayati raj institutions. But the devolution of functions, finances and functionaries to these institutions in the undivided state was far from adequate when compared to the other Southern states. The Gram Jyothi campaign launched recently in Telangana by the government could hopefully lead to greater empowerment of *panchayats* and *gram sabhas*.

Based on the presentation at the Panel Discussion on "Development of Telangana: Policy Concerns", at the 98th Annual Conference of the Indian Economic Association, at Prof Jayashankar Telangana State Agricultural University, Hyderabad, 29 December 2015; published in *The Hans India*, Hyderabad, 1 January 2016.

PART TWO

II-A

Some Reflections on Inclusive Growth

1

Crisis in Economic Theory

Implications for Indian Economy[1]

Functioning of the economy mirrors, among other things, the strengths as well as the gaps in the theory and practice in economics. Global financial and economic crisis that broke out four years ago was the worst that the world faced since the Great Depression of 1930s. This is the most recent instance of the crisis in economics as a discipline when economists not only failed to predict the economic crisis, but many of them actively worked with a theory and policy that in fact precipitated the crisis.

Market fundamentalism (the belief that markets are self-correcting, allocate resources efficiently and ensure full employment) has now been called into question as never before after the Great Depression of 1930s. This is because an important factor behind the current global financial crisis is a serious underestimation of the potential for market failures.

Further, state or government failure has been no less glaring. Y.V. Reddy (2009), former Governor of the Reserve Bank of India, calls it 'regulatory capture': financial markets developed far more rapidly than the real economy and the process fostered considerable linkages with the political economy, that drove the actions and inactions of both the central banks and governments, leading to the failure of both the market and the state (Reddy 2009).

---

1. The essays in this section are in continuation of my earlier work on Inclusive Growth (Rao 2014).

The mainstream opinion now among economics profession and other policymakers is in favour of continuing with market orientation with a greater role for the governments. But the idea of 'regulatory capture' goes deeper and points to the need for structural changes, as pump priming or public investments may not be a sufficient remedy and indeed, by itself, may have the effect of postponing the required structural changes.

What are these structural factors? Robert A. Johnson, another scholar who made an in-depth study of the crisis, says "the incentives faced by public officials, regulators, and elected officials and the role of money in politics are important antidotes to romantic notions of the efficiency of regulation to correct for the market failures. In addition, the role of expertise, and the incentives of experts who themselves are incentivised by considerations of power, prestigious awards and compensation should be thoroughly examined" (Johnson 2009).

There is yet another policy lesson for both the developed and developing economies: the rising inequalities in income have led to insufficiency of global aggregate demand exacerbating the present crisis. Hence the emphasis is on inclusive growth and measures for social protection. For large developing economies like India and China, an inclusive growth strategy for raising domestic demand could provide a safety net against the vagaries of global markets.

The question whether capitalism can survive the present global financial crisis is being debated fiercely in certain quarters. Nearly 70 years ago, in the wake of Great Depression, Joseph A. Schumpeter in his classic work, *Capitalism, Socialism and Democracy* had predicted the demise of capitalism and the rise of socialism. But thanks to Keynesianism and other developments, capitalism has survived so far, and socialism is nowhere round the corner. When Schumpeter wrote the above treatise, socialism appeared like a rising sun, the former

Soviet Union showing a promise of a viable alternative to capitalism.

Since then socialism and centralised economic planning had a sway for well over half a century and economic planning as a discipline in economics has had a great appeal in large parts of the globe. However, in a period when technological change and rise in productivity became the predominant source of accelerated economic growth in Western capitalist economies, the socialist economies lagged way behind on account of closed nature of their economies, lack of competition and absence of incentives for innovation and enterprise.

Economics as a discipline, in particular 'Economics of Socialism', failed to see the consequences from such a tardy progress on the productivity front under socialism. In retrospect, the demise of centralised bureaucratic planning since the 1980s and the 1990s can be attributed basically to the inefficiency and low productivity that the system had perpetuated over a long period. The system collapsed under its own weight without any outside intervention.

So, what is the way out? It seems we are back to some variant of Keynesianism as a via media between purely market-oriented development and a model of state-led development.

The experience of the last two decades following the implementation of economic reforms in India when poverty reduction was slower than expected and economic inequalities increased significantly with various deprivations e.g. undernutrition, lack of adequate health care and education coming to the fore, the idea of inclusive growth has become popular among policymakers.

The 12th Five Year Plan has come out with a blue-print of inclusive growth. But welfare schemes like employment guarantee and public distribution of foodgrains do not, by themselves, make for inclusive growth. After all, several such schemes have been there in India throughout the planning era. Economists have yet to formulate a theory of inclusive growth and economic policymakers need to present alternative models of such a growth, where equity and social justice are built into the growth process itself.

Based on the lecture delivered at the inaugural session of the National Economics Conference on "Crisis in Economics as a Discipline and its implications for the Indian Economy", organised by the Young Economist School, University of Hyderabad, on 10 May 2013; published in *The Hans India*, Hyderabad, 14 May 2013.

2

Marginalised Groups and Inclusive Growth

Implications for Indian Economy

The Concept of Inclusive Growth

The concept of inclusive growth, as stated in the 12th Plan document, focuses on the growth process, that is broad-based or in which wider sections of population, especially those hitherto excluded, participate. This implies, among other things, stepping up GDP (gross domestic product) growth rate in the slow growing or less developed regions through the development of infrastructure; greater priority to agriculture which contributes to food security and provides livelihood for nearly half the labour force in the country; and high priority to manufacturing so as to generate greater employment opportunities and ensure rise in wages.

It is recognised that setting sectoral priorities right is not sufficient for achieving inclusive growth. Marginalised groups can avail the opportunities for setting up enterprises and securing jobs in these sectors only when they have access to the resources like land and capital, education and skills without being subjected to various forms of discrimination.

Inclusive growth, so defined, needs to be distinguished from welfare programmes such as employment guarantee, public distribution of foodgrains to the poor at subsidised rates, etc. Such welfare programmes are, nevertheless, necessary to ensure inclusiveness in development. In fact, the need for such schemes increases when there is a failure to generate adequate employment and income for the poor in the process of economic growth.

Emerging Characteristics of Indian Agriculture

Agricultural landholdings are becoming smaller and unviable. Over 85 per cent of farmers are now small and marginal (below 2 hectares) accounting for a little over 40 per cent of cultivated area. Net area sown, as distinct from gross cropped area, will continue to decline because of increasing competition for land for non-agricultural uses like industrialisation, urbanisation and housing.

Redistribution of land to the landless in India, in the 1950s and 1970s, through the imposition of ceiling on agricultural landholdings was not significant as the land so distributed did not exceed 2 per cent of total area owned; even this meager land was of low quality and marginal. However, a major contribution of ceiling on agricultural landholdings has been to prevent the concentration of landholdings in the hands of a few large landowners and agri-business corporations.

Similarly, water resources are becoming increasingly scarce for agriculture on account of rising demand for non-farm uses. All this underscores the importance of TFP (total factor productivity) or productivity of all the inputs combined, e.g. land, labour and capital, as a predominant source of agriculture growth in future.

The younger and educated labour force is leaving agriculture depriving this sector of the possible demographic dividend or the productivity advantage arising from the lowering average age of labour force.

The resulting feminisation and ageing of the agriculture labour force necessitates better extension services to improve the skill and knowledge base of the farmers.

Agriculture is becoming capital-intensive and risk-prone due to increasing diversification of agriculture at a time when 'credit-worthiness' of farmers, as traditionally understood, is declining on account of their shrinking land base. There is a technology fatigue leading to sharp deceleration in TFP growth in agriculture during the 9th and 10th Plan periods, and only a modest recovery during the 11th Plan period.

Greater market uncertainties are emerging: farmers are suffering significant losses of perishable output like vegetables and fruits due to insufficient storage facilities. Price uncertainty is increasing, because, with increasing diversification of agriculture, the MSPs (minimum support prices) fixed by the government effectively leave out the prices of a large proportion of high value output, to be determined by the market forces.

Inclusive Agriculture Growth

Inclusiveness in agriculture growth is determined by the Economic Organisation of Agriculture for small and marginal farmers, that is, their access to land, capital, technology, modern marketing or pricing systems and institutions to cope with yield and price uncertainties.

In view of the existing ceiling on agricultural land holdings, rising income inequalities in the Indian economy, in the recent period, are attributable mainly to rising rural-urban disparities, and rising intra-urban inequalities in income and not so much to income inequalities within agriculture.

Since the size of labour force dependent on agriculture in India is going to be quite high for the next few decades, the existing ceiling on agricultural landholdings needs to be continued for preventing the concentration of agricultural land into a few large holdings or agri-corporations. This is a necessary precondition for ensuring inclusiveness in agriculture growth, especially because there is no evidence, as yet, that small farmers can not raise total factor productivity in agriculture as effectively as large farmers, when adequate public support systems are in place.

However, given the existing ceiling on ownership holdings, tenancy needs to be liberalised so that those wanting to leave agriculture—whether large or small land owners—are free to lease out their land without fear of losing their ownership. This would enable those choosing to remain in agriculture to become viable by enlarging their operational holdings, provided tenants have adequate access to institutional credit through the loan eligibility cards issued to them, as recommended by the Koneri Ranga Rao Committee for Andhra Pradesh (AP) in 2004.

It is clear from the Report of this Committee that a promising source for strengthening the land base of the most marginalised group like tribal population is to restore land that was illegally alienated from them which was estimated to be as high as 50 per cent of their land in AP. According to the Committee, if alienation of land continues at the present rate, tribals would soon become landless.

Under such conducive land relations, high agriculture growth by itself can contribute to inclusiveness through the rise in rural employment and wages and incomes of the small and marginal farmers. This explains why in India the phases of high agriculture growth have been associated with significant reduction in rural poverty.

Yet, there is considerable unexploited potential for more effective participation of the lagging regions like dry land areas and smallholders in agriculture growth for achieving greater inclusiveness and thus strengthening food and nutritional security.

In the present phase of high investment under greater uncertainty and risk, there is a need for much greater role of the government than in the green revolution days for the provision of irrigation, research and extension, institutional credit, and marketing infrastructure. As the 12th Plan document admits, public investment in irrigation during the 11th Plan period which would have benefited all classes of farmers, fell considerably short of the targets: public investment target of 4 per cent of agriculture GDP was not achieved. There is also a considerable shortfall in the outlay on agricultural research and extension which now stands at 0.7 per cent of agriculture GDP as against 1 per cent recommended by the Indian Council of Agricultural Research (ICAR) 20 years ago and a high figure of nearly 2 per cent for China.

But stepping up public investment alone is not enough. Public support needs to be supplemented in a major way by the increasing participation of the organised private sector like agro-processing firms and organised retail for the provision of these services including insurance to the farmers with appropriate regulations by the government. Such participation by the private sector would contribute not only to strengthening the resource position and knowledge base of farmers but would also create an environment of greater certainty in regard to prices and yields.

However, to be able to deal with the organised private sector on favourable terms, the small farmers need to be organised into cooperatives or groups for specific purposes, especially for marketing and insurance. Hopefully, the high profitability of collective endeavour in the ensuing phase of agriculture development will provide enough incentives for small and marginal farmers to organise themselves into such groups.

Food Security: The Issue of Direct Cash Transfers versus Public Distribution of Foodgrains

The avowed objectives of PDS (public distribution system) are three-fold: First, to provide implicit income support to the beneficiaries to the extent of the difference between the PDS price and the market price; second, to ensure sufficient availability of foodgrains in periods of scarcity, particularly in remote areas; and third—rarely brought in the present debate but, nevertheless, crucial for ensuring nutritional security—to alter the relative prices in favour of foodgrains for the poor consumers so that they may end up by consuming more foodgrains than they would if they have to buy whole of their requirements at free market prices.

Direct cash payments to the beneficiaries in lieu of price subsidy can, at best, meet the first objective of income support. Even this is doubtful in periods of inflation because of the need to keep track of the rising market prices for fully compensating the consumers. Besides, there is the well-acknowledged difficulty of such compensations reaching the women who run the household. Availability of foodgrains in the market on private account in sufficient quantity in periods of scarcity, especially in remote areas, is highly problematic. The third objective—perhaps the most important one—of ensuring nutritional security through the substitution effect by making foodgrains cheaper, can not be met through direct cash payments.

However, direct cash payments in the case of subsidy on fertiliser like urea may be desirable, as the resulting higher market price may discourage its excessive use.

Social Inclusion: The Present Status

The incidence of poverty has been most pronounced among the SCs (scheduled castes), STs (scheduled tribes), and Muslims. According to the India Human Development Report 2011 (Institute of Applied Manpower Research 2011), the SCs, STs and Muslims suffer the most on account of poor health status: the most striking shortcoming of our public health system has been the failure to reach out to the bottom of the pyramid, to the 300 million people who are often excluded.

The problem of illiteracy in both rural and urban areas was most pronounced among SCs, STs, and Muslims, and relatively more pronounced among females. The Report points out that the combination of low public expenditure on both health and education has had serious, long-lasting adverse consequences for India's human development levels, and suggests that establishing publicly funded educational institutions alone can ensure greater participation from among the educationally disadvantaged communities.

Some Recent Developments

However, of late, there are certain encouraging developments in regard to social inclusion—a ray of hope, so to say—pointing to the possible factors responsible for such favourable outcomes and the direction in which policies can be focused for accelerating desirable changes.

One good news according to the *Human Development Report 2011*, is that all the three groups, that is, SCs, STs, and Muslims have been converging towards the national average in terms of literacy rate. Health indicators for these marginalised groups are also converging with the national average, although in absolute terms, the overall situation continues to be worrisome. Over the same period, that is, between 2004-05 and 2009-10, the unemployment rate among the workers belonging to these three groups declined in both rural and urban areas. Poverty has declined for these groups at an accelerated rate between 2004-05 and 2009-10—which is higher than the overall or average annual rate of decline.

Basing on the data from the same source which covers a decade beyond what was captured in the *Sachar Committee Report*, the gaps between Muslims and the national average on most human development outcomes are narrowing, reflecting their improving condition.

These encouraging developments should not come as a surprise. The year 2004 was a watershed after 15 years of economic reforms, when the government at the centre made an explicit commitment, for the first time, to implementing economic reforms with human face. Among many policy initiatives taken in the social sector, two major ones are Mahatma Gandhi National Rural Employment Guarantee Programme and the Programme for the Welfare of Minorities. On all accounts, these two programmes had a distinctly better impact.

At the state level, according to *HDR 2011*, "the experience of Kerala and Tamil Nadu demonstrate that the 'destiny' of population can be changed through appropriate policies that address the needs of the marginalised communities. The analysis makes a strong argument for all state governments to act as agents of change to make the development process truly inclusive." It may be noted that in both Kerala and Tamil Nadu, the system of public distribution of foodgrains has been functioning successfully. These states also ensure better accountability of programme performance through Panchayati Raj Institutions.

Governance

The observations on governance in the 12th Plan document are worth mentioning as they are based on an in-depth analysis of past performance:

> The experience with Plan programmes has clearly established the central role of a socially mobilized and aware community as a decisive determinant of success....The states that have emphasized the role played by social mobilisation and have made specific financial and human resource provisions have, invariably, succeeded. It is the participation of users in planning, implementation and social audit of these programmes that has proved critical to their success.

But the basic issue is a political one of ensuring much quicker response of our democratic system to the needs and aspirations of the poorer and marginalised sections of society. The shift in policy towards economic reforms with human face and the strategy of inclusive growth adopted in the 11th and 12th Plans did represent the response of our democratic system to the growing discontent among the poorer sections. But the pace of change has been too slow, halting and even retrogressive sometimes because of the resistance from the vested interests.

Based on the inaugural presentations made at the National Seminars on "Inclusive Agriculture Growth and Food Security", at the Department of Economics, Osmania University, 15 March 2014; and "Economic Growth and Marginalized Groups: A Search for Inclusive Policy" at the School of Economics, University of Hyderabad, 24 March 2014. Published in *Mainstream* LII(38), 13 September 2014.

3

Future of Indian Children

In spite of steady economic growth, India is home to one-third of the world's undernourished children. Young Lives panel study on children carried out at the CESS for 2002, 2006, and 2009 has highlighted that about one third of younger children are stunted and did not register much progress in the last decade.

According to *Save the Children Report* of 2012, India is ranked amongst the bottom three countries in respect of government commitment in addressing undernutrition. Deficiency of micronutrients is common in India, because

The author speaking on the occasion of the Distinguished Lecture by the Chief Guest Dr A.P.J. Abdul Kalam, Former President of India, at the CESS on 28 March 2014.

diets rely predominantly on staple grains. Studies by the Centre for Economic and Social Studies (CESS) on women empowerment, and Young Lives study on childhood poverty have revealed that parental education, safe motherhood practices, dietary habits influence child nutrition.

Since agriculture plays a dominant role in our rural economy even today, public investment in agriculture along with innovative interventions like organic farming, due importance to small millets, and crop diversification may enhance the returns to farmers resulting in reduction of poverty and improving food and nutrition security. According to the International Food Policy Research Institute (IFPRI) initiative on Tackling Agriculture and Nutrition Disconnect in India (TANDI), the pathways between agriculture and nutrition are child feeding practices, nutrition knowledge among women and women's control over income and assets, all of which have a positive impact on nutritional outcomes. Young Lives study at the CESS too confirmed these findings.

National Family Health Survey (NFHS) data show that between 1998 and 2005-06, the incidence of malnutrition (underweight) below three years old increased for the bottom three deciles as against a decline for the top three deciles. This finding underscores the need for achieving inclusive growth in agriculture.

National Food Security Mission, Rashtriya Krishi Vikas Yojana, National Mission for Sustainable Agriculture, Pulse Village Scheme and Nutri-Farm Initiative are designed for improving agriculture and reduce malnutrition. Thus nutrition sensitive agriculture is gaining predominance in policy. In view of this, the Division for Child Studies (DCS) at the CESS can take initiative to collaborate with agriculture scientists, scientists from National Institute of Nutrition (NIN) and explore the characteristics of nutrition sensitive agriculture and link such evidence with policy. In this context, another area where DCS can work is on the impact of change in nutrition related behaviour, effective use of communication technologies in arresting malnutrition, and document good practices.

Observations made on the occasion of the Distinguished Lecture on "Future of Indian Children" delivered by the Chief Guest Dr A.P.J. Abdul Kalam, Former President of India, at the Centre for Economic and Social Studies, Hyderabad, on 28 March 2014.

4

A Study on Young Lives

The fourth series of 'fact sheets' just released give a preliminary overview of some of the key data emerging from Round 4 of the Young Lives household and child survey relating to the state of Telangana.

The most encouraging finding from this survey of Young Lives in Telangana is that as many as 96 per cent of 12-year-old children, whether boys or girls, were enrolled in elementary schools in 2013. This represents a

Prime Minister Prof Manmohan Singh declaring open the Auditorium before inaugurating the Silver Jubilee Seminar at the CESS on 7 January 2006.

substantial increase since 2006, the rate of increase being even higher for girls. STs (scheduled tribes) children of this age showed the highest rate of enrolment of 99 per cent in 2013. All this is in keeping with the huge increase in enrolment at elementary level across the country, especially following the ratification of The Right to Free and Compulsory Education Act, 2009 (RTE Act).

However, the educational outcome in terms of the learning levels of these 12-year-olds in 2013 is extremely worrisome. Their scores in maths tests show that their learning levels have declined, scoring significantly less than the children of the same age in 2006. A test involving simple division ranks lowest among the learning levels tested in maths. This picture of declining levels of learning is common to both the government and private schools, the government schools showing greater deterioration. The decline in performance is worse among children from rural areas and from poorer households.

Apparently, the causes for the observed deterioration in educational outcomes are two-fold: the decline in the effectiveness of learning or absorption by students and teaching processes. The first involves, among other things, nutritional status of children; and the second, training of teachers and their attendance, especially in government-run schools. In any case, as rightly observed in these fact sheets, the focus in education has to move now from 'access' to 'learning outcomes' giving due attention to quality teaching processes and the learning environment in schools.

One of the driving forces towards private schooling, according to these fact sheets, is the parental aspirations for better standards. However, the poorer households could afford to send only about 21 per cent of their children to private schools as against over 80 per cent of children from the richest third of households. Therefore, equity in access to education requires improving quality in government schools.

The findings of the survey on nutrition and health of children are highly relevant in this context. The fact sheets note that there has been little improvement in nutritional status of the younger cohort children in Telangana in terms of both stunting and thinness, and argue for the need to tackle malnutrition among the poorest children, SC and ST children, and children in rural areas in general.

Strengthening accountability mechanisms for performance of various programmes is central to ensuring appropriate educational outcomes. The existing top-down accountability mechanisms are far from being sufficient. The new bottom-up accountability mechanisms have to be built into the institutional framework for decentralisation of development, especially in rural areas, by empowering *panchayats* and *gram sabhas* and by raising awareness of parents in matters related to education and nutrition.

Observations made at the launch of "Putting Children at the Centre of Development Planning: Some Preliminary Findings from Young Lives Longitudinal Study: Telangana State and new State of Andhra Pradesh", Centre for Economic and Social Studies, Hyderabad, 22 September 2014.

5

Division for Sustainable Development Studies at the CESS

It is a privilege for me to have been associated with the Advisory Committee for Studies in the Research Unit for Livelihoods and Natural Resources at the Centre for Economics and Social Studies (CESS). These studies tried to examine the livelihoods and natural resources in an integrated manner by understanding the complex links and interactions between the two in the larger socioeconomic context subjected to fast changes. The research, in particular, looked at a wide spectrum of natural resources, both renewable and non-renewable, which are significant for livelihoods directly or indirectly. The faculty in this unit carried out their studies in collaboration with other reputed research institutes in the country, NGOs, and government agencies which turned out to be quite a rewarding experience.

Increasing loss of forests, land degradation and decline in freshwater quality and quantity undermine the already fragile livelihoods of people, especially the poor. With growing inequality, those least resilient to withstand the decline in the natural resource base will fall further behind. Poor women, representing the majority of the underprivileged, constitute one such group with limited resilience.

Over the last two decades of globalisation and acceleration in GDP (gross domestic product) growth in the country, one witnesses unprecedented pressure on natural resources owing to their unregulated exploitation by corporate interests with scant regard for its adverse impact on the livelihoods of the marginalised sections. Therefore, a major challenge of development in the coming decades will be to integrate environmental protection with economic development and social progress in ways that reduce poverty, narrow inequalities including gender inequalities at all levels, address the root causes of environmental degradation, social exclusion and development gaps by subjecting them to greater accountability so as to realise a sustainable future for all.

What has been the experience so far with the implementation of government schemes for better management of natural resources and improvement in the livelihoods of those dependent on such resources? 'An Anthology of Research Studies' completed under the Research Unit for Livelihoods and Natural Resources, being released by the Chairman, CESS, at this function contains valuable information on the implementation of several schemes including Forest Rights Act and Rehabilitation and Resettlement of those displaced by the development projects. In general, the implementation of schemes is far from satisfactory owing to the lack of political will reflected in the failure to resist pressures exerted by corporate interests and unwillingness to ensure the participation of the affected people in the implementation process. A ray of hope in a democracy like ours is that, as brought out by these studies, the awareness of the relevant issues among the stakeholders has been rising and there is some evidence of growing capacity among vulnerable sections to organise and resist injustices.

I am glad that the CESS having worked for six years between 2008-2014 in the three core areas of forest, dry land and river basin ecosystems and their linkages with livelihoods of the communities, has now decided to take forward the pool of knowledge base created by expanding it to other related frontiers of knowledge by starting a Division of Sustainable Development Studies. This decision to broaden the scope of studies necessitates that besides RULNR core faculty, CESS faculty working in the areas such as sustainable agriculture, industry, gender issues are also involved, forming the core research team for the new division. Their collaboration with a number of research institutions of repute in the country is bound to enrich the work envisaged.

I wish the CESS Faculty and those from the collaborating institutions all the best in their endeavours.

Opening remarks made while inaugurating the Division for Sustainable Development Studies (DSDS) at the Centre for Economic and Social Studies, Hyderabad, on 26 May 2014.

6

India Labour and Employment Report 2014

Workers in the Era of Globalisation

India Labour and Employment Report 2014: Workers in the Era of Globalization, prepared by the Institute for Human Development in collaboration with the Indian Society of Labour Economics, analyses changes in the labour markets in India in the post economic reform period and highlights the major employment challenges.

Let me start with certain positive developments brought out by the Report. There has been significant increase in real wages at an average rate of over 3 per cent per year during the three decades between 1983 and 2012. The growth of organised sector employment was high since 2004-05 with its share rising by a little over 5 percentage points to 17 per cent by 2011-12. For the first time, the share of regular formal employment also registered some increase reaching 7.5 per cent.

Thanks to the reservation policy, the access to quality employment for the deprived groups has also increased. These favourable developments led to a decline in poverty, the largest decline being among the SCs (scheduled castes), STs (scheduled tribes), OBCs (other backward class) and upper section of Muslims. Further, the pro-poor programmes such as Mahatma Gandhi National Rural Employment Guarantee Act (MGNREGA) implemented during this period contributed to worker awareness and improved their bargaining power.

These favourable developments notwithstanding, a little over 90 per cent of workers are still engaged in informal employment, a large majority of them having low earnings with limited or no social protection. Disadvantaged social groups are mostly concentrated in low-productivity sectors. The Report affirms the position often observed that the level of open unemployment in India is quite low (2.7%) showing that most workers being poor cannot afford to remain unemployed. As such, the problem is not primarily of unemployment but lack of productive employment.

Good quality 'formal' employment being rare, access to it is extremely unequal. Workers in the southern and western states have much better access to good quality employment when compared to those in the central and eastern regions. A dismal feature brought out by the Report is the substantial decline in the work participation of females during 2005-2012, even after accounting for their enrolment in educational institutions and the income effect. This decline in work participation has much to do with the lack of appropriate opportunities for females.

Notwithstanding the favourable impact of some of the pro-poor programmes on the bargaining power of the poor, the Report points out that increasing 'informalisation' of employment has eroded the strength of trade unions. This, by itself, seems to have increased the bargaining power of employers relative to that of workers, as indicated by the sharp decline in the percentage of work days lost due to strikes, even as there was considerable increase in closures.

Thus while the acceleration in the GDP growth rate in the post-economic reform period did result in some improvement in the employment situation, it could not bring about structural transformation of the economy characterised by widespread poverty, inequality and deprivation. On the contrary, it appears that the prevailing inequitable social structure in India has had a significant influence on the decision-making processes leading to a pattern of GDP growth which continues to be non-inclusive as indicated, among other things, by the declining share of wages and rising share of profits.

Against this backdrop, the most important challenge on the employment front, according to the Report, is the large number of 'working poor' and underemployed engaged in low productivity activities in the unorganised sectors. Youth unemployment, particularly that of educated females, is also becoming a major concern. The Report advocates rapid growth of organised sector, particularly manufacturing, provision of education and skills to the growing young population, and a minimum level of social security to all workers.

Comments made following the release of *India Labour and Employment Report 2014: Workers in the Era of Globalization* (prepared by the Institute for Human Development, New Delhi, in collaboration with the Indian Society of Labour Economics) at the Council for Social Development, Hyderabad, 27 August 2014.

7

Dynamics of Rural Labour Markets in India

Recent Trends and Policy Concerns

As pointed out in the background note for this seminar by S.R. Sankaran Chair at the National Institute of Rural Development and Panchayati Raj (NIRD&PR), the ongoing structural changes in Indian economy are leading to significant changes in rural labour market affecting their livelihoods and prospects for future. These developments call for discussions among social scientists for stock-taking and reflecting on policies for improving the livelihoods of rural labour.

The subject is important and interesting and is also quite wide-ranging. The major developments in the rural labour markets that have acquired prominence in the recent period in large parts of the country are: first, a significant rise in wages of agricultural labour and of rural labour in general; second, emergence of rural non-farm sector as an important source of employment for those dependent on agriculture; and third, increasing feminisation of agriculture consequent to male labour moving out, even as there has been a decline in the rural female labour force participation.

Rural Wages

Let me take up the rise in rural wages first. They are driven basically by the rising demand for labour emanating from the growth in agriculture as well as overall GDP. Agricultural wages are particularly sensitive to the growth in agriculture GDP (gross domestic product). Real wages of male as well as female agricultural workers showed a marked rise in several states during the decade of 1980s and later during 2005-06 to 2010-11. In both the periods, agriculture growth rate in the country had accelerated to a little over 3 per cent per annum. Growth in real agricultural wages slowed down during the post-reform period of 15 years between 1990-91 and 2005-06 when agricultural growth decelerated to below 2 per cent per annum, despite an acceleration in overall GDP growth. Real wages of rural casual labourers, both males and females, rose significantly in the country during 12 years ending 2011-12 (Jose 2016, Binswanger-Mkhize 2012).

The rise in rural wages, particularly a significant rise in quite a few states during 2005-06 to 2010-11, cannot be explained solely by the growth in agricultural and overall GDP. Rural labour being unorganised and consisting largely of those living below the poverty line have a low staying power and hence low bargaining power. Social security measures like pensions, public distribution of foodgrains, provision of healthcare, etc. targeted at them have a potential to raise their capacity for bargaining by improving their staying power. Mahatma Gandhi National Rural Employment Guarantee Programme (MGNREGA) launched during this period, and effectively implemented in quite a few states, is widely believed to have contributed significantly to raising the rural wages, especially agricultural wages, by improving the bargaining power of rural labour and raising their 'reservation wage'.

Farmers who depend essentially on hired labour have been quite vocal on being adversely affected by MGNREGA. Village studies such as the one by scholars from the International Crops Research Institute for the Semi-arid Tropics (ICRISAT) indeed confirm that this scheme has led to a rise in the share of labour cost in the total production cost, despite a decline in the number of labour days hired consequent to mechanisation (Nagaraj et al. 2016). Such a rise in wage share can be expected because the elasticity of substitution between labour and capital has, in general, been found to be less than unity in Indian agriculture under the given technology. But this is a static picture reflecting the immediate response by the farmers.

Over a period of time, however, farmers respond to the rise in the cost of labour by adopting capital-intensive technologies and practices, including diversification of agriculture, which raise profits by raising productivity and reducing the unit costs and, in the process, contribute to raising the growth rate of agriculture. This indeed seems to have happened, as diversification of agriculture towards high value products has, of late, been an important source of agricultural growth. The ICRISAT paper mentioned above does hint at such a possibility.

My own study, "Technological Change and Distribution of Gains in Indian Agriculture" done in the mid-1970s had brought out how in response to the rise in the cost of labour farmers reduce unit costs by raising productivity through increased application of fertilisers. In fact, a couple of years ago, another ICRISAT exercise had indicated a positive impact of wage rates on agricultural growth. Even if these results cannot be treated as conclusive because of problems of estimation, logical or a priori reasoning pointing to the positive relationship between wage rates and output growth cannot be given up altogether.

Even as they effectively cope with the rise in wage cost by adopting new technologies to raise productivity, farmers hiring labour may continue to express their misgivings about welfare programmes like MGNREGA which improve the bargaining power of labour. Such prejudices are inherent in a society characterised by inequalities of wealth and status. However, from the social point of view, the encouraging results of MGNREGA should prompt the policymakers to implement welfare measures targeted at the poor among the unorganised labour such as those recommended by the National Commission for Enterprises in the Unorganized Sector (2004-2007), headed by Prof Arjun Sengupta.

Rural Non-farm Sector

The emergence of rural non-farm sector as an important source of output and employment holds the prospects of spatially broad-based and environment-friendly growth conducive to the well-being of the rural poor. Spatially broad-based growth would reduce the costs and hardships associated with migration and urban congestion and can ensure larger volume of employment than when growth is limited to high wage pockets.

Non-farm wage income is less variable than income from farming which is subject to weather-induced fluctuations. Small, marginal, and semi-medium farmers may be receiving a larger proportion of their income as wage income and remittances from non-farm sources when compared to the medium and large farmers (Ranganathan et al. 2016). As the rural non-farm sector grows, this stable source of their income may predominate, thus drought-proofing their incomes. In view of the rise in land values, such farmers may prefer to continue as part-time farmers without alienating their land.

Agroprocessing which has strong linkages with agriculture and which has a large potential for sustained growth of output and employment in rural non-farm sector has yet to make a visible impact in India. Sustained growth of agriculture through the rise in TFP (total factor productivity) is indispensable for the growth of rural non-farm sector because of its strong backward and forward linkages. This requires strong policy measures to raise agricultural productivity and improve infrastructure for agricultural marketing.

Apart from raising agricultural productivity, the growth of rural non-farm sector requires broad-based development of physical and social infrastructure in rural areas such as roads, electricity, water, schools and health care facilities. In this context, it would be instructive to study inter-state or regional variation in the development of rural non-farm sector in India in relation to agriculture growth and development of rural infrastructure.

Feminisation of Agriculture

Feminisation of agriculture is largely a consequence of male labour in the household taking up non-farm work. Management of farms by women may become widespread among marginal, small and medium farms in course of time with the male members of households increasingly taking up non-farm work.

Management of farms by women should be regarded as an opportunity as well as a challenge. Opportunity, because it enables empowerment of farm women who have greater familiarity with enterprises like dairying and horticulture which are going to be the major sources of farm income. Challenge because women lack property rights on land, farming becomes an additional responsibility for them apart from household work, their lower literacy level and lack of experience in dealing with agricultural support systems, including extension services, which are male dominated.

As it is, small and marginal farmers fail to get adequate access to agricultural support systems because of their weaker resource position and various forms of discrimination against them within and outside the village. The seriousness of the challenge is underlined by the need to accelerate total factor productivity growth in agriculture where small and marginal farmers predominate cultivating a substantial proportion of area, including the area leased-in by them which is on the increase.

Nevertheless, a silver lining is that apart from their familiarity with and expertise in managing certain farm enterprises, women farmers have performed extremely well when adequately empowered, as exemplified by the work of women's self-help groups. This experiment needs to be extended for the provision of various services, including marketing, by organising small and marginal farmers into groups.

Since feminisation of agriculture is a major challenge, it calls for strong policy initiatives, right from the national level, for dealing with issues such as strengthening land inheritance rights for women, endowment of property rights on houses built with public assistance, improving literacy level and awareness among women farmers, measures to lighten the burden of their household work, and sensitising the agricultural support systems, including credit institutions, about the needs of women farmers and, in particular, inducting women in large numbers in agricultural extension system to assist women farmers.

Inaugural Address at the National Seminar on "Dynamics of Rural Labour Relations/Markets in India: Issues, Dimensions and Processes", S.R. Sankaran Chair (Rural Labour), National Institute of Rural Development and Panchayati Raj (10-12 March 2016), Hyderabad. Published in *Rural Labour in India: Processes and Policy Options*, S.R. Sankaran Chair (Rural Labour), NIRD&PR, Hyderabad, 2016; Also in *Mainstream*, 19 March 1916.

8

Some Major Issues Related to *Adivasis*

Major Issues

The socioeconomic condition of *adivasis* as the most marginalised section of our society has been extensively documented. I do not propose to describe their condition again. I would rather like to straightaway raise three major issues for policy action and further research: first, the restoration, to the extent possible, and protection of the existing land and other natural resource base of the *adivasis*; second, the prospects of raising agricultural productivity which is going to be their major source of sustenance for quite some time to come; and third, the issues of governance in tribal areas, including development administration in general, and *adivasis*' own political participation and their collective action towards making governance work for their betterment.

Land Base

The process of alienation of land, traditionally held by *adivasis* for cultivation, to the migrant farmers and moneylenders because of high indebtedness or other fraudulent practices which started in the colonial period continues unabated to this day. It is estimated that in the last two to three decades alone, nearly half of their land under cultivation has been alienated in different parts of the country. Such alienation has been quite high in the undivided state of Andhra Pradesh: according to the Land Committee headed by Koneru Ranga Rao, a Minister, in 2004, as much as half the land held by tribals had been alienated to non-tribal population and "if it is not checked with strong executive action, very soon the tribals may not have lands at all." The Committee recommended restoring lands to the tribals by reopening and re-examining of orders in favour of non-tribals and review of a large number of cases of illegal occupation by non-tribals. Thus the threat of erosion of land base of *adivasis* in the country looms large calling for the requisite political will to protect their major source of living.

Despite the continuing alienation of land, the remaining land base of tribals appears slightly better than the average for all the social groups in the country. According to the Report of the High Level Committee on Socio-Economic, Health and Educational Status of Tribal Communities in India (May 2014), the area owned by STs (scheduled tribes) per rural household in 2003 was 0.77 hectares when compared to the All India average of 0.73 hectares per rural household. The Report notes, however, that the alienation of tribal lands may not be fully reflected in the records. Besides, the quality of land under cultivation by the tribals is poorer than the average for the country because of degradation and smaller proportion of area irrigated.

There were high hopes from the enactment of the Scheduled Tribes and Forest Dwellers (Recognition of Forest Rights) Act, 2006, implemented since 2008. But its implementation by the states has been tardy. Only about half of the claims of individual ownership rights and very few rights on community forest resources have been accepted. Altogether, the impact of this measure on improving the land base of tribals has been minimal.

Conservation of natural resources like forests is critical for the protection of livelihoods of *adivasis* because of their greater dependence on these resources when compared to other social groups. There is a threat of their displacement on account of indiscriminate exploitation of minerals—abundant in tribal areas—as well as location of various projects in the tribal belt in the post-liberalisation era. Certain measures initiated by the United Progressive Alliance (UPA) government like the

Right to Fair Compensation and Transparency in Land Acquisition, Rehabilitation and Resettlement Act 2013 sought to provide safeguards such as getting the consent of the affected people as a prerequisite for undertaking such projects and liberal compensation to those affected. But the ordinances brought by the present government seek to dilute or do away with these safeguards. This issue has already evoked a fierce debate in the country and the outcome is eagerly awaited, especially by those interested in the well-being of the marginalised sections like *adivasis*.

Agricultural Productivity

The dependence of STs on agriculture as a major source of livelihood in 2009-10 was as high as 70 per cent—about 37 per cent of them as self-employed in agriculture and another 33 per cent as casual labour within agriculture. Because of their shrinking land base and low agricultural productivity, their dependence on casual labour within agriculture has been increasing and is next only to SCs. Their outmigration and dependence on non-agriculture as casual labour, though low at present, has been increasing. For example, their participation in Mahatma Gandhi National Rural Employment Guarantee Scheme (MGNREGS), in terms of number of days worked, was highest among all social groups in 2009-10.

It has been estimated that the value of agricultural output per hectare in central tribal districts of the country in 2007 was less than one-third of national average. Across the districts in Chhattisgarh in 2004-05, one finds an inverse relationship between the proportion of tribal population and yield per acre of paddy and pulses. In Odisha too, one finds a similar inverse relationship between yield rate of foodgrains and per cent of ST population across districts in 2005-06. In the tribal areas of the country, the proportion of area irrigated and the quantity of fertilisers used per acre are quite low when compared to the average for the country, despite the co-existence of tribal agriculture with that practiced by non-tribal migrants in the same areas who realise much higher yields by investing in minor irrigation and practicing input-intensive agriculture.

This shows the weaker resource position of the *adivasi* farmers and their inadequate access to public extension services and institutional sources of credit in an otherwise exploitative environment. My own field visits to several tribal areas in the country including Jhabua in Madhya Pradesh in the late 1970s and to Paderu in Andhra Pradesh in the early 1990s (this visit was kindly arranged by late S.R. Sankaran) clearly brought home the willingness of tribal farmers to use irrigation and yield-increasing modern inputs when access to them is ensured by public agencies.

But we do not know how productivity in tribal agriculture has been changing over a period of time in different parts of the country and the factors contributing to the observed changes. An intensive investigation into these aspects is essential for devising appropriate strategies for raising productivity. We do know, however, that in general water conservation through watershed development, minor irrigation and the use of high-yielding technology including fertilisers are the promising sources for tapping the existing high potential for raising productivity in tribal agriculture. Because of unsustainable use of chemical inputs in certain areas of green revolution, it would be tempting to romanticise the low-input agriculture and advocate organic farming for tribal areas. The products of organic farming have a price advantage but not the yield advantage—essential for achieving food security. Organic farming is profitable under a highly developed marketing framework for meeting the demand from the affluent sections of consumers. Nobel Laureate Dr Norman Borlaug's view that green revolution through the use of sustainable but input-intensive and yield-increasing technology is indispensable for food security cannot be overlooked.

The ongoing research study on agriculture in tribal areas in seven states of the country sponsored by the Indian Council of Social Science Research (ICSSR) and coordinated by the Centre for Economic and Social Studies (CESS) promises to throw new light on the critical issues bearing on the growth of productivity in tribal agriculture. Indeed, the importance of this subject emphasises the need for an officially constituted high level expert body at the national level for making a focused investigation in different parts of the country and recommending measures to restore and protect the existing land base of *adivasis* and to raise agricultural productivity.

Participatory Governance

Posting committed, competent and honest officials in tribal areas, is a necessary condition for efficient and responsive administration. This can be supplemented by the participation of well-trained tribal youth through their induction at different levels including in services like agricultural extension, supply of inputs, institutional credit and marketing, etc. This would make administration sensitive to the local needs and would fill up the large vacuum that exists in governance in remote tribal areas and would thus help to bring the people closer to administration by bridging the communication gap. While in the Planning Commission, my extensive visit to Bastar in 1982 had convinced me that the prevailing vacuum in administration and the communication gap was largely responsible for whatever encouragement that the extremists got for their activities in this area.

Effective community action is a well-known trait of tribal communities. This latent force can be harnessed to build up pressures from tribal population for redressing their grievances, among other things, through their effective participation in elected *panchayats*. Unfortunately, however, because of the way our democratic institutions are functioning, the needs of the small minority groups like tribals are not met through the effective ventilation of their grievances. According to Prof R. Radhakrishna, in the north-eastern states where tribal population is in majority and their leaders are in power, the socioeconomic condition of tribal population is much better than that of their counterparts in the rest of the country. In most of the remaining states, tribal population is a small minority at the state, district and even at block levels. This accounts for their low political clout, so much so, even the left parties are not quite visible in mobilising tribal population around their pressing demands.

A silver lining is the existence of quite a few committed NGOs without political motives of their own. Such agencies could be encouraged and supported from the highest policy level to take up the demands of tribal population and mobilise them for effective collective action. The feeling of alienation is bred when there is a sense of neglect and discrimination; and, worse, when there is no hope of redressing through democratic and peaceful means. This feeling creates a fertile ground for extremist activities with tacit support from the aggrieved population.

Inaugural Address at the National Seminar on "Labour Market and Issues Related to Adivasis", at NIRD&PR, Hyderabad, 22-23 January 2015. Published in *Adivasis in India: Issues of Livelihood and Labour Market, Public Action and Market Solutions*, S.R. Sankaran Chair (Rural Labour), NIRD&PR, Hyderabad, 2015; Also in *Mainstream*, 21 February 2015.

9

Governance, Resources, and Livelihoods of *Adivasis* in India

*Strengthening Tribal Leadership for Effective Implementation of PESA and FRA**

The Panchayats (Extension to Scheduled Areas) Act (PESA), 1996—applicable to Schedule V areas in 10 states—empowers *gram sabhas* to manage forest lands and community resources, including decision-making relating to land acquisition and development projects and implementation of social sector development projects. Forest Rights Act (FRA) of 2006 aims at correcting the historical injustice done to *adivasis* and forest dwelling communities by granting individual/community based tenurial rights over forest land.

This empowerment of *gram sabhas* at the hamlet or village level has aroused widespread expectations among *adivasis* and there are some encouraging cases of implementation of these Acts in some states because of civil society activism and the good work done by NGOs (non-governmental organisations). But the gap between promise from the extent of empowerment under these Acts and performance or achievements on the ground is very wide. In this sense, the implementation is far from satisfactory.

---

* Valedictory Address at the National Seminar on "Governance, Resources and Livelihoods of Adivasis in India: Implementation of PESA and FRA" organised by S.R. Sankaran Chair at the National Institute of Rural Development and Panchayati Raj, Hyderabad, 19 November 2016; Also published in *Mainstream*, Annual 2016, 24 December 2016.

A reading of the papers presented at this seminar clearly brings home the point that *adivasis'* own awareness of the relevant Acts, laws, rules and regulations, as well as their own initiative in taking up issues are critical for effective implementation of the provisions in these Acts. For instance, a paper presented in the seminar refers to a study done by the Planning Commission showing that not even in a single village, *gram sabha* was aware of the rights over natural resources. Therefore, better awareness and leadership from *adivasis* themselves become crucial.

Historian Ramchandra Guha in his essay on "Tribal Tragedies in Independent India" (*Democrats and Dissenters*, Penguin Random House India, 2016), attributes insufficient political clout and low bargaining power of tribals to their concentration in remote areas, unlike the Dalits who live in mixed villages alongside other castes and communities. With 10 to 20 per cent of vote, Dalits can have a decisive impact in elections even in constituencies not reserved for them. Tribal vote may matter only in 50 or 60 constituencies whereas Dalit vote matters in as many as 300 constituencies.

Discussing poor leadership capabilities among *adivasis*, Guha mentions how jobs under ST (scheduled tribe) quota as well as reserved seats in prestigious colleges go to tribals in north-east, because of their better schooling through English medium. Due to their inadequate representation in higher level civil services, tribals are subject to harsh treatment by other officials of forest, police, revenue and various other departments.

It is in recognition of insufficient awareness and low bargaining power of *adivasis* that the Governors have been conferred with significant powers for Schedule V areas in 10 states in matters affecting the livelihood and empowerment of *adivasis*. But, surprisingly, the interventions by the institution of Governor in such matters have been very few. The gap between the powers given to the governors by PESA and their actual exercise is very wide indeed. It was expected that *adivasis* and their leaders approach the governors seeking their intervention under the Act for rescuing and helping them. But such instances are not visible in many of these states because of lack of necessary awareness and initiatives from the grassroots.

For developing tribal leadership, we need to look at the problem with a long-term perspective of 2-3 decades, in view of increasing rural-urban migration among tribal population and feminisation of tribal areas. Livelihood prospects from natural resources are shrinking and becoming increasingly uncertain for tribals. While policies have to be strengthened for protecting the existing sources of livelihood for them, bold and far-reaching measures are needed to explore new avenues of livelihood.

Access to the development of human resources in general and quality education in particular through residential or *ashram* schools holds the key to their prospects in future. This should enable many of them to find remunerative jobs including in higher level services. Those of them remaining in rural areas with some education or choosing to come back would prove to be invaluable assets for providing good leadership. The present approach focusing on area development rather than human development needs to be radically changed. Also, replacing top-down approach by micro-level planning would provide opportunities for the development of local-level leadership. Towards this end, *gram sabhas* should be entrusted with the implementation of Mahatma Gandhi National Rural Employment Guarantee Act (MGNREGA) and such other programmes.

In the meantime, awareness building among the tribal youth with existing literacy levels and augmenting their skills for inducting them in various services in rural areas would better connect the administration with the tribal population and their problems by facilitating the development of local leadership. Way back in the early 1980s, in the course of my visit to the areas in Bastar when I was in the Planning Commission, I found this disjunction to be quite large primarily due to the jobs at the local level being filled by those from the plains, leading to the alienation of administration from the people at large.

Increasing feminisation of tribal agriculture calls for providing better access to services like agricultural extension and credit to women farmers by inducting women officers and workers for the provision of such services. Although in many such areas agriculture is mostly carried on by women, it is not uncommon to find male extension workers belonging to plains spending their time by talking to men. It would also be beneficial to upgrade the skills of women engaged in certain vocations having a good market potential.

10

Poverty as an Element in Priority Setting for Agricultural Research at International Research Centres' Level

Poverty Weighted Congruence Analysis

According to the existing method of allocating resources for research among countries by the Consultative Group on International Agricultural Research (CGIAR), certain low income countries which have been able to reduce inequalities in income significantly through appropriate socio-economic measures are at a disadvantage when compared to certain high income countries where income inequalities are glaring. It is true that the existing inequality and poverty cannot simply be wished away while allocating research resources, especially because research in such situations can make a positive contribution towards alleviating poverty. However, since a country's own capacity to finance research and alleviate poverty is influenced by the level of its per capita income, the existing inequality for countries with high per capita income need not be given full weight in the formula as it would adversely affect the share of those with low per capita income and low income inequality.

Two alternatives for modifying the existing formula may be considered. The Gini Coefficients or measures of inequality used in the present formula for adjusting purchasing power parity per capita income range widely from 55.7 per cent for Latin America to 35.4 per cent for Asia. One way could be to bring down the upper end of the Gini Coefficient to around 45 per cent which would still be higher than 40 per cent used for sub-Saharan Africa. If this procedure is considered arbitrary, an alternative free from subjective judgement could be to estimate the upper end of Gini Coefficient through the regression by relating the Gini Coefficients of individual countries with purchasing power parity per capita incomes for 1991.

Research Agenda

Congruence analysis modified by the locus and level of poverty, as proposed, ensures larger research allocations for crops and regions characterised by greater incidence of poverty. This process enables the research centres to better address poverty concerns by carrying out research focused on the alleviation of poverty than would be possible in the absence of such poverty weighted allocations. However, if the research agenda at the centres' level is not specifically oriented to the goal of alleviating poverty, then the allocations based on poverty weighted congruence analysis may not make any difference to the contribution of research towards poverty alleviation. An attempt is made in this note to indicate the type of research needed for addressing the poverty concerns. However, each centre will have to formulate its own research agenda in the light of its specific circumstances.

From the available evidence, it is clear that the poor in the world at large have so far benefited from agricultural research both as consumers through the attainment of food security and the decline in the relative prices of food, and as producers from a significant rise in their incomes. The experience so far suggests that the prospects for evolving technologies for the benefit of poor farmers are bright and that agricultural research so designed can result in alleviating rural poverty significantly without sacrificing productivity.

In countries where urban poverty predominates and the poor are largely divorced from agriculture as producers, as seems to be the case in certain parts of Latin America, they are affected by technological change in agriculture basically as consumers. In such a situation, agricultural research focused on productivity increase—albeit, consistent with sustainability—will result in alleviating poverty on account of the achievement of food security and the decline in the relative prices of food. If high wages and labour supply bottlenecks inhibit the adoption of productivity-increasing techniques, it may even be desirable to encourage labour-saving technologies. These may, on balance, prove to be beneficial to the poor on account of high growth in food output and the decline in its prices.

Agricultural research in such a situation may be guided by the interests of poor consumers by focusing on the increase in productivity in respect of commodities which predominate their consumption basket and the demand for which is inelastic, so that the increase in the supplies of such commodities results in a significant decline in

Members of the Technical Advisory Committee (TAC) of the CGIAR, meeting at the International Food Policy Research Institute, Washington, D.C., 24-27 September 1997.

their relative prices. Consumers are likely to gain more than the producers from such research. As a consequence, producers may even shift some of their resources away from these products but, on balance, the poor consumers may stand to gain.

The challenges for agricultural research are daunting for countries where a large proportion of the poor live in rural areas and derive their livelihood directly or indirectly from agriculture as small and marginal farmers and landless agricultural labourers. In the Asia-Pacific region, for example, nearly 75 per cent to 80 per cent of the poor live and work in rural areas. Labour-intensive and broad-based agricultural growth, covering fragile and less developed areas and small and marginal farmers, together with conservation of natural resources alone can make a dent on rural poverty in such countries by increasing employment and income for the poor producers. Given the favourable policy environment such as the development of physical infrastructure and ensuring access to productive assets like land and capital for the poor, agricultural research can make a significant contribution towards increasing the incomes of the poor farmers by raising the productivity of their resources and by imparting stability to yields.

The technologies suitable for the poor farmers need to have a labour-using bias by saving on land and capital resources. Technologies to conserve soil and water in degraded or marginal areas would also be necessary to make a dent on poverty. The trade-offs between the objectives of productivity, sustainability and poverty alleviation, if any, need to be minimised.

These objectives pose quite a few challenges in the field of agricultural research. Scientists have to increasingly address the concerns of the less endowed and difficult environments and resource-poor farmers. Such situations are typically characterised by diverse conditions such as moisture stress under low rainfall that is highly variable, and low lying areas under floods. In socio-economic terms, agricultural research has to take into account the low investible capacity as well as the limited risk-bearing capacity of small and marginal farmers. In view of these highly variable agro-climatic and socioeconomic situations, the recommend packages have to be location specific.

For achieving broad-based, labour-intensive and environment-friendly agricultural growth, the following strategies may be necessary in the field of agricultural research. First, the research base may be widened to cover a large number of new crops grown in diverse agro-climatic situations. Secondly, the emphasis may be shifted from yield raising practices for individual crops taken in isolation, to maximising the combined income from all the crops grown in an agricultural year. This would necessitate strengthening research in intercropping, cropping intensity and farming systems suited to different agro-climatic conditions, so as to ensure maximum use of poor farmers' own resources such as land and labour by fully tapping the natural resources like ground water, sunshine and precipitation throughout the year. Thirdly, adequate emphasis may be placed on research to conserve and save on inputs. Research on water management including water-harvesting techniques, biological fixation of nitrogen, minimising wastages in the use of chemical fertilisers, evolving high-yielding seeds incorporating multiple resistance to pests and diseases and adverse environmental conditions, and integrated pest management belong to this category.

With the increase in the outmigration of male labour from rural areas in low income countries in the wake of growth in GDP (gross domestic product) and the rising demand for labour in industry and services, the female labour participation in farm operations is on the increase. This emerging trend provides an opportunity to address the problems of women farmers more effectively. Since, traditionally, the participation of poor women is greater in post-harvest operations and in transplanting and inter-culturing, special attention would be needed for evolving technologies to reduce the drudgery for women and raise the productivity of their labour in such operations. Technologies which reduce drudgery at home can also result in raising their incomes by releasing labour for farm operations. Improved technologies for regeneration of environment through soil and moisture conservation and afforestation would be particularly beneficial to poor women as these will result in better access to fuel-wood, fodder and drinking water.

Experience has shown that socioeconomic measures for the conservation of soil and moisture in marginal areas can become attractive, if technologies for raising crop yields and reducing their variability are available for such unfavourable areas. It is thus necessary to integrate the task for genetic improvements in seeds with the measures for soil and moisture conservation.

Biotechnologies can contribute immensely to the protection and regeneration of environment and alleviation of poverty because of their scale-neutrality at the farm level, their saving on chemical inputs, imparting stability in yields, improved prospects for raising yields in unfavourable areas and by facilitating large-scale afforestation through tissue culture techniques. However, the realisation of this potential depends on the priorities for research. For, biotechnologies present a wide range of options and they can be engineered equally to suit the entrenched interests to the detriment of the poor and the environment.

The new priorities in agricultural research require greater interaction with field situations involving effective participation by poor farmers in setting research agenda as well as in testing out the results of such research. Greater collaboration between agricultural scientists and social scientists would also be needed for understanding the socio-economic rationale of the prevailing farming systems which would help to tailor technology to suit the resource endowments and needs of the poor farmers.

Written as member of the Technical Advisory Committee (TAC), of the Consultative Group on International Agricultural Research (CGIAR), 1995-1997.

11

Key Aspects of State-level Planning

Prologue

The Press Note issued by the Government of India on 1 January 2015, while replacing the Planning Commission with a new Institution named NITI Aayog (National Institution for Transforming India) says that there is a need for setting up an institution that serves basically as a think tank of the government. An important change from the past, says the Press Note, will be replacing the centre-to-state one-way flow of policy by a genuine and continuing partnership with the states, as the States of the Union seek a decisive say in determining the architecture of economic growth and development of the country. However, unless the planning process at the state level is strengthened, by similar think tanks at the State level, it would not be possible to ensure the two-way policy flow and genuine partnership with states. Nor would it be possible to ensure decentralisation of development below the state level envisaged by the NITI Aayog.

This paper on the "Key Aspects of State-Level Planning", written in 1985 indicates the nature and magnitude of the tasks involved in this respect. It appears, in retrospect, that with the exception of some of the developments listed in the section on 'major improvements in methodology', the position has not changed much in many states since then. A number of states have dispensed with the practice of bringing out plan documents. As a result, there is hardly any work done by the planning departments with regard to goal setting, macro projections and project selection. Allocation of resources is also done in an ad hoc manner at the time of annual budget making. With the proposed removal of plan and non-plan distinction, there is an uncertainty with regard to the shape of planning in future.

Planning Machinery

The States' awareness on the issues and problems connected with State planning became perceptible only since the Fourth Plan period when major changes were introduced in regard to the allocation of Plan finances to the states. This induced them to set up suitable planning machinery in their states to take up the challenging tasks in state planning. In order to enable the States to build up suitable planning machinery, the Centre introduced a scheme for strengthening of planning machinery at State level. Under this scheme, the Planning Commission meets two-thirds of the costs incurred on the induction of professional personnel in the State Planning Departments. While recommending the schemes to the State Governments, the Planning Commission also suggested a model for a State planning organisation on the following lines:

(a) There should be an apex body at the State level with the Chief Minister as Chairman, and the Finance Minister, the Planning Minister, and technical experts representing various departments and disciplines.

(b) The work of the apex bodies should be supported by steering groups set up under the chairmanship of technical experts, preferably from outside the Government, in the fields of agriculture, industry, irrigation and power, social services, transport, manpower, and employment and other important functional fields. The Chairmen of these steering groups should be members of the apex planning bodies described above.

(c) To ensure that the apex planning body is effective in guiding Plan formulation as well as the monitoring of Plan implementation, a non-official full-time Deputy chairman will operate through the State Planning Department which should function as the secretariat of the apex planning bodies.

(d) In order to enable the Planning Departments to adequately discharge their secretariat functions for the apex planning bodies, their strength should be suitably augmented with experts drawn from various disciplines and these should also be functionally reorganised into different units which should mainly be the following: (i) Perspective Planning Unit, (ii) Monitoring, Plan Information and Evaluation Unit, (iii) Project Formulation Unit, (iv) Regional/District Planning Unit, (v) Plan Coordination Unit.

Most of the States have taken advantage of the Central scheme and set up apex planning bodies along with necessary technical and administrative staff to support them.

However, from the information received about functioning of the State Planning Boards, it is apparent that these bodies are not very active in most States. They have not been brought close to the planning process operating in the State. Sometimes, some isolated functions like preparation of perspective plan for the State or guidelines for decentralised planning, etc, have been given to the State Planning Board. On the whole, there appears to be considerable scope for enlarging the planning functions at the level of the State Planning Board.

So far as the Planning Departments in the States are concerned, they have been strengthened by setting up functional units on the lines envisaged in the Planning Commission scheme. In some States, the technical machinery available for planning is quite good. For example, Uttar Pradesh has a big State Planning Institute with a number of functional units. Similarly, in Karnataka, Kerala and Gujarat also, there has been considerable strengthening of the planning machinery at the State level.

Major Improvements in Methodology

With the strengthening of planning machinery, the methods and techniques of Plan formulation and implementation have also greatly improved at the State level. The major areas in which the States have improved their methods and techniques are in regard to goals and targets setting, the determination of priorities among sectors and sub-sectors, the criteria for project selection and measurement of Plan/programme/project performance. Some of these details are discussed below:

(a) *Goals and target-setting*: The State Plans have shown consistent improvement in regard to specificity of goals and realism of targets. Apart from the general goals in terms of reaching a particular State domestic product or per capita income, other goals such as employment, growth rate, etc., are now being quantified in the State Plans. Considerable refinements have been introduced in the system of National and Regional Accounts and in the collection and compilation of data which form the basis for target-setting. All these have infused the State plans with a sense of realism and have enabled the planners to indicate realistically the limits within which they can influence the pattern of development.

(b) *Projection of macro parameters*: Techniques of projection used in the State Plans for setting macro-framework are becoming increasingly sophisticated. In the beginning, simple linear methods were used to determine the aggregate income in the terminal year. Currently, many states are employing econometric methods including detailed input-output models for this purpose. The latter are particularly being used in perspective planning exercise. While, as a rule, all States in the country draw up their annual and the medium-term (five-year) Plans, some States which have built up sufficient expertise also undertake perspective planning exercises. In other specific purpose projections made for the medium-term and perspective plans also (that is, population and commodity projections), one finds steady progress in the use of increasingly sophisticated techniques. Thus, for population projection, for instance, a few States, who have built up the expertise, have adopted the component method, and in such cases the estimates have been based on assumptions relating to fertility, mortality, etc. In some other aspects of planning too, there is a keen desire on the part of the States to improve their methods and techniques of estimation. This is particularly true of employment where the projections currently made by the States are based on capital-labour ratios. These methods are being further refined by introducing different components of manpower and sub-sectors of industry and doing the exercise on varying assumptions.

(c) *Allocation of resources*: The methods used by the various States to allocate resources to the different sectors are of varying degrees of refinement. While the past trends in expenditure and the criterion of implementation capability continue to guide the pattern of allocations, a few States have been using sophisticated methods involving the use of capital-output ratios to determine the sectoral allocations. In regard to the methodology for inter-regional (that is, the district level) allocations, a significant improvement has been made by adopting the concept of 'divisible outlay' and by disaggregating this through a method of weighted indicators. More refinements are being introduced in the selection of indicators and in assigning weights to them.

(d) *Criteria for project selection*: With the setting up of project formulation units in the State Planning Departments, a system of methods and procedures for project planning is evolving in India. Major and medium projects in all key sectors of the State economy are now being appraised by the State governments and decisions are taken only after such appraisal. This has improved the quality of planning in the public sector. So far as the private sector is concerned, guidelines and manuals have been prepared by the Centre and State governments for preparing feasibility reports for projects and for scientifically identifying, formulating and implementing projects. From experience derived in the past, certain aspects of project planning are now receiving special attention. These relate to: (i) the optimal timing of investment; (ii) the attention to and or consideration of required investment in associated projects; (iii) the desirability of making available a package of infrastructural facilities and other critical inputs; and (iv) examination of cost-effectiveness including social cost-benefits. The last mentioned aspect is becoming an increasingly important tool in project selection. Some State governments like Madhya Pradesh and Tamil Nadu, are widely using this technique for the selection of irrigation projects. To impart knowledge relating to scientific project planning in the country, a massive training programme on PIME (project implementation, monitoring and evaluation) has been organised by the centre with the assistance of selected institutions in the country.

(e) *Measurement of reporting of plan programme project performance*: Major strides have been made in the States in organising a monitoring and concurrent evaluation system and in making post facto studies on programme evaluation. Monitoring and evaluation units have been established in the States which are measuring and watching the progress of selected Plan schemes against the time and resource schedules during their implementation stages. The States have evolved their own formats for this purpose. The shortfalls and lagging areas are identified and suitable correctives are being applied from time to time. During the current Plan, the monitoring and evaluation systems in the States have been further strengthened with emphasis on the priority areas in agriculture, provision of minimum needs and the implementation of the 20 Points Programme.

Possible Areas for Further Improvement

There are of course many directions in which State planning can show improvement. Some of them have been listed in the 'theme paper' circulated by the Indian Econometric Society. Particular mention may be made of the need to improve perspective planning exercises in the States. A long-term perspective worked out in sufficient detail will bring out clearly the interdependence between different sectors of the economy and would help in a clear understanding of the possibilities for the growth of the economy as well as the constraints inhibiting growth. It would also enable consistent and timely decisions to be made regarding the optimum use of the State's resources, economies of scale and location and regional distribution of economic activities. Long-term sectoral plans for important sectors would be an essential component of such perspective plans. Such sectoral perspective plans would provide a framework for a meaningful dialougue between different levels of policymaking at the State level, so that the role of each agency can be defined.

With a view to improving the quality of a perspective plan, it would be necessary to strengthen the quality of statistical and technical information available. The 'theme paper' has also referred to the updating of natural resources inventory in the State to provide more and better information for planning. The use of aerial photographs and remote-sensing techniques has now provided a tool for quickly updating such data. In some states like Uttar Pradesh, already use is being made of such techniques for updating of the natural resources data. The Department of Science and Technology is also seeking to provide better information on natural resources through its programme of Natural Resources Data Management Systems (NRDMS). During the Seventh Plan, it is proposed to set up information systems on pilot basis in selected districts under this programme.

Regional plans for problem regions in the State would be another essential component of the perspective plan which would strengthen State planning. Systematic regional planning in the country is yet to receive due attention, although we have made some progress in this direction in the context of planning for certain special programmes like Hill Area Development Programme, Tribal Development Programme and the Western Ghats Development Programme. We are also entering into an important phase of decentralised planning at the district level. The methodology of local level planning has been clearly spelt out and the States are expected to adopt a 'stages-approach' to district planning during the Seventh Plan period. Some beginnings have already been made in the States in this regard.

The regional plans and the district plans, which I mentioned, relate to developments at the sub-State level. So far as State Planning is concerned, there is the basic problem of integration. It is necessary to ensure that the plans at the various levels are properly linked and meaningful balance and consistencies are achieved in this process. There is also the problem of integration of the State Plans with the National Plan. After the State plans are finalised by the Planning Commission, the sectoral outlays for State Plans undergo necessary revisions in the light of the alterations in the total outlays decided for the State. Every care is taken to see that sectoral targets as well as outlays for all States add up to corresponding national aggregates embodied in the Plan. But it is necessary to check whether the State plans so aggregated conform to the national objectives in terms of the target rate of growth of GDP and its principal components as well as in regard to the achievement of certain national goals like the reduction in regional disparities, growth in employment and removal of poverty. The achievement of the above goals presupposes a pattern of State-wise or regional allocation of resources which may not necessarily conform to the allocations finally decided upon. This is a major lacuna in our planning process at present. An examination of this would bring us face to face with several questions like the distribution of financial resources between States from public as well as institutional sources, Central sector investments, capability of individual States to implement certain programmes, etc.

Another direction in which, I think, important changes are needed is in regard to the role of States in national policymaking connected with planning. At present, there is no mechanism by which States can make effective contribution towards national planning, excepting in regard to what they wish to be done at their own State-level and what they discuss at the National Development Council. There is thus an important gap to be filled. The Plan has to be seen as the outcome of a 'partnership approach' in planning in which the States have to make substantial contributions. Here is perhaps a vital role for the State Planning Boards in the country. Towards this end, suitable conventions and rules of the game need to be evolved.

Inaugural address delivered at the Regional Conference of the Indian Econometric Society at Tirupathi, 25-26 October 1985 (Published in *Mainstream*, 14 December 1985). The conference was a part of the Society's Silver Jubilee Celebrations.

12

Language Question

*A Key to Educational Reform**

There seems to be a storm blowing in the country on the question of different languages and their future position in our education. 'National pride' and patriotism is sought to be demonstrated by strong denunciation of English and by showing complete indifference towards it. Some protagonists of 'Hindi' plead for the immediate introduction of Hindi all over the country and in all branches of life. The 'defenders' of regional languages go to the extent of exhorting the people to unite against 'Hindi imperialism', while the so-called 'internationalists' assert that English alone can unite the whole country; and even now people are not lacking who suggest that 'Sanskrit' must be made the national language. It is unfortunate that some of us tend to go extreme and claim what is not due for us and seek to deprive others of their due. This problem must be viewed in an unbiased and dispassionate way and in a scientific manner taking into consideration the objective position of different languages in our country and the larger interests of our people.

Teaching through mother tongue as the most scientific and the easiest possible way of imparting knowledge has been recognised by educationists all over the world. In our country although vernaculars have been introduced as the

---

* As a graduate student and Vice-President of the College Union in Nizam College in 1954, I was a participant in the then raging debate on the Language Question. This paper published in the college magazine is being reproduced, as some friends who read it recently told me about the continued relevance of some aspects of this debate.

media of instruction up to the secondary stage, English continues to be the principal medium of instruction in all stages of higher education. A student of intermediate who had completed all his courses through the medium of mother tongue finds it extremely difficult to assimilate the knowledge through English. The results of intermediate examinations have been quite discouraging in recent years; in certain colleges those passing exams being even less than 10 per cent. The difficulty of expression through English is in fact one of the major causes for this wastage of thousands of academic years and funds and is also one of the major causes for the existing lack of coordination between secondary and higher education.

Language is a vehicle of thought and not entirely an end by itself. And for a student, no other means of communication can be easier than one's own mother tongue. It must be realised that it is only through vernaculars that the youth can assimilate even the most difficult knowledge in the easiest possible way and can attain capacity and efficiency for original thinking. It is only through this that an effective coordination between acquired knowledge and original thinking is possible in a greater measure and one can express oneself in the most clear and direct terms with utmost vigour and confidence. "We recognise," the University Education Commission in their Report observed, "that in near future, the regional languages will be the principal media of instruction at all stages and in all provinces." But, unfortunately, the recommendations of the Radhakrishnan University Education Commission have been shelved and the energies of youth are being diverted towards mastering and learning everything through a language which is completely foreign and therefore unknown to the overwhelming majority of our people, with the result that after such a hard struggle with the language when a student comes out of the institution, he finds a big wall between himself and the entire people. He can neither fully understand his own people nor can he make them understand his views. 'We have become foreigners in own country', once remarked Mahatma Gandhi discussing the position of English and asserting that 'our languages are the reflection of ourselves', he maintained that a foreign language cannot represent the true national culture and as such it cannot impart to our youth the best from our national culture and traditions.

The process of replacement of English by our vernaculars should of course be gradual but a beginning must be made in that direction. Certain practical problems relating to teaching and translation of textbooks can be solved very easily if only a bold step is taken by effecting a change in language policy and initiative is given to cultural and literary organisations. It would be nothing short of degrading ourselves if we consider our languages and literature to be conservative and static, incapable of enriching themselves with newer and advanced knowledge. Human knowledge is transferable. And it has spread through the process of its transfer from one language to another. No language in the world can claim to have treasured in it all the knowledge or even a considerable part of it. Even English had to enrich itself much from German and French and from other languages, and there is no reason why the same process should not continue in the matter of our vernaculars if by doing so many people can benefit. The fear of standards falling as a result of introduction of vernaculars is unfounded. On the other hand, the pitiable state of affairs in the matter of examination results will no longer assume serious proportions. The gradual diminishing of the percentage of failures is bound to be associated with the gradual attainment of higher standards also.

Instruction through mother tongue in the multilingual states, such as we have, may, in the long-run, create certain obvious difficulties not only in regard to the organisation of education but also in the matter of employment in the administrative and other fields. There should be no hesitation to assert that such a scheme of things can fit in best only with the homogeneous structure of states re-adjusted on the basis of the spoken language of the great majority of the people in the areas concerned. It is only under such reorganisation that the present language barrier between the administration and the people can be removed and greater participation of people in the affairs of administration and the government can be ensured which is so essential for the success of a democracy. Cultural variety should not be confused with political division. And, the encouragement of vernaculars and the reorganisation of states, drawing more and more people in the sphere of social and political activity, will positively contribute to the greater political unity and consolidation of our country.

Hindi is the only language which is spoken and understood by a considerable number of people in different parts of our country. By Hindi, we generally mean its easier form which does not obviously exclude the easier form of Urdu. We sometimes call it Hindustani also. As provided in our constitution, Hindi has to be developed as a lingua-franca gradually and in a natural way by making it a compulsory second language for study in all stages of education and also by providing opportunities in those non-Hindi speaking areas who would like to receive education through the medium of Hindi. It has to be developed consciously by all Indians in the spheres of inter-state communication and All India business transactions, etc. But constitutional position guaranteed to Hindi should not be misinterpreted and no attempt should be made to introduce Hindi in a way detrimental to the development of other regional languages. It is only through such a positive and democratic attitude that Hindi can be developed gradually without giving any room for prejudices or hatred.

The only language which at present serves as the easier means of communication with the rest of the world is English. The exit of the British does not necessarily require the exit of English also. Language is not like cannon fodder which can be withdrawn at any moment. Despite all political disadvantages that followed the British rule and despite the fact that English was introduced to the detriment of our languages, we cannot minimise certain positive contributions made by it as a language and as a vehicle of advanced knowledge. To this extent its importance cannot be minimised even now, and all narrow tendencies of crusade against English should be fought and it should be introduced as a subject for study in different stages. Also, opportunities should be provided for those willing to study through the medium of English. Such a position will also facilitate higher learning and research for all students. It is equally important to fight certain erroneous trends which seek to restore and maintain the unnatural position occupied by English, hitherto, in our national life. We cannot falsify the historical fact that English was not learnt by our people voluntarily but it has been forced on us. Same has been the case with the countries under the British Empire. It is therefore wrong to call English as an accepted international language not only because of the very nature of its imposition but also because of the simple reason that just the British Empire does not constitute the whole world. It is equally wrong to assert that English united the whole country. The fact is that unity has been brought about in spite of it and the presence of Hindi as national language would have accelerated this process by drawing millions of common Indians in closer touch with the developments in the country.

Published in *Torch*, the Nizam College Monthly Magazine 3(3), December 1954 (Editor: Bashiruddin Ahmed; Assistant Editor: Shyam Sunder Benegal).

Bashiruddin Ahmed became Vice-Chancellor, Jamia-Millia Islamia, New Delhi; and Shyam Benegal is a leading filmmaker in the country who pioneered a progressive trend in film making in the 1970s.

Epilogue

Currently, two major issues have come to the fore on the language question not anticipated six decades ago. One is the rising demand in the country for education through English medium and the other is the deterioration in the quality of education in the government schools and colleges, particularly through English medium.

The rising demand for education through English medium is traceable basically to the rapid rate of globalisation in the last three decades. This has led to the increase in the mobility of students and skilled personnel across countries in response to the expansion of employment opportunities for them. Government has been very slow in responding to the changing demand. Besides, low quality of education in government schools and colleges has been driving even the poorer sections of students to private institutions by incurring heavy costs.

While government should provide equal opportunities for students opting for any of the three languages as medium of instruction—mother tongue, Hindi and English—it needs to undertake a major drive to improve teaching capabilities, especially through English medium. It is equally important to ensure proper accountability for their performance.

II-B

Comments on Some Books and Papers

1

Michael Lipton: Why Poor People Stay Poor

Urban Bias in World Development

This important contribution from Michael Lipton comes at an opportune moment. There is now widespread dissatisfaction with the past two and a half decades' economic performance in many of the less developed countries. The initial enthusiasm and effort for import substitution and emphasis on basic and heavy industries has led to some distortions in resource allocation resulting in the relative neglect of agriculture and the rural sector as a whole. The concern for greater employment and reduction of poverty is reflected in the renewed emphasis on rural development.

Lipton's contribution is particularly relevant for India where the debate on these issues has been conducted with the greatest vigour in the last one year. Interestingly, Lipton's diagnosis comes very close to what the politically dominant sections in India have been suggesting recently: that the rural sector has been neglected in the last quarter century of planning in India and that public investment in agriculture and the rural sector in general should be stepped up substantially.

Less Persuasive

Some of the basic propositions in this book were put forward by Lipton more than a decade ago and have been pursued by him consistently. He had drawn attention to the deficiency of public investment in agriculture and to the urban bias in agricultural planning at a time when it was fashionable to regard agriculture essentially as a source of surplus—marketed surplus, tax revenues and manpower—for economic development. Agriculture in itself was seldom regarded as a potent source of national income growth and employment. The ideas such as those Lipton put forward came as a necessary corrective to the distortions in evidence. In this book, however, these ideas have taken a shape far less persuasive in their entirety than one would have encountered in his earlier writings. The rural versus urban focus he now gives renders the diagnosis unreal and consequently some of his prescriptions are quite ineffective and even harmful.

Lipton points out that "the past 25 years in the LDCs (least developed countries) have seen more growth in real output per person than the previous 20 centuries." However, according to him, this growth hardly had any impact on the heartland of mass poverty as, for instance, "...the proportion of Indians below a fixed (and very modest) 'poverty line' almost certainly rose between 1950 and 1970." Another important point which he repeatedly tries to bring home is that "the disparity between urban and rural welfare is much greater in poor countries than in the rich countries during their earlier development".

While Lipton is impressed by the phenomenal growth in the last 25 years when compared to several centuries past, he does not analyse the factors behind such a breakthrough. This lack of perspective is responsible for the alarming view he takes of the prevailing structures and the rural-urban disparities which are found to be different from those obtaining in the presently developed countries in the comparable stages of their development. The spurt in real output per person in LDCs in the last 25 years can be explained by the freedom from colonialism and several institutional changes brought about in the wake of freedom. Technological changes and the spread of education have immensely contributed to this growth.

Colonial Legacy

Lipton nowhere mentions that the LDCs had the great initial disadvantage of starting with the structures and institutions inherited from the colonial period. These structures are typically characterised by the urban enclaves over the vast rural heartland of mass poverty. The prevailing institutions, administrative set-up and educational system were oriented to serving colonial interests and certain limited sections in these urban enclaves. Given these initial conditions, the kind of disparity between urban and rural welfare which Lipton mentions is quite plausible. In the developed countries, economic growth was a spontaneous process under a set of institutions far more progressive than those inherited by the LDCs. Economic development in the LDCs, on the other hand, has largely been an imitative process. Highly sophisticated capital-intensive industrial technology could be readily imported from the developed countries. These were quite unlike the techniques available in the comparable stages of development in the developed countries. Agricultural technology, on the other hand, owing to its biological character and climate-specificity, could not be so readily transferred. Such a process could understandably perpetuate and even accentuate the rural-urban differential. But the important question is whether the institutional changes effected in the post-Independence period have by themselves contributed to the reduction of such disparities. Lipton does not formulate his issues in this light. Nor does he examine the experience accordingly. In India, for instance, the abolition of princely states and intermediaries in land, the development of physical and institutional infrastructure, adoption of democratic political framework and the spread of education and skills have contributed towards the reduction of intra-rural as well as rural-urban disparities which would have otherwise accentuated.

Another basic factor which Lipton overlooks while comparing the performance of LDCs with that of developed countries in the comparable stages of development is that the structures, both in terms of institutions and the availability of mass consumption goods, were saving-oriented in the developed countries whereas in many of the LDCs the inherited attitudes, the democratic framework, the demonstration effect and the availability of the most up-to-date technology give a consumption orientation to these economies even in the earlier stages of their development. The existing potential for mass consumption in the developed countries and the near disappearance of rural-urban differential are, therefore, attributable to the rapid economic growth made possible by these structural factors.

The evidence presented by Lipton is not conclusive so far as his proposition regarding the decline in the absolute level of living of the poor is concerned. In India, for example, if we take the time series instead of any arbitrarily selected period between two years, there is no evidence of an increase in the proportion of the poor below poverty line. Lipton asserts that:

> Despite some vulgar Marxisants, the basic conflict in the Third World is not between capital and labour, but between capital and countryside, farmer and townsman, villager (including temporarily urban 'fringe villager') and urban industrial employer-cum-proletarian elite, gainers from dear food and gainers from cheap food.

According to Lipton, workers in urban modern industry who seldom form more than 5 per cent of labour force "have much more to lose than to gain from sharing their benefits with rural masses. Hence organised labour in today's LDCs is likely to fight equalising measures. In yesterday's, it spearheaded them." They are pitched against the rural poor, who according to him, "constitute an almost voiceless, largely illiterate, dispersed, unorganised rural mass. It seldom combines, articulates its needs, or backs them with effective political or trade-union power".

Urban-Rural Conflict Exaggerated

Lipton exaggerates the so-called rural-urban conflict and underestimates the bargaining power of the rural poor. In the process, he understates the conflict of interests between the rich and the poor in urban as well as rural areas. Indeed, some of his prescriptions, as we shall see, would undermine the bargaining power of the poor both in the urban and rural sectors. It is not clear from Lipton's analysis whether the industrial workers have not gained at the expense of the surplus which the capitalists could have accumulated in the absence of the trade union movement and with the existing allocation of resources which, according to him, is biased in favour of the urban sector. The trade union movement in India has undoubtedly enabled the working class to share part of the increase in industrial productivity and thus contributed to the reduction of intra-urban inequality which, as Lipton rightly observes, is greater than rural inequality.

The model of rural-urban conflict presented by Lipton ignores the strong complementary relationships between the two sectors which outweigh the conflicting interests. Incidentally, Lipton's analysis amounts to identifying the urban sector with urban rich and the rural sector with rural rich. This is because, according to his analysis, the interests of the rich and the poor in each sector converge more than they conflict. Anything that benefits the rural rich either through higher prices of food or through greater investment allocations would percolate to the poor through greater employment and higher wages. Hence, in his model, the unionisation of labour is harmful to the interests of the poor themselves. Even institutional changes like land reforms are harmful to the rural poor.

This urban-rural dichotomy arises from several wrong assumptions and the treatment of these two as mutually exclusive and closed sectors. The urban rich as well as bureaucracy are increasingly recruited from the class of rural rich through the process of education and migration. Similarly, the urban poor, as Lipton admits, consist of the migrant rural poor, to a significant extent. This partly accounts for lower inequality in the rural sector than in the urban sector. Thus viewed, urban sector serves as a 'safety valve' for the rural sector. In the course of economic development, even with sufficient or optimal allocation for agriculture, the proportion of labour force in the agricultural sector as well as output contributed by this sector declines. Both the rural rich as well as the rural poor get increasingly absorbed in the growing urban sector. Given this process, it would appear that the linkages and complementarities predominate over the conflict of interests. In fact, by pleading for greater allocations for the rural sector, one is seeking greater urbanisation of rural areas and for better integration of the two so that the rural-urban distinction gets obliterated.

Farm Prices and Investment

Lipton is at fault in assuming that the rural rich actively favour greater investment for the rural sector at the expense of the urban sector. The experience in India shows that the rural rich have not been interested in public investments which benefit all classes of farmers proportionately. Instead, they are more interested in, and actively working for, higher prices for farm products which benefit them proportionately more than the small farmers because of their greater surplus. They have also been appropriating a greater share of institutional credit and inputs like fertilisers. Lipton grossly underestimates the emergence of the rural sector as a significant force. In India, for example, the political processes have brought the rural rich at the helm of state power and decision-making. At least at the state level, in the last 25 years, they have been able to use state power and resources largely for the benefit of the rich farmers. The rural poor have also gained, though not to the same extent as the rural rich. Their predominance in terms of votes has contributed to several shifts in policies favouring them. The increase in literacy and education among them, their political awareness and their voting power cannot be underestimated.

The dominance of the rural elite in the political processes should be obvious to any observer of the political scene in India. Lipton is, therefore, very much off the mark when he says:

> Even when there are quinquennial elections and massively rural electorates, it is townsmen who write the papers and put out the radio programmes. ...fund political parties, pick candidates, own or frequent 'political' coffee-houses and bars.

On agricultural prices, Lipton thinks that:

> Less obviously, the whole interest of the rural community is against cheap food. This is clear enough for the farmers who sell food to the towns (largely big farmers, bought off by input subsidies): but even the 'deficit farmer' or net food buyer (who grows too little to feed himself from his land alone) often gains when food is dear, except perhaps in the very short term.
>
> Whether they work for crop wages or for cash it pays the big farmer to hire more labour when food is dearer and this bids up farm wages as well as rural employment.....Moreover, the richer farmers have more cash to lend out when food is dear and their income high, so the interest rate to the poor borrower is reduced as lenders compete.

If investments for agriculture in the rural sector have been lower than desirable, then one should expect a rise in the prices of agricultural commodities. Such a rise confers disproportionately larger benefits on the surplus producers or the intra-marginal regions and farmers. Lipton's arguments assume a high responsiveness of agricultural supplies to prices. However, the available evidence for India shows that the aggregate supply elasticity is much less than unity and since the employment elasticity to output is also less than unity, the derived demand for labour as a result of price rise would be much lower whereas for any given rise in prices, the fall in real incomes of the rural poor would be much greater. It is clear, therefore, that for the rural poor, the negative real income effects of the rise in food prices outweigh the possible employment and income effects. Public investment in agriculture could benefit at least proportionately different sections of farmers whereas high output prices would essentially benefit the rural rich. Hence growth via the former would be more broad-based than from the latter.

Lipton does not go into this question of the relative efficiency of public investments and higher prices for the farm sector. This explains why he relies on the high cash income of the rich farmers as a source of credit at low interest rates to the rural poor instead of a direct increase in their share in the institutional credit at low interest rates. Also, it is difficult to reconcile this case for higher liquidity via higher prices with his statement elsewhere, that the rural rich divert much of their cash income to investments in non-agricultural and non-rural pursuits. He also overlooks the possibility of higher consumption by the rural rich resulting in greater inequalities. Indeed, he asserts the opposite when he says that better rural prospects (or dearer food) will pull the poorest back to the village which would reduce inequality in the towns.

The experience in India shows that rising agricultural prices or improved terms of trade were the consequence of the deficiency of public investment in the agricultural sector to match the rise in demand. Whereas private investment, particularly by affluent farmers and in the developed regions, was stepped up in response to higher prices, the overall impact on growth has not been appreciable. In fact, the rate of the growth of agricultural output during the period of rise in prices has been slower than in the first decade of planning when the terms of trade were not favourable to agriculture but public investment was rising at a faster rate. Also, there is evidence to show that the inequalities in the distribution of income both in the urban and the rural sectors have increased during period of rise in farm prices and low rate of public investment.

Lipton tries to fortify his thesis of deficiency of investments in the rural sector by referring to social prices or true prices of farm products as also of capital inputs:

> Farm output is undervalued not only because of selective intervention in favour of (and greater monopoly power within) the non-farm sector, but also by the great inequality of most LDCs. Since it is poor people who spend most of their incomes on food, this inequality reduces demand for farm products (relative to others) and hence cuts their prices compared to the valuation placed on them in a less unequal society.

The argument is persuasive in so far at it makes out a case for higher investment in the rural sector than is warranted by the prevailing prices. However, the conclusion is not straightforward in so far as this means high food prices for the rich farmers as also lower interest rates for them. Since insufficient public investment in agriculture would, by itself, result in higher market prices of food, the divergence between the market prices and social prices can be explained in terms of inequalities in wealth and income. If this is so, the solution should be to correct these disparities as well as raise public investment. However, raising market price of food and lowering the cost of the capital would only reinforce the existing inequalities and thus perpetuate the distortions in prices.

Questionable Propositions

The false rural-urban dichotomy leads Lipton to several questionable propositions on subjects like rural education, rural taxation and public procurement and distribution of foodgrains. On the one hand, Lipton suggests that rural education has been neglected, in that it has a very small share of the existing educational facilities. In the same breath, he blames urban bias in education in so far as it contributes to the migration of the educated rural children to urban areas.

The following statement suggests how insufficient are educational facilities allotted to the rural sector:

> The fact that a first rate and rurally-aware university like Delhi had only 22 per cent of students from rural areas, as against 34 per cent for all Indian places of higher learning, reveals a hidden component of urban bias in educational provision; ...the rural child seldom gets even half the town child's chance of an education... Also, inadequate in quantity and quality, is the village educand's share of teachers.

That Lipton would like to have it both ways is evident from the following:

> Given the excessive incentives and directives for educated persons to work in cities, the share of education allotted to the rural sector is more than enough to harm both its prospects of development and the efficiency with which educated resources are allocated.

The above observations on education ignore the complementarity between the rural and the urban sector and the inevitable trend of the outflow of rural population to the urban areas, in the course of economic development. Lipton is right in so far as the content of the education is not oriented to the rural needs but, to believe that the migration to urban sector constitutes a drain would be to overstate the capacity of the rural sector to absorb educated persons over a period of time. A lot can be said against the existing educational system which is divorced from the needs of the poor whether in the rural or urban sector. And, there is lot of overinvestment in certain lines reflecting misallocation of resources. But there is little basis for the argument in terms of rural-urban conflict in this respect. For instance, it can be rightly said about the health resources and facilities that they are highly biased towards the rich and ignore the needs of the vast majority of poor people whether in the urban or the rural areas. However, Lipton would prefer to dramatise this in terms of rural-urban conflict:

> ...but it is not cant to stigmatise as violence the diversion of health resources to kidney machines, while villagers suffer infant mortality rates as high as one in five for want of the simplest medical care.

On the taxation of agricultural sector, while one would be inclined to agree with Lipton that the revenue prospects from agricultural taxation have been overplayed by development economists in the last three decades, he casts the whole question in terms of rural-urban conflict ignoring the need to tax the rural rich for ensuring intra-sectoral as well as inter-sectoral equity. According to him:

> Just as the rural sector pays too large a share of taxation relative to `capacity' even if we ignore non-tax burdens, so in most poor countries does it probably pay out more in taxes than it receives in public benefits, even if we ignore the outflow of private benefits induced by public action.

He ignores that many prosperous farmers pay hardly 2-3 per cent of their income as direct taxes, which is very much lower than what their urban counterparts pay. Also, he implicitly sets up wrong criteria for taxation or for that matter for investment by passing judgements on the burden of taxation by comparing it with what the sector concerned receives in terms of public benefits. The criteria governing taxation are different from the criteria governing investment. There is no logical basis to determine the relationship between the taxes received from a sector and the investment allocations made. Following the concept of taxable capacity, one would measure the burden in terms of the income levels whether they are rural or urban.

In regard to prices, public procurement and distribution of foodgrains, Lipton follows the same line:

> Around 1967-68, about a quarter of Indian cereal marketing were publicly procured, at prices about 25 per cent lower than were obtainable, in the market, by sellers better placed to select the time and place of sale.... Rural people do not even gain as consumers, though government intervention in food pricing has been overwhelmingly motivated by cost-of-living considerations.

One would agree with Lipton that the incidence of lower procurement price falls proportionately on all classes of farmers and the benefits of this accrue to the poor as well as rich in urban areas while the rural poor are not adequately cared for. However, the whole issue can be cast in different terms keeping in view the objective of equity. In fact, rural-urban dichotomy evades the equity issue in procurement and distribution of foodgrains. It is open to the government to procure the necessary quantities at lower than the market prices only from large farmers through a system of compulsory levies and distribute the grain so procured only to the poorer sections both in the urban as well as the rural areas. The benefit of higher market prices can then go to the poorer farmers (sellers) and the benefit of subsidised grain to the urban as well as rural poor leaving the urban rich to buy at market prices.

Class Disparities Ignored

Following his analysis, Lipton naturally pleads for the removal of rural-urban inequalities, ignoring explicitly the inter-class inequalities and conflicts in both the sectors:

> The best path to intra-rural equalisation may well be first to weaken the urban forces that rely on rural inequality to obtain surplus food, savings and educands from the village elite.

He, in fact, feels that attempts to ensure intra-rural equalisations directly may not be desirable as, according to him:

> Rural labourers, and their organising capacities, would often gain more from . . . increases in the share of 'labour-enhancing' resources allocated to agriculture, than from direct attempts at rural unionisation in advance of such increases.

Lipton is more explicit when he suspects in land reform measures, the effort to divide the rural folk with a view to serving the urban interest:

> Without some sort of theory—or ideology—to guide it, a 'peasant movement' is likelier to divide rural people among themselves than to confront the urban sector that exploits them all ... In the Indian state of Kerala, landless labourers probably lost as a result of

> the distribution in the late 1960s of land from large farmers, who hired most of their workers, to small family farmers who did most of the work themselves. Other measures of rural redistribution, benefiting mini-farmers at the cost of medium and big farmers, often have similar effects.

As pointed out at the very outset, Lipton makes a useful contribution in so far as he focuses on the deficiency of public investment in the rural sector. His case for more investment in terms of growth as well as equality is persuasive in view of the undoubtedly labour-intensive nature of most rural output and the fact that capital and land are distributed much less unequally in the village than in the town.

But his recommendations that "in a country with 70 per cent of its population and workforce in agriculture, it would be reasonable to expect the share of public investment there to rise, from currently normal levels around 20 per cent to 35 to 45 per cent in 5 to 10 years" is based on intuition rather than on any concrete exercise. A hard empiricist would expect him to come out with a model giving the optimal rate of investment for agriculture which could at once indicate deficiency of investment, if any, as well as the desirable rate at which investment should be stepped up.

Unfortunately, the overall impression that this work gives is that the rural rich should be provided unfettered opportunities for development through state aid. The prescriptions of the book, if implemented, would undoubtedly lead to greater rural development but also to greater inequalities, both in the rural and urban sectors because of the absence of appropriate institutional framework and policies to ensure that gains of development accrue adequately to the poor.

"Rural vs Urban or Rich vs Poor?", *Economic and Political Weekly*, 7 October 1978.

2

K.N. Raj: Organisational Issues in Indian Agriculture

This is a collection of a set of brilliant and extremely well-written papers on Indian agriculture by K.N. Raj which he contributed over a span of nearly four decades, from the early 50s to the late 80s. Each one of these essays focused on an important issue evoked considerable interest because of the relevance of the topic when it was written, and the message conveyed each time made a significant impact on academic as well as policymaking circles.

The essays in their entirety bring out the major structural features of Indian agriculture including the way the economic activity is organised in this sector and their bearing on the efficiency of resource-use, the distribution of income and the prospects for agricultural growth. The analysis acquires sharpness and evokes special interest in view of Raj's effort to bring in the comparative experience of agricultural growth in Mexico, China, East Asia and Sri Lanka. The book would, however, interest the reader more for the light it throws on the structural features and their implications for resource-use efficiency and income distribution in agriculture. There are, of course, quite a few flashes on strategies and policies for agricultural growth but such issues are not in the forefront. At any rate, they have not been worked out as anything like a coherent package.

And this is not accidental. Delving deep into the structural aspects and constantly appealing to the ideal structure as a frame of reference for efficient and equitable growth, Raj steadfastly stuck to the first best model of agricultural growth. He derives inspiration from the East Asian and Chinese experience where thoroughgoing land reforms and development of rural infrastructure by taxing agriculture and by deploying surplus labour (as in China) laid the foundations for rapid growth of agriculture consistent with efficiency and equity. This is not to suggest that Raj totally subscribes to the Chinese model of growth. Indeed, he is quite critical of the distortions in resource-use in China following the introduction of communes, under-pricing of agricultural produce and the command system in labour-use and decision-making in general.

It is noteworthy that despite sticking to the first best model, Raj appears, by and large, either silent or ambivalent on issues of agricultural growth such as technology and infrastructure, particularly on the role of planning and public effort in these spheres, and does not project any definite viewpoint on growth as is usually the case with the proponents of structural change. It would be fair to say that from a position of assertion in the early years that drastic land reforms are a prerequisite for efficient and equitable growth through technological change, his position gets softened and somewhat diluted towards the 80s. He leaves the options open and the alternatives leaning on technological change and public investments in agricultural infrastructure can be quite consistent with the changes in agrarian structure and organisation visualised by him. Indeed, such of the structural changes as are feasible would be desirable as they would reinforce the beneficial effects of technology and infrastructure.

Raj's treatment of agrarian structure in the less developed countries is much more than an empirical presentation of prevailing structures. It is really an effort to understand the prevailing structures in terms of received theory and, what is more, to question the received theory where it is found inadequate and to project an alternative framework for better understanding of the agrarian structure in such societies. For example, after analysing the manner in which the different factors of production are remunerated in traditional societies, he notes:

> Not only are market and social power in these societies generally exercised by a very small minority but members belonging to this minority often occupy dominant positions in a number of factor and product markets simultaneously, with the result that these markets are interlocked by price as well as non-price links ... when markets are inter-locked in this way through price or non-price links, the differential bargaining positions of the participants in a particular market cannot be fitted into the conventional models of monopoly or monopsony and absorbed into the framework of general equilibrium analysis.

In Raj's framework, distribution of land ownership is basic to the understanding of other features of agrarian structures. Some of these features may be noted. The quantum of land that could be leased in is governed by the size of ownership holding so that the distribution of operational holdings follows the distribution of ownership holdings. This effectively limits the prospects for the landless to make a living by leasing in land. High interest rates on loans paid by smallholdings are traceable to the ability of large owners to extract surplus. The uncertainties of hiring labour by large farmers as well as the risks of leasing out land account for low absorption of labour in agriculture. More than underpricing of scarce resources, e g, capital and foreign exchange, such imperfections in land market are responsible for mechanisation resorted to by the large farmers. While the case for taxing agricultural land is reinforced by its inequitable distribution, the failure to tax is explained by the power wielded by the well-off farmers.

In view of such pervasive impact of land ownership, Raj concluded in his presidential address to the Indian Society of Agricultural Economics in 1974 that "mobilisation of social and political forces on the basis of radically-conceived programmes of land redistribution is perhaps a necessary condition for the transformation of such societies, whether or not such programmes satisfy the requirements of economic viability." However, by 1986 Raj appears to have become more realistic:

> On the practical plane, there are of course problems in bringing about such changes. Attempts at radical land reform have been seldom found politically feasible except when carried through after major upheavals accompanied by substantial changes in power relationships within society (as in China, Japan, South Korea and Taiwan after the Second World War).

On issues concerning the development of infrastructure and technological change in Indian agriculture, Raj has been either ambivalent or at best pessimistic even as he is greatly impressed by the achievements in China, Taiwan and South Korea. As recently as 1986, he thought that "the magnitude of the basic infrastructural investment needed for accelerating agricultural growth are therefore likely to be very much higher in most countries of South Asia than would appear from the experience of Japan, Taiwan and even South Korea. This could require substantial resource transfers into the agricultural sector for a while unless some methods of mobilisation of rural labour are devised for this purpose as in China." He appears to have shared this pessimism from the very beginning: "In a country like India that has had a long tradition of irrigation, and where past investments have already exploited a large part of the more easily available water resources, not only is the scope for further extension more limited than in some other countries but it is likely to be much more costly." It may be noted, however, that when this essay was written, almost half the irrigation potential still remained to be exploited in India and a good part of this potential consisted of medium and minor irrigation, including ground water in the eastern part of the country where the water table is high.

It is revealing to see the most recent perceptions of Raj appearing in the last para of his last essay where he notes that in Kerala, despite changes in rural power structure through moderate land reform, organisation of rural labour supported by measures for formal and non-formal education for the entire population, "there has been no evidence of growth in agricultural productivity as a result of such social transformation ... the failure on this account has been largely due to inadequate understanding, on the political plane, of the imperative need for productive investment and technological change to support processes of social change".

It is indeed heartening that Raj has at last given us a glimpse of a viable strategy for agricultural growth: productive investment and technological change together with such of the changes in rural social structure as are politically feasible. But the groping has been too long. He has been unduly deterred by 'structural constraints'; expected for too long replication of certain basic elements of the Chinese model under a diametrically different socio-political framework; underestimated the potential for growth as well as for wider distribution of benefits through well-conceived infrastructural investments and technological changes; and was probably not favourably inclined to a significant resource inflow into agriculture which, according to received wisdom, was expected to generate surpluses for overall economic growth.

In fairness, however, insufficient attention to growth issues cannot perhaps be regarded as a deficiency of the work which is explicitly concerned with organisational issues. On such structural issues, Raj's book is highly illuminating as well as persuasive and is among the best that this reviewer has seen.

Economic and Political Weekly, 19 October 1991.

3

Deepak Nayyar: Economic Liberalisation in India

Analytics, Experience and Lessons

Seeing the title of the book, one would be curious to know whether the author, Deepak Nayyar, is pro or anti liberalisation and what direction he would like the economy to take at this stage. Nayyar is not against liberalisation of the economy as such, but is critical of the manner in which economic reforms have been pursued in India since the early 1990s. To put it in his own words, he is averse to caricature perceptions: either state can do nothing wrong or state can do nothing right. Yet he is not as critical of the 'pre-reform' paradigm of development. In an otherwise forthright and non-dogmatic treatment of the subject, one would look for a frank appraisal of the earlier strategy, especially in view of the telling evidence accumulated on the breakdown of the centrally planned economies. This is perhaps explained by his uneasiness about the current cynicism that state can do nothing right. This prompts him to emphasise the positive aspects and the achievements of the earlier strategy of development, which provide a basis for a series of suggestions regarding the content, sequencing and speed of reforms with a view to effectively addressing the problems of poverty and development.

According to the author, the most important achievements under the earlier paradigm of development were the significant step-up in savings, investment and growth, development of a diversified industrial sector and ensuring food security. Among the important shortcomings of the earlier period are neglect of exports, human resources, agrarian reforms and slow reduction in poverty. The author asserts that the economic crisis that erupted at the beginning of 1990s is traceable not to the 'misplaced' strategy of development since the mid-1950s, as alleged by some, but to the soft options adopted by the government in the second half of the 1980s to sustain import liberalisation.

The author argues quite persuasively that the deflation associated with the orthodox stabilisation programme may lead to contraction of output, due to a squeeze in investment and working capital, rather than a reduction in demand and prices, the outcome being stagflation instead of stabilisation. Further, the orthodox approach is static rather than dynamic as it tends to ignore inter-temporal considerations and does not quite incorporate increasing returns, market structures or externalities inherent in any process of industrialisation. Thus success at industrialisation, he says, is not only about resource allocation and resource utilisation at a micro level. It is as much about resource mobilisation and resource creation at a macro level.

The author cites the experience of Latin America and sub-Saharan Africa with the implementation of the standard package of economic reforms and shows how they resulted in stifling long-term growth by overestimating export prospects and the availability of external finance. Inflation redistributed incomes, even as there was a squeeze on public expenditures in the social sectors, so that the impact of these reforms on poverty was invariably adverse. Thus, according to him, 'adjustment with human face' is an illusion for the added reason that economies in crisis simply do not have enough resources for providing the so-called 'safety nets'.

In India, over the five years following economic reforms, inflation remained at 10 per cent, despite five good monsoons in a row and despite no significant exogenous shock. This could be considered a success, he says, only if Latin American economies are a reference point, but a failure if India's own past record is the norm.

The author points out that total external debt rose from less than one-fourth of GDP (gross domestic product) at the end of 1990-91 to one-third of GDP during the period of stabilisation, so that the proportion of export earnings pre-empted by debt servicing rose to 40 per cent. Insofar as a reduction in fiscal deficit does not always translate itself into a corresponding reduction in current account deficit on the balance of payments, a sustainable reduction in current account deficit, he argues, may be easier to attain through a reduction in the trade deficit rather than in the fiscal deficit. Macroeconomic adjustment conducive to growth needs to raise the investment-GDP ratio by raising the saving rate and export-GDP ratio instead of allowing a compensatory increase in the import-GDP ratio supported by external borrowing.

The focus of adjustment being on fiscal deficit rather than on revenue deficit of the government, budgets relied on a surplus in the capital account to finance a deficit on revenue account. Such a process of fiscal adjustment meant a massive squeeze on public investment. The author shows that budget support for key infrastructure sectors, e.g. energy, transport and communications registered a significant decline even in nominal terms leading to a decline in total investment, as public investment crowds-in rather than crowds-out private investment.

According to the author, the contraction in public expenditure had an adverse effect on rural non-agricultural employment and urban informal sector employment. In an effort to contain subsidies, the issue prices of food grains were raised steeply which led to a significant decline in their off-take. Inflation was thus concentrated in the prices of wage goods which redistributed income away from the poor. As a result, the incidence of poverty rose, rural poverty rising steeper representing a reversal of previous trends.

The author favours dismantling of the complex regime of controls. Such a step, according to him, was both necessary and desirable. However, the author's assertion that there is no concrete evidence so far to validate or refute the hypothesis that structural reform would impart efficiency and dynamism to the process of economic growth may be a bit premature. Also, the author's fears that a rapid liberalisation of the import regime may force a de-industrialisation, especially in the capital goods sector, may be exaggerated in the light of the more recent evidence in regard to the growth of this sector. He also strikes a pessimistic note when he says that direct foreign investment is likely to be modest even as he is right in saying that it cannot be an important source for financing current account deficit or investment in the economy. Further, he underestimates the impact of reforms launched so far on the fortunes of agriculture: "the reforms proceeded as if agricultural sector does not exist or, if it exists, it does not matter." It is true that reforms directly affecting agriculture have not been conspicuous, but the experience elsewhere shows that the impact of economy wide reforms on agriculture has been far more powerful than of those directly affecting agriculture.

The author echoes the widely shared feeling that it would be desirable to use capital receipts from disinvestment to retire public debt or to mop up excess liquidity, and use it for restructuring public enterprises, and fears that the sale of government assets and privatisation "may instead of resolving the real problems of efficiency can end up socialising costs and privatising benefits!" The financial system remains undergoverned because the institutional and legal frameworks that would govern the markets have not yet been put in place. He is also not happy with freeing interest rates as it would no longer be possible to use them as a strategic tool for guiding the allocation of scarce investible resources in a market economy. Further, a significant rise in interest rates on government securities would increase the burden of public debt.

One could not agree more when the author says that "industrialisation is not only about getting prices right; it is also about getting state intervention right." As he puts it, in a world of uneven development, rapid technical progress, ever-changing comparative advantage and imperfect market structures, the role of government in industrialisation remains vital. Human resource development, acquisition of technological and managerial capabilities and the creation of institutions that would regulate, streamline and facilitate the functioning of markets are some such areas. The reform process neglects the possibilities of building on past strength in this regard.

This monograph reveals the author at his best as a teacher: informative, analytical and, not the least, eloquent. Balanced as his presentation is, one wishes he was a little more forthcoming on the failures of centralised bureaucratic planning.

"Beyond Getting Prices Right", *Economic and Political Weekly*, 15 June 1996.

4

Ester Boserup: The Conditions of Agricultural Growth

The Economics of Agrarian Change under Population Pressure

Ester Boserup in this book, has analysed the factors governing the agrarian change from the primitive method of forest fallow cultivation to the modern methods of multiple cropping. According to her, the changes in cultivation methods are induced and in fact made possible by the pressure of population. Technical change is thus treated as an endogenous variable and population growth as an exogenous variable. This is in sharp contrast with the Malthusian theory which says that the growth of population is limited by the supply of food. Critics of the Malthusian theory have been pointing out the possibility of counteracting the tendency towards diminishing returns through the application of improved techniques. But Boserup argues persuasively through an exhaustive analysis of historical data that technical change itself is induced by the growth of population.

The sequence of her argument is: primitive communities subsisting on forest fallow cultivation are characterised by a very low density of population. The actual work put in per man in terms of man-hours is very low and hence productivity per man-hour is high. As the population grows and food requirements increase, a shift occurs from root cultivation to crop culture, and, where crop culture is already in vogue, from long-fallow cultivation to short-fallow cultivation and from cultivation of a single crop during the year to multiple cropping where the proportion of land left fallow has already reached the critical minimum as a result of population pressure. Under the intensive methods, productivity per man-hour may decline in the initial stages, although the division of labour and urbanisation made possible by the pressure of population may ultimately lead to the introduction of techniques which increase productivity per man-hour. But even the decline in productivity per man-hour in the initial stages is compensated by the increase in the number of work hours per man made possible by the intensive crop culture. Thus the growth of population leads to the diminution of idle period and to more sustained employment throughout the year.

That population growth is not rigidly limited by the supply of food is amply borne out by the experience of many underdeveloped countries in recent decades. It is also understandable that the pressure of population should lead to progress in techniques of a labour-intensive type, induced by the increased needs of subsistence as well as facilitated by the availability of labour. This may in fact explain much of the growth in the volume of agricultural output that has recently taken place in some of the densely populated underdeveloped countries including India. Boserup makes it clear that a continued high rate of growth of population in such countries may lead to the diminution of investible surplus necessary to stimulate agricultural growth further.

However, she is not equally clear about the causes of the progress in agricultural technology in the modern context where new inputs are almost invariably introduced from outside of agriculture. Their relationship to population growth is too indirect and dubious to provide a neat causal relationship. If agricultural growth in the modern context is conceived as the growth of productivity per man-hour through the application of modern techniques with higher capital-intensity, then technical progress should largely be regarded as independent of population growth. In regard to the absorption of new techniques, however, Boserup's arguments are again quite persuasive: certain modern inputs which are not labour-displacing but which increase output per unit of land may be more readily accepted by communities with greater population pressure than by those with stationary or declining populations.

Ester Boserup analyses the process of agrarian change from an entirely new angle. Her findings constitute, therefore, an original contribution to the analysis of the process of economic growth.

"Population Pressure and Economic Growth", *Eastern Economist*, 3 September 1965.

5

Yujiro Hayami: Japanese Agriculture under Siege

The Political Economy of Agricultural Policies

It is paradoxical that post-war economic development in Japan has been characterised by the rapid growth of protection of domestic agriculture despite sharp increases in imports of food and the associated decline in the self-sufficiency rate. The level of agricultural protection in Japan is among the highest in the world giving rise to strong external pressure for agricultural trade liberalisation, particularly in view of the country's large trade surplus. Yujiro Hayami, a leading agricultural economist of international repute, investigates in this book the roots of this agricultural trade friction which is embedded, according to him, in the social and economic structure of Japan. This book is part of the series *Studies in the Modern Japanese Economy* edited by Malcolm Falkus and Masao Baba.

The rapid economic development of Japan in the post-war period, based mainly on the borrowing of industrial technology, has led to a sharp decline in the comparative advantage of agriculture because of extreme scarcity of land and the usual limitations to the borrowing of agricultural technology. Because of such rapid changes in comparative advantage, the agricultural adjustment problem became more severe in Japan than in other industrial countries. According to Hayami:

> This very severe adjustment problem may be called the 'agricultural problem of the *nouveaux riches*',

> because it is rooted in the fact that Japan rose (within only two decades) from a developing country to an industrial superpower with per capita income among the highest in the world.

As in the case of developed western economies, consumer resistance to agricultural protection became weak in Japan because a very small proportion of income is spent on food and, with the rapid growth in per capita income, the capacity of the society at large to subsidise agriculture increased. This is a fertile ground for the emergence of vested interests as rent-seekers. The most notable of such institutions which came to wield political clout in Japan are the agricultural co-operative associations—commonly called 'NOKYO', an abbreviation of Nogyo Kyodo Kumiai—engaged in marketing of all farm products and inputs together with credit and insurance business. Further, even though the farm population declined, electoral districts changed little, leaving the political weight of farm votes intact.

The rest is a familiar story but with more dramatic overtones for Japan: the ratio of agricultural subsidy to total agricultural budget was as high as 80 per cent in 1984. The ratio of current subsidies to agricultural GDP in 1983 was 9 per cent (more than 60% higher than the EC average). The ratio of capital subsidies to agricultural fixed capital formation was 41 per cent in 1980 (about 50% higher than the EC average). Of course, as Hayami explains, these higher rates of current and capital subsidies reflect the more severe agricultural adjustment problem corresponding to declining comparative advantage of agriculture in Japan relative to other industrial countries.

Among agricultural products, rice is subject to the strongest protection reflecting the severe adjustment problem. Export of rice is made on concessional terms, the real price of exports being less than half the nominal price which itself is less than half the domestic producer price. According to Hayami, "it is likely that well over one-half of rice-farming income was really a transfer from consumer-cum-tax payers to producers".

As elsewhere, the casualty of such huge subsidies is productive investment which could raise agricultural productivity and eventually obviate the need for subsidies. Investment in the education of rural people and in agricultural research and development have been too little relative to their returns, because a major portion of government budget is eaten up by protection policies.

Underlying the declining comparative advantage of agriculture is the failure of labour productivity in agriculture to rise corresponding to the rise in non-farm productivity. Japan has surpassed other industrial countries in respect of output per hectare. However, because of the meagre endowment of agricultural land relative to the labour force, average farm size is still only a little over one hectare which is a chief constraint on raising labour productivity. With the rise in wages, economies of scale inherent in labour-saving technology have become important for Japanese agriculture which can be exploited only with the enlargement of farm size.

Here is another related paradox of recent Japanese economic growth: slow increase in farm size despite steep rise in non-farm productivity and wages. This is rooted in high population density or extreme scarcity of land, successful implementation of land reforms and a pattern of industrialisation leading to growth in non-farm employment opportunities for farmers within a commutable distance from their residence. This has resulted in a phenomenal increase in a class of part-time farmers whose farm income is smaller than their off-farm income (the latter, on an average, accounting for over 90% of total income) and who yet stick to their small and fragmented holdings, thus effectively blocking the concentration of farm land in the hands of viable farmers. This has been facilitated by the increase in the elderly labour force and the diffusion of power tillers. Because of protection of tenancy rights and fixation of rents at low levels, there is no incentive to lease out land to full-time farmers. Also, land values rose sharply due to high density and rapid economic growth so that it was unprofitable for full-time farmers to purchase land as its price exceeded the present value of the agricultural income stream. The nexus between part-time farmers (whose incomes from farm plus non-farm sources are higher than those of full-time farmers) and NOKYO in the matter of sale of inputs and marketing of produce, involving large commissions to the latter, is the key to the slow structural adjustment as they together dominate the rural economy and politics of Japan.

Despite these constraints there is, according to Hayami, a likelihood of a major decline in the number of farms within a decade or so. This stems from a sharp rise in wage rates comparable to advanced industrial economies and the emergence of significant economies of scale. Hayami suggests that policy should be oriented to increasing the comparative advantage of full-time farmers with high entrepreneurial and managerial abilities and by activating the land rental market through liberalising rental contracts. There should be a shift to land-saving and capital-intensive activities such as horticulture and livestock farming. Towards this end, there should be greater investment in research, education, training of farmers and land infrastructure. "Concerted efforts for such structural adjustments seem to be the best way to adapt Japanese agriculture to an open trade system in the long run".

The book is rich in data and analysis and the presentation is concise and lucid. The reader has much to learn and understand from this book and hardly anything to disagree with, mainly because the author has pursued his enquiry with total objectivity and has made no attempt to prove or disprove any pet propositions.

Economic and Political Weekly, 30 November 1991.

6

N. Subba Reddy: Cultural Diversity and Common Humanity

This book brings together papers written by N. Subba Reddy, noted anthropologist, who has been with the Centre for Economic and Social Studies (CESS) as Honorary Professor and whom we have the pleasure of honouring this morning. These papers were prepared over a long period for different occasions, including seminars and conferences in India and abroad. Not being an anthropologist, I am not in a position to offer expert comments on this book. Nevertheless, the nature of the issues discussed in these papers and their readability prompt me to make a few observations on their significance and on the policy implications brought out for social and economic development.

On a reading of this book, one is struck by three of its prominent features: a wide-ranging scholarship on each of the topics dealt with; deep concerns of a humanist in the choice of the subjects as well as in the search for solutions; and a multi-disciplinary approach in the analysis of these issues, true to the grand Lucknow tradition set by the great teachers like Radhakamal Mukerjee and D.P. Mukerjee.

On each topic that Subba Reddy sets out to analyse, he invariably begins with a critical discussion of the views of the acknowledged authorities on the subject with an astonishing range of his scholarship. While doing so, he is quite unsparing in his rejection of the views whose factual basis is deficient or the arguments lack logical rigour and consistency.

Reddy's quest centers round the issues of social harmony and social justice. On the complex issue of secularism in pluralist India, after discussing the views of well-known writers on the subject, while concurring with the views of Jawaharlal Nehru whom he calls a 'quintessential' secularist, Reddy says, "any label we use should reflect the plurality of our society and the inclusiveness of our culture. I should think that Bharatiyata fits the bill, not Hindutva." Reddy concludes this paper by drawing attention of the majority community to what Vivekananda said: "Hinduism sees all religions to be true. That should continue to be the world view of our national culture".

His paper on "Globalisation and Equitable World Order" covers the whole gamut of issues in the current debate on economic reforms and social justice, with the perspective of a social scientist. He gets into economic history and certain basic propositions of economists right from Adam Smith to Joseph Stiglitz. Reddy affirms that 'unregulated' or 'free market' is a myth; it never existed: even the growth of capitalism owes to state intervention and support in varying degrees. He believes that growing inequalities in income and wealth and the resulting social unrest in the wake of globalisation are harmful to human well-being which can be mitigated only through appropriate public intervention.

Reddy deals extensively with the crisis of confidence among tribal people and the naxalite movement in Parvatipuram agency where, according to him, the problem of land alienation reached a more acute stage than elsewhere. It is pertinent to recall, in this context, that Reddy led a team of researchers at the CESS in 1996 to prepare a report submitted to the government on resettlement and rehabilitation of tribals facing displacement on account of Polavaram Project. The Report suggested, among other things, that the magnitude of displacement should be minimised as much as possible, the oustees should have prior claim to the fruits of the project, and land-based programme has to be the mainstay of resettlement.

Public policies and strategies for poverty eradication have often failed to achieve the desired results on account of a narrow and exclusive focus on income generation and provision of certain physical amenities for the poor without the comprehension of what Reddy calls 'culture of poverty'. Poverty gives rise to conditions which tend to perpetuate poverty, for example, extension of short-term loans to the poor by moneylenders at usurious rates of interest. On the other hand, poverty leads to a style of life and community ethos among the poor serving as mechanisms to cope with poverty. Therefore, according to Reddy, sustainable reduction of poverty requires redressing conditions that perpetuate poverty, and the use of institutions of self-help and community action among the poor.

Reddy's last paper in the book delves deep into the debate among the economists initiated by Prof. Amartya Sen in the 1960s on the inverse relationship between farm size and productivity per acre in India. One can discern in Reddy's paper his own contribution towards taking this debate forward. Because of the dependence of a large population on agriculture in India, the pressure on land will continue for quite some time. Reddy thinks that a farm size of 10-25 acres is likely to be economically viable under the existing technology. Also, his suggestion on the need for service cooperatives for small and marginal farmers for ensuring productivity consistent with equity is well taken. This was indeed recommended by the Steering Group on Agriculture for the 11th Five Year Plan.

Observations made while releasing the book "Cultural Diversity and Common Humanity" at the Centre for Economic and Social Studies (CESS), Hyderabad, on 15 July 2014.

7

Indira Hirway: Abolition of Poverty in India, with Special Reference to Target Group Approach in Gujarat

THE major focus of this study by Indira Hirway is on Small Farmers' Development Agency (SFDA) and Small Farmers and Agricultural Labourers (SFAL) programmes, the target groups being small farmers, marginal farmers and agricultural labour households. The sectors under these programmes included agriculture, soil conservation, land development, minor irrigation, animal husbandry, rural artisans and training programmes. The study is based on field investigations conducted in four villages of Gujarat in 1980-81, the year when Integrated Rural Development Programme (IRDP) was started. Thus the study does not cover the major poverty alleviation programmes being implemented during the Sixth and Seventh Plans, such as IRDP, National Rural Employment Programme (NREP), Rural Landless Employment Guarantee Programme (RLEGP), etc. Nevertheless, since the study is basically concerned with the structural constraints to the successful implementation of target-oriented programmes for the rural poor, the findings have considerable relevance to the understanding of the prospects for the poverty alleviation programmes currently underway. The method of investigation followed was designed to facilitate a deeper understanding of the factors at play: apart from the usual method of data collection through structured questionnaires, the major emphasis was on personal discussions and participant observation.

'Target orientation' seems to have two connotations, one at the policymaking level and another at the implementation level. At the former level, it simply means the 'beneficiary-oriented' or 'target-group-oriented' nature of the programmes. At the field level, the implementing agencies seem to feel that since these are basically 'target-oriented' programmes, they should struggle hard to achieve the targets. The tendency, therefore, is to implement 'easier' schemes in 'progressive' or developed areas. In the process, quite a few from the non-target population, including the rural rich, are found to benefit from the schemes.

However, it would be simplistic to think that the poor are bypassed on account of the pressure to fulfil the targets. The real reasons, according to the author, are: "first of all, there is a constant danger of transfer if the *sarpanch* or other influential persons are not happy with any staff, especially the lower level staff. Secondly, the staff gets different types of favours from the rich such as food grains, free gifts, etc. Lastly, it is a very tough job to help the poor as they are not motivated enough and cannot get bank loans easily." The operation of banks in the selected villages reveals that the bank officials follow the easy and less risky course of lending to those who are already credit-worthy in the conventional sense. Consequently, the average share of lending to weaker sections was going down since 1978 reaching as low a figure as 13 per cent in 1981. It is difficult to trace in the area of study the positive and dynamic role of banks such as nationalised institutions identifying schemes suited to local conditions, selecting beneficiaries who are genuinely poor and following up cases for ensuring recovery. The net result is an extremely limited impact of the programmes in terms of area development and alleviation of poverty as "the administration is interested in reaching the targets, the banks are interested in the business and the village leaders are interested in maintaining their special position".

These attitudes explain why schemes like irrigation, improved tools, and extension of new technology for the poor, which are costly and involve efforts on the part of the extension staff have done poorly in the selected villages. There are significant leakages to the non-poor comprising mostly big farmers. The proportion of such leakages to total beneficiaries or wrong selection ranges from 21 per cent to 28 per cent in the four villages. Besides, the bulk of the poor who are entitled for the programmes are left out. Such non-participation by the poor is attributable not so much to lack of information about the programmes or to the unwillingness on the part of the poor to participate, as to the deliberate attempts on the part of the rural rich to prevent the poor from participation through various devices. This is done partly to grab these schemes for themselves and partly to perpetuate their hold on the rural poor who are a source of cheap labour and interest earnings on consumption loans. The author also thinks that non-participation of the poor is not rooted in lack of decentralisation, as, according to her, in a society dominated by the rural rich, any attempt at decentralisation of power will increase the power of the rich only.

The author highlights a number of interesting policy implications arising from her study. First and foremost, there is a need to reduce the dependence of the poor on the rural rich for borrowings for consumption and agricultural inputs by providing consumption credit and by "setting up of grain golas and fair price shops to provide consumption items at reasonable prices to the poor, and easy credit facilities for agricultural inputs (seed banks, for example)." Second, the allocation of funds should be done on the basis of micro level planning taking into account the resource potential of the area, the incidence of unemployment, the nature and extent of poverty, etc. Third, in view of the vulnerability of the poorest of the poor, the asset-based programmes should not be emphasised too much for them. Instead they should be encouraged to take up wage employment. Fourth, there should be exclusive VLWs (village level workers), field assistants and extension officers for the poor who should not be called upon to serve the rural rich. This would help to reduce the leakages to the non-poor.

The author also makes an extreme recommendation that 'target orientation' in terms of number of beneficiaries covered and the amount of money spent be done away with, as this encourages leakages and inefficiency. This formulation goes counter to the findings of her study where the domination of rural rich, conservatism of banks and inadequate planning seem to be the main factors behind leakages and inefficiency. Her findings should have indicated that if such targets are given up, whatever the alternative criteria for evaluation of the staff, banks would not readily come forward to lend money for the poor and the staff would be prevailed upon by the rural rich through various means to go slow on such programmes.

The author also suggests that decentralised or local-level elected institutions such as village panchayats should not be involved in the implementation of the programmes as these organisations are dominated by the rural rich. However, 'direct contact' of the staff with the poor without any involvement of elected institutions can expose the programme to greater risks such as faulty planning and absence of vigilance and checks. The dynamics of democratic polity are such that the poor can be expected to increase their influence in the working of elected institutions and exert pressure on the administration. It is significant to note in this context the author's own finding that as many as 70 to 80 per cent of beneficiaries selected are those who are entitled to the programmes according to the guidelines. Whereas she has painstakingly documented and rightly brought out the dominance of the rural rich, it is difficult to believe that the poor even in the developed areas of Gujarat, which has pioneered Panchayati Raj institutions and voluntary movements in the country, are dumb and helpless. One gets the impression that the rising consciousness of the poor and their capacity to resist exploitation and injustices in a democratic and highly politicised society like ours is underestimated. The poor can still be mobilised to become an active force in the planning and effective implementation of the programmes meant for them without having to give up target-setting or bypass the local-level elected institutions.

"Poverty Alleviation Programmes and the Poor", *Economic and Political Weekly*, 29 August 1987.

8

B.M. Bhatia: Indian Agriculture

A Policy Perspective

In his book, B.M. Bhatia presents a fairly comprehensive survey of agricultural performance and policy in India. The book would, however, interest the readers more for its critique of agricultural policies and suggested reorientations in them.

The author brings out the inadequate priority accorded to agriculture in India's development plans and strongly argues for an agriculture-oriented development strategy. While noting the successes of the green revolution after the mid-1960s, the author highlights the crop-wise and region-wise imbalances in the performance of agriculture and the inadequate impact of agricultural growth in mitigating unemployment and poverty in rural areas.

As for the future, he argues for greater attention to dry farming through the use of new biotechnologies than to the spread of irrigation and the known HYV (high yield variety) technologies. On price policy, he is against public procurement and distribution of foodgrains and argues for opening up the market for surplus producers who should be free to export foodgrains to other countries on a competitive basis. He is also against separate allocations for poverty alleviation programmes like Integrated Rural Development Programme (IRDP) and would like these amounts to be utilised for the development of agriculture by small and marginal farmers.

While it is possible to identify the author's position on the major questions of agricultural policy, there are several inconsistencies in his argument. And his own policy prescriptions, though unambiguous, are by no means persuasive and not without surprises. For instance, the plea for dismantling the public distribution system coming from an acknowledged authority on famines in India is not entirely on the expected lines, particularly when large parts of the country are still vulnerable to droughts and experience severe shortages of foodgrains and high prices during droughts despite the operation of the public distribution system. It must be pointed out, however, that the author would like the benefits of food subsidies to be confined to the poorer sections only, if the system of public procurement and distribution is to be continued.

Let me first deal with the infirmities and inconsistencies in the author's position on fertiliser subsidies. He points out, on the basis of simple coincidence of events, how the output of wheat and rice rose whenever there was a cut in fertiliser prices and a rise in procurement prices. He clearly underplays the impact of the secular growth potential which manifests itself in years of good rainfall. This is evident from his prediction of a rise in foodgrains output from the level of 150 million tonnes: "In keeping with past experience, the next jump of about 20 million tonnes may come in 1987-88 or 1988-89 depending upon when the government gives the next concession in fertiliser prices and, of course, upon the amount of rainfall in that year." As it now turns out, there was no change in fertiliser prices in 1987-88. Yet there was a significant decline in output due to bad weather. The steep rise in output in 1988-89 should be attributed essentially to good rainfall which has brought out the production potential built up.

While attributing the spurt in foodgrains production in 1983-84—weather-wise one of the best years—to a cut in fertiliser prices, he goes to the extent of affirming that "subsidisation of fertiliser consumption from the exchequer is a part of public investment in the agricultural production programmes of the plans". The author has apparently overlooked the available empirical evidence which shows that variation in fertiliser consumption is explained far more by variation in the proportion of sown area irrigated than in prices.

However, when the author discusses the growing regional disparities in agricultural development, he comes down heavily on subsidies on irrigation water, fertilisers and electricity, etc, which, according to him, had the effect of perpetuating a dualistic economy in agriculture. If it is contended that what is stated above does not amount to an inconsistency in the author's position, it can be maintained only on the basis that although subsidies did in fact help to boost output, they are not needed as the producers are likely to get incentive prices as a result of the dismantling of public procurement and distribution.

While there is much to be said for scaling down food and fertiliser subsidies, it is not clear that opening up of the market by itself will ensure incentive prices and reduce regional imbalances, especially because the author is not in favour of extending infrastructure, such as irrigation through major and medium irrigation projects, to new areas and would instead opt for 'low cost' biotechnologies to be extended to the less developed and dry regions. Because of regional concentration of surpluses, the possibility of prices crashing in the surplus regions in the absence of public procurement is very real in good years. For these reasons, public intervention in foodgrains procurement has become an essential ingredient of public policy even in the advanced capitalist economies.

Maintaining that in India "agricultural price policy, judged by the terms of trade that agriculturist has got since the beginning of planning, has been inimical to the growth of agriculture," the author asserts that in China, "the terms of trade between agricultural produce and factory products were deliberately kept tilted in favour of the former. The result has been the achievement of a respectable 4 per cent annual compound growth rate in agriculture by that country over a 30-year period from 1952-53 to 1982-83." The author does not present any evidence to substantiate this proposition but the consensus of expert opinion on China is that the terms of trade were deliberately turned against agriculture in China up to 1978 and that the growth rate of foodgrains output has been no higher than in India throughout the 1960s and 1970s. It is amusing to find the author quoting his version of the Chinese experience to refute the view that "the growth of agricultural production is more responsive to public investments in irrigation and other agricultural improvements than to favourable price policy". It is well known that the overall rate of public investment in agriculture in China has been higher than in India, so that the proportion of cultivated area irrigated there is much higher as compared to India. It should not be overlooked, therefore, that the favourable response of Chinese agriculture to the recent economic reform was made possible by the strong infrastructure built over three decades of economic planning.

As mentioned earlier, while on the one hand, the author records with some concern the emergence of dualism in Indian agriculture with regions like Punjab, Haryana and western Uttar Pradesh forging much ahead of the rest of the country, which he attributes, among other things, to input subsidies, he is equally emphatic in asserting that "the per hectare income of land under wheat cultivation in Punjab declined from ₹328 in 1970-71 to ₹193 in 1978-79, while in Haryana the corresponding figures were ₹611 and ₹(-)46" (p.123). The author is not too sure of the negative figure and suspects it to be a computational error but is quite convinced about the "declining trend of income per hectare from the cultivation of wheat over the period in the two states".

The author should have seen that the particular methodology underlying the study he quotes is responsible for the declining as well as the negative figure. If 'net income' is obtained by deducting from the sale value of the commodity produced, cost C which includes factor income, and if, 'net income' so obtained is deflated further by the index of wholesale prices of all commodities, as is done in the study quoted, declining or even 'negative income' is to be expected, particularly when the price of wheat relative to the wholesale price index has been declining.

What is showing a decline is really the deflated net profit after the remuneration to own as well as hired factors of production—land, labour and capital—valued at market prices is taken out. On this basis, the surplus rice and wheat producers even in the developed regions can be shown to be experiencing negative incomes, even as they are flooding the market with their surpluses.

The author rightly points out that the emergence of dualism in agriculture, because of the `bimodal' pattern of agricultural growth that we have followed, is responsible for the widespread rural unemployment and poverty in the less developed regions. Hence his advocacy of a 'unimodal' growth pattern in agriculture involving effective participation of the less developed regions. However, it is difficult to reconcile this with his assertions elsewhere in the book on the favourable impact of mechanisation including the use of harvest combines on employment in Punjab-Haryana through the increase in cropping intensity.

There is a need to clearly distinguish the impact of the choice of technology as such on employment from the increase in employment arising from the high rate of growth itself. The evidence even on the positive impact of tractorisation on employment is not conclusive. Harvest combines are clearly labour-displacing. This explains why employment per unit of output and even per hectare for wheat and rice has gone down recently in Punjab-Haryana. However, the total employment in terms of person days seems to have increased somewhat until recently because of a high rate of growth of output. This suggests that under a 'unimodal' strategy when growth is more dispersed, the same overall rate of growth can generate greater employment in the aggregate because of a more labour-intensive technology adopted in the less developed regions. Under such a strategy, the highly labour-saving mechanisation now resorted to in high growth pockets because of 'shortages' of labour becomes no longer attractive to the farmers.

These inconsistencies apart, the author's own position is unambiguous: (i) give up public procurement and distribution of foodgrains and open up the market for surplus regions which have experienced green revolution on the basic foundations of irrigation from major and medium sources in the past; (ii) no further expansion of such irrigation to new areas through public investment but give greater attention to biotechnologies and minor irrigation wherever possible.

The consequences of the author's prescriptions are clear: first, further accentuation of dualistic pattern of growth in agriculture, which is bound to follow from the slow extension of irrigation to the new areas and the consequent rise in foodgrain prices, particularly when there is no evidence that new biotechnologies will not be more readily adopted in the already developed agricultural regions. Second, and a far more serious consequence is the jeopardising of our food security itself which has been built up in the post-green revolution period through the use of HYV technology as well as through the creation of infrastructure including, particularly, irrigation from all sources.

"Dispensing with Food Security?", *Economic and Political Weekly*, 20 May 1989.

9

Pulapre Balakrishnan: Economic Growth in India

History and Prospect

Much of the recent literature on economic growth in India concentrates on the comparison of the performance in the period following 1991 when economic reforms were launched with the preceding plan period since the early 1950s, identified as the Nehru era. These analyses conclude that the 1990s mark a major break in performance, with the GDP (gross domestic product) growth showing an acceleration. Some variants of this approach discern a break earlier in the late 1970s or early 1980s. This book by Pulapre Balakrishnan breaks new ground by showing that the dominant break in GDP series occurs at the dawn of independence with the launching of economic planning under Nehru's leadership. He identifies Nehru era as the 15-year period between 1950-51 to 1964-65, which experienced a GDP growth rate of 4 per cent as against a mere 0.9 per cent in the first half of 20th century under colonial rule. Furthermore, this growth rate of 4 per cent compares favorably with the growth rate of 4.1 per cent achieved in the second half of 20th century which includes the post-reform decade of 1990s.

Thus the release of 'animal spirits' usually attributed to economic reforms of the early 1990s was experienced first—perhaps far more vigorously—way back in the 1950s in the Nehru era. According to Balakrishnan, this is evident when viewed against the neglect of banking, denial of tariff protection to Indian industry and neglect of mass education by the colonial government. His figures show that in the Nehru era, there was a reversal of the decay of agriculture in the first half of 20th century. This comes out as one of the great achievements in independent India in the Nehru era affecting the well-being of the wider sections of population. Another specific achievement of the Nehru era having a bearing on growth, cited by him, is the unprecedented mobilisation of resources by the Indian state enabling a hike in public investment. However, he is critical of the severe neglect of primary education in this period.

If Balakrishnan was able to highlight the achievements of Nehru era which remained obscure in most analyses, it is because he has shunned looking at the growth performance through the ideological lenses, whether of the rightist or the Leftist vintages, and scrupulously followed a 'historical approach', or what he calls "'analytical growth narrative' guided by economic theory and alert to empirical reality to be explained".

The second period identified by the author for his growth story is 1965-1991 when Indira Gandhi was at the helm of affairs during much of the period. It is in this period at the end of 1970s that he sees another major economy-wide transition occurring in GDP growth. His quest for an explanation of this break provides valuable insights. Improvement in public savings rate from mid-1970s is no doubt a favorable factor. But, in his judgement, agricultural transformation of mid-1960s trumps all other factors in explaining this transition, as the green revolution not only raised permanently the rate of growth of agriculture but via forward and backward linkages energised the rest of the economy. This looks highly plausible because green revolution in this period became broad-based covering the states in the Eastern Gangetic plains, which resulted in moderating the disparities in growth rates between the richer and poorer states. Thus growth achieved in this period became more inclusive, especially because there was a decline in the relative prices of foodgrains. Indira Gandhi gave full fledged political support to the project of raising agricultural production but in the author's view hostility shown towards private investment and politicised governance of public enterprises in this period may have delayed growth acceleration by at least a decade.

According to Balakrishnan, the reforms of 1991 were characterised basically by the integration of the Indian economy with the rest of the world with a radical shift in policy towards openness to foreign capital. Services sector growth in this period acquired an autonomy of its own emerging as independent of agricultural performance, while continuing to be independent of manufacturing. Growth in Indian agriculture, which had shown dynamism since the mid-1960s, slowed down after 1991. Another break in GDP growth performance is discernible only from the year 2003-04 when there was an increase in both private and public investment.

The rest of the book discusses the prospects for growth and its inclusiveness. Based on the history of growth across nations as well as growth experience in India, Balakrishnan identifies slow growth of agriculture and lack of educational preparedness as the most significant constraints. The discussion of policies for these sectors is, therefore, a logical extension of his earlier analysis of growth in different phases. Overcoming these constraints is also critical for achieving inclusive growth, underlining closer interdependence between growth and inclusiveness in the ensuing phase of development. Realising them, the author believes, is related more to better governance than increased public expenditure.

The author emphasises the need for continuously raising agricultural productivity which would result in cheaper food, as wage goods constraint is still with us. Mere economic incentives would not be sufficient for realising increased productivity. The major constraints needed to be addressed in this sector are: declining farm size, slow expansion of public capital, especially for irrigation, and land degradation.

Balakrishnan highlights the gross neglect of primary education in India, showing that the skewness in public expenditure towards higher education in India is greater than elsewhere in the world—such expenditure in India exceeding that on primary education by a factor of six. In particular, the neglect of women's literacy may have cost India dearly in terms of human capital. Balakrishnan is right when he says that it is political economy rather than capacity to spend that better accounts for this skewness. He attributes this political bias to the prevailing social structure when he quotes J.P. Naik's astute observation made in 1975 that expansion of education in India would require mobilisation of community for radical structural change in society.

The basic conclusions of the book are: expanding the reach of the markets or purely liberalising reforms are insufficient for accelerating permanently the rate of growth of economy. Thanks to higher growth and rise in tax-GDP ratio, financial capacity of the government to invest in physical and social infrastructure is no longer a binding constraint. Governance or ability to enforce the performance as intended, notably in sectors like agriculture and education, is the binding constraint. I may add, since the crux of good governance is its accountability to the people, their participation in decision-making and implementation through their empowerment in a decentralised framework becomes crucial.

Presented at a Seminar at the Centre for Economic and Social Studies, Hyderabad, 23 September, 2010; published in *Indian Economic Journal*, October-December 2010.

10

Raj Krishna: A Study on the Marketable Surplus Function for a Subsistence Crop

In his study of marketable surplus for a single subsistence crop, Raj Krishna found the marketable surplus function to be linear in the case of majority of the samples analysed. These results would imply that "the marginal propensity to sell out of the output of a subsistence crop is constant over the wide range of output above the minimum subsistence output." From these findings relating to a single subsistence crop, Raj Krishna proceeds to question some of the widely held beliefs regarding the consumption behaviour of poor farmers as well as the effect of farm size structure on the marketable surplus. He says:

> These findings should weaken the widely held belief that output increases on relatively small farms are always likely to be swallowed up in consumption whereas those on large farms are likely to flow into the market. The truth seems to be that in many areas, the small as well as the large producers producing more than a minimum output sell (consume) the same additional quantity out of every additional unit of output... it follows that the usual discussions about changes in the farm size structure having a favourable or unfavourable effect on the marketable surplus of a subsistence crop have a lean empirical basis ... The overall policy implication of the analysis is that it is best for Governments to concentrate on inducing increases in farm output without any special discrimination in favour of small or large farms.

The study of a single subsistence crop does not warrant the above inferences regarding the consumption behaviour of the farmers and the policy implications regarding the influence of farm size structure on the marketable surplus. These conclusions can be justified only if the nature of the marketable surplus function for total output of the farmer consisting of all crops can be shown to be similar to that for a single subsistence crop. That these two may turn out to be dissimilar is supported by a number of considerations.

If the small farmers allocate a relatively larger proportion of farm area to food crops other than the crop under study and (or) if a larger proportion of output of these crops is consumed by the small farmers as compared to the large farmers, then the marketable surplus function for subsistence crops would exhibit a non-linear relationship as the amount sold would increase with every unit increase in the output of food crops. This is quite conceivable as small farmers are known to grow and consume relatively more of inferior cereals whereas Raj Krishna's study relates only to a single superior cereal, viz, wheat or rice.

Marketable surplus of small farmers is a function not merely of output on the farm but also of other kind receipts. Many small farmers supplement their incomes in a substantial way through kind receipts by working on large farms. Since such kind receipts as a proportion to total output decline with the increase in income, the marginal propensity to sell would show an increase with the increase in output, if such kind payments are included in their total output. Incidentally, by treating kind payments by the large farmers (which are in fact the kind receipts of the small farmers) as marketable surplus, Raj Krishna has overestimated the elasticities of marketable surplus because the number of hired labourers and consequently the amount of kind payments increase steeply with the increase in farm size. These elasticities may represent the behaviour of 'potential' surpluses when the wages will have been completely monetised. They do not reveal the marketed supply behaviour for a partially monetised stage.

The usual hypotheses regarding the consumption behaviour of small versus large farmers concern the per capita changes in consumption in response to the changes in per capita income. Raj Krishna could not hold the family size factor constant. According to him "in the economics of subsistence farming, the peasants determine the size of output of the subsistence crop itself keeping their family needs in view. The output variable itself reflects family size." This explains why in most of his functions, family size when included as another independent variable turned out to be non-significant. The problem of inter-collinearity between independent variables signifies only the limitation of the particular method followed. Since this method fails to eliminate the effect of the changes in family size, these findings cannot disprove the usual hypotheses relating to the behaviour of marketable surplus with the changing per capita output.

If the proportion of farm area allocated to food crops declines with the increase in farm size or farm income, that for non-food crops increasing correspondingly, as is often found, then the total marketable surplus function (food as well as non-food crops) would show a distinct non-linear relationship because non-food crops are almost entirely marketed. It does not follow, therefore, that the changes in the size structure of holdings cannot have any effect on the marketable surplus.

A more equitable structure of landholdings may, other things remaining the same, lead to a larger allocation of area for subsistence crops for the purposes of consumption and to a corresponding decline in the overall marketable surplus. Of course, this does not necessarily imply that equitable distribution is either desirable or undesirable or that the marketable surplus cannot be increased through any other method, e.g., by increasing productivity, whatever be the structure of holdings. What is suggested here is that the usual hypothesis regarding the effect of size structure of holdings on the marketable surplus is not disproved by Raj Krishna's findings from the study of a single subsistence crop.

In the case of certain samples, Raj Krishna found marketable surplus behaving in a non-linear way. These, according to him, belong either to extremely poor or extremely wealthy villages. One wonders whether in the case of such samples, the subsistence crop under study is not a predominant crop or whether some of these samples are not characterised by mono-culture. In cases where the above suspicion turns out to be true, the output of the subsistence crop under study would be a proxy for total output and the non-linear behaviour can be explained in terms of the usual income hypothesis. Raj Krishna suggests that "after a certain level of income has been reached, the cultivation of the subsistence crop becomes highly commercial and the marginal propensity to sell rises with output." A priori there is no reason to believe that the subsistence crop under study should alone become highly commercial after a certain level of income has been reached. Any other crop could become commercial, depending on the relative profitability of crops. The fact that the subsistence crop under study is found to be commercial indicates that it may be a predominant crop owing presumably to its high profitability and the non-linear behaviour of marketable surplus can be explained by the variations in income without bringing in the mean income levels of samples.

For the so-called 'linear zone', the hypothesis of constant marginal propensity to consume (or sell) would be meaningful only if it can be shown that the crop under study is the only crop grown in these areas or is at least the predominant crop. Alternatively, it has to be shown that the crops other than the one under study exhibit a similar behaviour in regard to their marketable surplus. In the absence of such evidence, the hypothesis of "constant marginal propensity to consume (sell) over a wide range of income for a single subsistence crop" cannot have any analytical or policy significance. In any case, one must justify such a hypothesis on theoretical grounds as well, if one is serious about its implications. Conclusions drawn from empirical findings having a lean theoretical basis could be as meaningless as those flowing from a priori notions lacking in factual evidence.

"The Marketable Surplus Function for a Subsistence Crop", *The Economic Weekly*, 17 April 1965.

11

Dharm Narain: Distribution of the Marketed Surplus of Agricultural Produce by Size Level of Holding in India in 1950-51

In this study, Dharm Narain makes a courageous exploration into what was hitherto considered an intractable field. The author's findings unravel some of the most obscure aspects of rural economy which have a considerable bearing on the formulation of appropriate developmental and price policies.

The estimates of 'marketed' surpluses are arrived at by deducting from total receipts the total retentions of various holding size groups. The apportioning of total agricultural produce and retentions between different holding size groups constitutes, therefore, the core of this work. But it is here that the author encounters the most difficult problems concerning the method. The basic difficulty arises from the fact that the information on the relevant variables, viz., size distribution of operational holdings, size-holding-wise variations in per acre output, retentions for inputs such as seeds and animal feeds, kind payments and receipts as rents and wages (which involve the complications of inter-group and intra-group receipts and payments), and retentions of agricultural produce for household consumption, is not available from the same sources or where available, the data relating to different variables do not lend themselves to a desired integration through the normal exercise of ingenuity. The task of 'marrying' and 'tying them up', to use the phrases from the book, must have given the author the moments of utmost despair as well as excitement.

The information on the distribution of total areas held for agricultural purposes by size level of operational holdings is taken from the National Sample Survey (NSS) on land holdings. For apportioning output between different size groups, the variations in per acre output between different size groups, as revealed by the Farm Management Studies, are made the basis. The retentions for seed and bullock-feed are also apportioned on the basis of the data given in these studies. For arriving at values retained for family consumption the author had to depend on NSS data on consumer expenditure of rural households by size levels of consumer expenditure. For identifying the levels of consumer expenditure associated with different holding size groups, the author 'marries' the two series, viz., per capita consumer expenditure according to expenditure level and size distribution of holding. This method rests on the assumption that the rise in the levels of per capita expenditure will be associated with increasing size of per capita holding. The author runs up against a more serious difficulty in estimating net amounts of kind rents received or paid out by different groups. The difference between total operated area and owned area, if available for each size group of operational holding, could give the net area leased in or leased out. But whereas total operated area is available by size groups of operational holding, total owned area is available by size groups of ownership holdings. Since there is no reasonable way of marrying these two, the author looks for a more manageable pair of data. Total area owned by owner-operators being available according to size groups of 'owned area self-operated' holdings, the author sets out to relate 'owned area self-operated' with 'operational size groups' for arriving at the required figures. For the global magnitudes in regard to output, rent and wage payments in kind etc. The author draws upon diverse sources such as the Final Report of the National Income Committee, The All India Rural Credit Survey, and The Agricultural Labour Inquiry.

The main findings of the author are: the marketed surplus as a ratio to output is significantly higher (33.6%) for the size group below five acres; the ratio declines significantly for the next two size groups (27.4% and 28.1% for group 5-10 acres and 10-15 acres respectively), and then rises reaching 51.4 per cent for the size group 50 acres and above; secondly, size groups below 10 acres contribute as much as 46.5 per cent of the total marketed surplus. Such a high contribution from smaller size groups is explained by the pressures in regard to their cash commitments relative to their incomes. These pressures seem to ease for the size groups of 15 acres and above.

In an effort to arrive at the levels of expenditure associated with different holding size groups by relating per capita expenditure of rural households with the size distribution of operational holdings, the author includes landless agricultural labourers in the lowest holding size group with a view to making the estimates of per capita consumption of cultivators in the larger holding size groups bear a closer approximation to reality. But on the same account, this technique is likely to have underestimated the per capita expenditure for the lowest holding size group as the lowest categories in the NSS expenditure groups represent landless labourers and other poorer sections whose expenditure level is known to be lower than that for the lowest size holding group. In apportioning kind wages, the author implicitly assumes a proportionate relationship between the number of agricultural labourers and the payments made to them. Although about 50 per cent of agricultural labourers are landless, they cannot be assumed to account for only 50 per cent of kind payments, partly because over two-thirds of attached male labourers who claim the bulk of kind payments are landless and partly because the number of days worked in the year are invariably higher in the case of landless labourers, whether attached or casual. Instead of 1:1 ratio in regard to the kind payments for agricultural labourers with and without land, 1:2 ratio would perhaps be more reasonable. The author also assumes a uniform rate of kind rent per acre between different groups on the grounds that the difference in per acre rents is more likely to be a regional phenomenon rather than size-holding-wise phenomenon and that rents in question relate to kind payments. However, rents especially those paid in kind may vary in sympathy with the size-holding-wise variations in output per acre. The variations in per acre output between different size-holding groups derive partly from the difference in the quality of lands in which case the assumption of a uniform rate is not realistic. Again, to the extent rents are fixed as a proportion of gross output—as is very often the case in regard to kind rents—they should vary with size even where the variations in per acre gross output are purely a size phenomenon. If the points raised above are correct, the marketed surpluses of small size holding groups—particularly of the lowest group—are likely to have been overestimated somewhat through an overestimation of receipts and underestimation of retentions.

It must be pointed out, however, that in view of the distinctly higher ratio of marketed surplus for the lowest size groups revealed by the study, the behaviour of this ratio between different size groups is unlikely to be modified significantly if due adjustments are made. For, the author's findings very largely rest on the well accepted facts, viz., output per acre declines steeply as the size of holding increases (almost a 50% decline between the lowest and the largest size-holding groups) and per capita expenditure on agricultural products rises over two-fold between the lowest and the largest size groups.

The book is highly rewarding both in respect of its findings and as an exercise in empirical analysis.

Indian Economic Review, February 1963.

References

Aiyar, Swaminathan S. Anklesaria (2010). "Fast Growth Trickles Up from the States", *Economic Times,* 6 January.

Ambedkar, Babasaheb (1979). *Writings and Speeches, Vol.I* (Part II: On Linguistic States). Education Department, Government of Maharashtra.

Baru, Sanjaya (2016). *1991: How P.V. Narasimha Rao Made History.* New Delhi: Aleph Book Company.

Binswanger-Mkhize, Hans P. (2012). *India 1960-2010:Structural Change, Rural Non-Farm Sector, and the Prospects for Agriculture.* Stanford University.

Dhar, P.N. (1958). *Small-scale Industries in Delhi: A Study in Investment, Output and Employment Aspects.* Bombay: Asia Publishing House.

ESCAP (Economic and Social Commission for Asia and the Pacific) (1996). *Rural Poverty Alleviation and Sustainable Development in Asia and the Pacific,*(ST/ESCAP/1617). New York: United Nations.

Guha, Ramachandra (2016). "Tribal Tragedies in Independent India", in *Democrats and Dissenters.* Penguin Random House India.

Institute of Applied Manpower Research (2011). *Human Development Report 2011: Towards Social Inclusion.* New Delhi: Oxford University Press.

Institute of Human Development in collaboration with the Indian Society of Labour Economics (2014). *India Labour and Employment Report 2014: Workers in the Era of Globalisation.* New Delhi.

Johnson, Robert A. (2009). "Failure of an Economic Philosophy and Implications for Financial Regulation", *Economic and Political Weekly,* 5-11 September.

Jose, A.V. (2016). "Factors Influencing the Growth of Wages in Rural India", Paper presented at the *National Seminar on Dynamics of Rural Labour Relations/Markets in India: Issues, Dimensions and Processes,* S.R. Sankaran Chair (Rural Labour), National Institute of Rural Development and Panchayati Raj, Hyderabad, 10-12 March.

Mohanty, Manoranjan (2015). *Red and Green: Five Decades of the Indian Maoist Movement.* Kolkata: Setu Prakasham.

Nagaraj, N., Lalmani Pandey, Cynthia Bantilan, Namrata Singh (2016). "Impact of MGNREGA on Rural Agricultural Wages in SAT India", Paper presented at the *National Seminar on Dynamics of Rural Labour Relations/Markets in India: Issues, Dimensions and Processes,* S.R. Sankaran Chair (Rural Labour), National Institute of Rural Development and Panchayati Raj, Hyderabad, 10-12 March.

Planning Commission (2008). *Eleventh Five Year Plan (2007-2012).* New Delhi: Government of India.

Raj, K.N., Amartya Sen and C.H. Hanumantha Rao (ed.) (1988). *Dharm Narain: Studies on Indian Agriculture.* New Delhi: Oxford University Press.

Ramesh, Jairam (2016). *To the Brink and Back: India's 1991 Story*. New Delhi: Rupa Publications India Pvt. Ltd.

Ranganathan, Thiagu, Amarnath Tripathi, Bisla Rajoriya (2016). "Changing Sources of Income and Income inequality among Indian Rural Households", Paper presented at the *National Seminar on Dynamics of Rural Labour Relations/ Markets in India: Issues, Dimensions and Processes*, S.R. Sankaran Chair (Rural Labour), National Institute of Rural Development and Panchayati Raj, Hyderabad, 10-12 March.

Rao, V.K.R.V., A.M. Khusro, C.H. Hanumantha Rao, P.C. Joshi, K. Krishnamurty and Ajit K. Dasgupta (1973). *Inflation and India's Economic Crisis*. New Delhi: Institute of Economic Growth and Vikas Publishing House.

Rao, C.H.H. and Ashok Gulati (1994). "Indian Agriculture: Emerging Perspectives and Policy Issues", *Economic and Political Weekly*, 31 December.

Rao, C.H.H. (1996). "Economic Reforms, Agricultural Growth and Rural Poverty: Some Reflections on the Relevance of East and South-East Asian Experience for India", *The Indian Economic Journal* 43(4), April-June.

————. (2005a). "Agriculture in India and China: A Comparison", in *Agricultural Growth, Farm Size, and Rural Poverty Alleviation in India*. New Delhi: Academic Foundation.

————. (2005b). *Agriculture, Food Security, Poverty and Environment: Essays on Post-Reform India*. New Delhi: Oxford University Press.

————. (2009). "Regional Disparities, Smaller States and Statehood for Telangana", *Mainstream* XLVII(2), 7 March.

————. (2010a)."Statehood for Telangana", *Economic Times*, January 9.

————. (2010b). *Regional Disparities, Smaller States and Statehood for Telangana*. New Delhi: Academic Foundation.

————. (2014). *Essays on Inclusive Growth and Some Reminiscences*. New Delhi: Academic Foundation.

Reddy, Ravi Narayan (1992) *Naa Jeevana Pathamlo*. Ravi Bharathi (ed.). Hyderabad: Moosi Publications. p.91.

Reddy, Y.V. (2009). *India and the Global Financial Crisis: Managing Money and Finance*. New Delhi: Orient BlackSwan.

World Bank (2007). *Jharkhand: Addressing the Challenges of Inclusive Development*. Rural Poverty and Economic Management, India Country Management Unit, South Asia.

Index

A

adivasi(s) 205-14

agrarian/agriculture/agricultural 45, 61, 65, 76, 77, 119, 175, 176-79, 184, 192, 199, 200, 201, 202, 214, 216, 218, 222, 227, 239, 240, 244-46, 250, 251, 253-57, 262, 266, 275, 277, 283-88, 290-92,
- ageing 176
- change 265-67
- development 179
- feminisation 203, 204
- growth 80, 200
- landholdings 82, 176, 177, 295
- planning, urban bias 240
- nutrition sensitive 184
- performance 283, 291
- productivity 207-09
- public investment in 96, 184, 239, 246, 247,
- research 178, 215-20, 271
- support systems 203, 204
- Telangana 154, 157-62, 164

Aiyar, Mani Shankar 66

Alexander, P.C. 63

Aligarh Muslim University 23

All Hyderabad Students' Union (AHSU) 23, 32, 36

All India Congress Committee (AICC) 61, 66, 114

Ambedkar, B.R. 142, 148

Andhra Pradesh 12, 115, 139, 140, 143, 144, 149, 151-54, 158, 160-62, 165, 178, 205, 208
- Andhra Mahasabha 20, 29, 35
- Jai Andhra 143, 144

Arora, Gopi 58

Arthur, Mac 44

Azmi, Kaifi 31

Ayodhya 105

B

backward regions 142

Balakrishnan, Pulapre 289-92

balance of payments (BoPs) crisis 71, 74, 75, 88, 110, 113

Bhargava Committee 51

Bhatia, B.M. 283-88

Bhattacharya, B.B. 122

Biksham, Dharma 25

Boserup, Ester 265-67

C

Centre for Economic and Social Studies (CESS) 183, 184, 187, 191-93, 209, 273, 274
- Division of Sustainable Development Studies 192
- Research Unit for Livelihoods and Natural Resources 191, 192

Chakravarthy, Sukhamoy 135

Chanchalguda jail 24, 30

Chandra Shekhar 69

Chandramma 26

Chandrashekar, B.K. 66

Chelliah, Raja 69

colonialism 93, 240

Communist Party of China 37

Communist Party of India (CPI) 36, 37, 40, 43

Communist Party of the Soviet Union (CPSU) 37, 38, 41,
Comrades' Association 24
Consultative Group on International Agricultural Research (CGIAR) 215, 217, 220
cropping
  intensity 160, 219, 287
  multiple 265, 266
  system 160

D
Dalam 26-28,
Dandekar, V.M. 67
debt
  external 261
  public 262
Delhi School of Economics 11, 33, 42, 119, 131-33
democratic
  centralism 12, 38, 40, 41
  socialism 43-46
Desai, Nitin 63
development/developmental 30, 32, 36, 39, 42, 45, 55, 57, 59, 60, 66, 83, 84, 91-103, 105, 107, 111, 117, 135, 142, 143, 145, 148, 149, 158, 172, 173, 175, 179, 180-82, 189, 195, 199, 202, 205, 213, 218, 224, 228, 235, 242, 248, 251, 256, 259, 260, 263, 283, 285, 291, 299
  economic 82, 84, 106, 108, 221, 240, 241, 244, 248
  equitable 44, 45, 88, 89
  Nehruvian model of 12, 45, 46, 71-80
  rural 13, 65, 115, 117, 239, 251, 254
  social 61, 88, 107, 111
  socioeconomic 11, 81
  sustainable 191-93
Dhar, P.N. 120, 127-29, 132, 135
disadvantaged sections 142, 180, 196
Dutt, V.P. 46

E
Economic Administration Reforms Commission (EARC) 55, 66, 71, 75, 79, 88, 91, 109
economic
  crisis 89, 171, 260
  dualism 107
  reforms 12, 64, 67, 71-80, 88, 107-18, 123, 135, 158, 162, 173, 181, 182, 259, 260, 274, 289
Economic Organisation of Agriculture 177
Emergency 40, 46-48, 51, 52
expenditure, public 165, 180, 260, 261, 291

F
fallow cultivation 265
farmer(s)
  marginal 58, 83, 96, 177-79, 203, 218, 219, 275, 277, 283
  women 161, 203, 204, 214, 219
Finance Commission(s) 12, 67, 76-78, 151
For a Lasting Peace, For a People's Democracy 37
Friedman, Milton 120
fundamentalism, religious 105-08

G
Gandhi, Indira 12, 40, 45, 47, 55-61, 65, 76, 88, 97, 106, 109, 115, 290
  20-Point Programme 40, 68, 110
  Green Revolution 45, 96
  nationalisation of major commercial banks 40, 45
Gandhi, Rajiv 12, 61-69, 88, 109, 113, 115, 117, 152, 154,
Gandhi, Sanjay 47
Gandhi, Sonia 80
Ganguli, B.N. 132
Ghaffar, Qazi Abdul 23
Gorbachev, Michael 41, 72

Goud, Raj Bahadur 21
government securities 262
Grewal, Sarla 68
growth
export-dependent 92
export-led 92, 95
inclusive 13, 80, 88, 123, 135, 151, 171-236, 291
Guha, Ramchandra 212
Gulati, Ashok 77
Gulati, S.C. 122

H

Hayami, Yujiro 269-72
Hill Area Development Programme 228
Hirway, Indira 277-81
Hindi 34, 140, 142, 231, 234-36
Hussain, Syed 32

I

Ibrahim 24
Indian Council of Agricultural Research (ICAR) 161, 179
Indian Council of Social Science Research (ICSSR) 39, 72, 73, 208
Indian National Congress 46
industrialisation 161, 176, 260, 262, 263, 271
Institute of Economic Growth (IEG) 11, 45, 46, 55, 67, 68, 119-26, 127, 129, 130, 132, 134, 135
Institute for Social and Economic Change (ISEC) 132
Integrated Rural Development Programmee (IRDP) 58, 65, 277, 283
Integrated Tribal Development Projects (ITDP) 58
International Monetary Fund (IMF) 111, 114, 154
International Rice Research Institute (IRRI) 55

J

Jain, L.C. 66
Japan 44, 256, 269-72
Jawaharlal Nehru University 43
Jayashankar, K. 157, 164
Jha, L.K. 55, 66, 67, 71, 75, 88, 109
Johnson, Robert A. 172
Journal of Political Economy 120
Joshi, P.C. 37, 43, 46
P.C. Joshi Archives 43

K

Karimnagar 19, 20, 21, 23, 26, 30
High School 22, 23, 28, 35, 36
Keynesianism 172, 173
Khan, Waheeduddeen 32
Khrushchev, Nikita 41
Khusro, A.M. 32, 33, 119, 131, 132, 134
Khundmiri, Alam 24
Kokil 25
Koneri Ranga Rao Committee for Andhra Pradesh 178
Krishna, K.L. 135
Krishnamurthy, B.V. 132
Krishnamurthy, K. 135
Kurian, George 132

L

labour force 175-77, 199, 242, 244, 271
Ladejinisky, Wolf 44
land
redistribution 44, 176, 255
reforms 44, 45, 58, 79, 243, 254, 271
least developed countries (LDCs) 240-42, 247
Leftist 20, 33, 94, 99, 100, 108, 113, 290
liberalisation 66, 67, 68, 71, 72, 74, 77, 79, 88, 109, 110, 206, 259-63, 269
Lipton, Michael 239-51

M

malnutrition 184, 185, 189
Malthusian theory 265
marginalised groups/sections 40, 102, 175-82, 192, 205, 207
marketable/marketed surplus 240, 293-97, 299-302
Mahatma Gandhi 29, 106, 232
Marxist 25, 42, 128
    Marxist-Leninist 11
Minimum Needs Programme (MNP) 58
Mishra, Vikas 119
Mission Kakatiya 152, 160, 163
Mohiuddin, Makhdoom 21, 24, 27, 28, 31
Mukerjee, D.P. 273
Mukerjee, Radha Kamal 273
Mukherjee, Pranab 56, 164
Mulki agitation/rules 143, 157
Musheerabad jail 30

N

Nagar, A.L. 135
Nahata, Amrit 31
    Kissa Kursi ka! 31
Narain, Dharm 127, 129, 130, 299-302
Narain, Jaya Prakash 40
National Commission for Enterprises in the Unorganized Sector 91, 201
National Commission on Rural Labour 68, 69, 110
National Food Security Mission 184
National Institute of Nutrition (NIN) 184
National Institute of Rural Development 117
National Mission for Sustainable Agriculture 814
Natural Resources Data Management Systems 228
National Rural Employment Programme (NREP) 58, 277
Nayyar, Deepak 110, 259-63
Nehru, Jawaharlal 11, 29, 30, 35-47, 69, 81, 106, 110, 274, 289
    era, post 60, 81-87
New Times 37
NITI Aayog 152, 153, 221
Nizam College 13, 31, 32, 36, 74, 231, 235
non-farm sector 202, 247
Nutri-Farm Initiative 184

O

Osmania University 11, 24, 30, 32, 33, 131

P

Panandikar, Pai 66
Panikkar, K.M. 142
Pandit, V.N. 135
Paranjape, Bhalchandra 21
Payam 23, 29
Peoples' Daily 37
Planning Commission 12, 13, 55-69, 75, 76, 91, 113, 115, 141, 152, 209, 212, 213, 221-23, 228
population growth 83, 143, 265, 266,
Prasad, Omkar 23
proletarian
    dictatorship 12, 38, 39, 41
    internationalism 38, 41,
Pulse Village Scheme 184

R

Radhakrishna, R. 13, 209
Radhakrishnan University Education Commission 232
Raj Krishna 135, 293-97,
Rajeshwara Rao, Ch. 24, 40
Raj, K.N. 132, 135, 253-58
Rao, A. Prabhakar 20
Rao, Burgula Narsing 13, 30
Rao, C.R. Krishnaswamy 63
Rao, Chandra Rajeshwara 21, 37, 40
Rao, J. Anand 26, 30

Rao, Kondapalli Gopala 25
Rao, M.S.A. 132
Rao, P.V. Narasimha 75, 88, 110, 111, 113-17
Rao, P.V. Prabhakar 109
Rao, N. Dharma 26
Rao, Srinivasa 25
Rao, V.K.R.V. 33, 45, 46, 119, 122, 123, 127, 131, 135
Rao, V.L.S. Prakasa 132
Ranadive, B.T. 25, 27, 37
Rashtriya Krishi Vikas Yojana 184
Rathia, U.S. 47
Raychaudhuri, Tapan 132
Razvi, Jawad 21, 31
Reddy, Baddam Yella 20, 21
Reddy, Ravi Narayan 21, 28, 29, 37
Reddy, N. Sanjeeva 69
Reddy, N. Subba 273-75
Reddy, Y.V. 13, 171
Ricardo, David 129
Rural Landless Employment Guarantee Scheme 58

S

Sachar Committee Report 181
Sankaran, S.R. 115, 199, 208
Sardar, Ali 31
Satyamma 26
Scheduled Caste Component Plan (SCP) 58
Schultz, T.W. 120
Schumpeter, Joseph A. 172
Sen, Amartya 73, 134, 135, 275
Sen, Mohit 40
Sengupta, Arjun 55, 91, 201
Shroff, Govindas 23
Shukla, Amrit Lal 26, 27
Siddharthan, N.S. 122
Singh, Manmohan 65, 67, 88, 110, 113, 115, 124, 135, 187
Sivasubramanian, S 132
Small Farmers' Development Agency (SFDA) 277
Small Farmers and Agricultural Labourers (SFAL) 277
Smith, Adam 274
Srikrishna Committee Report 155
Stalin 28, 37, 41
    de-Stalinisation 41
States Reorganisation Commission 142, 157
states, smaller 12, 141-43, 151
Stigler, George 120
Stiglitz, Joseph 274
Srinivas, M.N. 132
Swaminathan, M.S. 55

T

Tackling Agriculture and Nutrition Disconnect in India (TANDI) 184
Teerth, Swami Ramanand 23, 117
Telangana 12, 20, 29, 30, 31, 35-37, 113, 139-45, 147-49, 151-55, 157-66, 187, 189,
Telangana State Agricultural University 157, 161, 162
Tribal Development Programme 228

U

untouchability 35, 36
University Grants Commission 132
University of Chicago 120
Urdu Progressive Writers' Association 31

V

Venkataraman, R. 61
Venugopal, K.R. 115
Vyshempayen 23

W

Western Ghats Development Programme 228
World Bank 44, 111, 141

Y

Yugandhar, B.N. 115